LLEWELLYN'S

# 2017

# MOON SIGN BOOK

# Llewellyn's 2017 Moon Sign Book®

ISBN 978-0-7387-3763-8

Cover design by Kevin R. Brown
Cover images: iStockphoto.com/4468602/©ANGELGILD
  iStockphoto.com/23088297/©DavidGoh
  iStockphoto.com/12271763/©Magnilion
Editing by Aaron Lawrence
Stock photography models used for illustrative purposes only and may not endorse or represent the book's subject.
Copyright 2016 Llewellyn Worldwide Ltd. All rights reserved.
Typography owned by Llewellyn Worldwide Ltd.

Weekly tips by Penny Kelly, Nicole Nugent, Robin Ivy Payton, and Charlie Rainbow Wolf.

Any Internet references contained in this work are current at publication time, but the publisher cannot guarantee that a specific location will continue to be maintained.

Astrological data compiled and programmed by Rique Pottenger. Based on the earlier work of Neil F. Michelsen.

You can order Llewellyn annuals and books from *New Worlds*, Llewellyn's catalog. To request a free copy of the catalog, call toll-free 1-877-NEW-WRLD, or visit our website at www.llewellyn.com.

Llewellyn Publications is a registered trademark of Llewellyn Worldwide Ltd.
2143 Wooddale Drive, Woodbury, MN 55125-2989 USA
Moon Sign Book® is registered in U.S. Patent and Trademark Office.
Moon Sign Book is a trademark of Llewellyn Worldwide Ltd. (Canada).
Printed in the USA

Llewellyn Publications
A Division of Llewellyn Worldwide Ltd.
2143 Wooddale Drive
Woodbury, MN 55125-3989
www.llewellyn.com

Printed in the United States of America

# Table of Contents

# What's Different About the Moon Sign Book?

Readers have asked why *Llewellyn's Moon Sign Book* says that the Moon is in Taurus when some almanacs indicate that the Moon is in the previous sign of Aries on the same date. It's because there are two different zodiac systems in use today: the tropical and the sidereal. *Llewellyn's Moon Sign Book* is based on the tropical zodiac.

The tropical zodiac takes 0 degrees of Aries to be the Spring Equinox in the Northern Hemisphere. This is the time and date when the Sun is directly overhead at noon along the equator, usually about March 20–21. The rest of the signs are positioned at 30-degree intervals from this point.

The sidereal zodiac, which is based on the location of fixed stars, uses the positions of the fixed stars to determine the starting point of 0 degrees of Aries. In the sidereal system, 0 degrees of Aries always begins at the same point. This does create a problem though, because the positions of the fixed stars, as seen from Earth, have changed since the constellations were named. The term "precession of the equinoxes" is used to describe the change.

Precession of the equinoxes describes an astronomical phenomenon brought about by Earth's wobble as it rotates and orbits the Sun. Earth's axis is inclined toward the Sun at an angle of about 23½ degrees, which creates our seasonal weather changes. Although the change is slight, because one complete circle of Earth's axis takes 25,800 years to complete, we can actually see that the positions of the fixed stars seem to shift. The result is that each year, in the tropical system, the Spring Equinox occurs at a slightly different time.

## Does Precession Matter?

There is an accumulative difference of about 23 degrees between the Spring Equinox (0 degrees Aries in the tropical zodiac and 0 degrees Aries in the sidereal zodiac) so that 0 degrees Aries at Spring Equinox in the tropical zodiac actually occurs at about 7 degrees Pisces in the sidereal zodiac system. You can readily see that those who use the other almanacs may be planting seeds (in the garden and in their individual lives) based on the belief that it is occurring in a fruitful sign, such as Taurus, when in fact it would be occurring in Gemini, one of the most barren signs of the zodiac. So, if you wish to plant and plan activities by the Moon, it is helpful to follow *Llewellyn's Moon Sign Book*. Before we go on, there are important things to understand about the Moon, her cycles, and their correlation with everyday living. For more information about gardening by the Moon, see page 61.

# Weekly Almanac

**Your Guide to Lunar Gardening & Good Timing for Activities**

*Bread and beauty grow best together.*

~ALDO LEOPOLD

# ♑ January

## January 1–January 7

*Fill your paper with the breathings of your heart.*

~WILLIAM WORDSWORTH

| Date | Qtr. | Sign | Activity |
|---|---|---|---|
| Jan 6, 3:18 pm–<br>Jan 8, 5:06 pm | 2nd | Taurus | Plant annuals for hardiness. Trim to increase growth. |

Start a small library of books to inspire you and provide excellent references for health and healing, gardening, developing your consciousness and intuition, or any book that feeds your passion for something good in your life. Don't lend these out! Create a shelf just for your library, and be choosy about what you put there. Every so often, branch into a new area and explore a new subject. You don't have to go to college in order to get a good education. You just need to be willing to read—and think about what you read!

_____

_____

_____

_____

◑

*January 5*
*2:47 pm EST*

### JANUARY

| S | M | T | W | T | F | S |
|---|---|---|---|---|---|---|
|  | 1 | 2 | 3 | 4 | 5 | 6 | 7 |
| 8 | 9 | 10 | 11 | 12 | 13 | 14 |
| 15 | 16 | 17 | 18 | 19 | 20 | 21 |
| 22 | 23 | 24 | 25 | 26 | 27 | 28 |
| 29 | 30 | 31 |  |  |  |  |

# January 8–14    ♑

*Life itself is the proper binge.*    ~JULIA CHILD

| Date | Qtr. | Sign | Activity |
|---|---|---|---|
| Jan 6, 3:18 pm–<br>Jan 8, 5:06 pm | 2nd | Taurus | Plant annuals for hardiness. Trim to increase growth. |
| Jan 10, 5:49 pm–<br>Jan 12, 6:34 am | 2nd | Cancer | Plant grains, leafy annuals. Fertilize (chemical). Graft or bud plants. Irrigate. Trim to increase growth. |
| Jan 12, 6:34 am–<br>Jan 12, 7:08 pm | 3rd | Cancer | Plant biennials, perennials, bulbs, and roots. Prune. Irrigate. Fertilize (organic). |
| Jan 12, 7:08 pm–<br>Jan 14, 10:52 pm | 3rd | Leo | Cultivate. Destroy weeds and pests. Harvest fruits and root crops for food. Trim to retard growth. |
| Jan 14, 10:52 pm–<br>Jan 17, 6:16 am | 3rd | Virgo | Cultivate, especially medicinal plants. Destroy weeds and pests. Trim to retard growth. |

Personalize your own coffee table with a collage on glass. Acquire a piece of glass the same size as your table and gather cutouts from greeting cards, calendars, and invitations, along with paint brushes and decoupage. Following the decoupage directions, place the images facedown on the glass and paint their backs and sides with the paste. Overlap images to create a collage effect. Let it dry for a few days, then flip it over for a unique coffee table top.

2016 © HalfPoint Image from BigStockPhoto.com

○

*January 12*
*6:34 am EST*

JANUARY

| S | M | T | W | T | F | S |
|---|---|---|---|---|---|---|
| 1 | 2 | 3 | 4 | 5 | 6 | 7 |
| 8 | 9 | 10 | 11 | 12 | 13 | 14 |
| 15 | 16 | 17 | 18 | 19 | 20 | 21 |
| 22 | 23 | 24 | 25 | 26 | 27 | 28 |
| 29 | 30 | 31 | | | | |

# ♉ January 15–21

*The best way to cheer yourself up is to try to cheer somebody else up.*

~MARK TWAIN

| Date | Qtr. | Sign | Activity |
|------|------|------|----------|
| Jan 14, 10:52 pm–<br>Jan 17, 6:16 am | 3rd | Virgo | Cultivate, especially medicinal plants. Destroy weeds and pests. Trim to retard growth. |
| Jan 19, 5:09 pm–<br>Jan 19, 5:13 pm | 3rd | Scorpio | Plant biennials, perennials, bulbs, and roots. Prune. Irrigate. Fertilize (organic). |
| Jan 19, 5:13 pm–<br>Jan 22, 5:45 am | 4th | Scorpio | Plant biennials, perennials, bulbs, and roots. Prune. Irrigate. Fertilize (organic). |

Drain a roof ice dam by cutting off the bottom ten inches of a panty hose leg. Fill the hose with ice-melting salt and tie off. If you have good aim, try throwing the hose so it lands on top of the dam, perpendicular to the roof line; alternately, carefully use a ladder. The salt will melt a channel in the ice dam, allowing excess water to run off the roof. Be sure to fix your attic issues once winter passes.

◑

*January 19*
*5:13 pm EST*

### JANUARY

| S | M | T | W | T | F | S |
|---|---|---|---|---|---|---|
|   |   |   |   |   |   |   |
| 1 | 2 | 3 | 4 | 5 | 6 | 7 |
| 8 | 9 | 10 | 11 | 12 | 13 | 14 |
| 15 | 16 | 17 | 18 | 19 | 20 | 21 |
| 22 | 23 | 24 | 25 | 26 | 27 | 28 |
| 29 | 30 | 31 |   |   |   |   |

## January 22–28 ~~~

*Those who contemplate the beauty of the earth find reserves
of strength that will endure as long as life lasts.*

~RACHEL CARSON

| Date | Qtr. | Sign | Activity |
|------|------|------|----------|
| Jan 19, 5:13 pm–<br>Jan 22, 5:45 am | 4th | Scorpio | Plant biennials, perennials, bulbs, and roots. Prune. Irrigate. Fertilize (organic). |
| Jan 22, 5:45 am–<br>Jan 24, 5:43 pm | 4th | Sagittarius | Cultivate. Destroy weeds and pests. Harvest fruits and root crops for food. Trim to retard growth. |
| Jan 24, 5:43 pm–<br>Jan 27, 3:37 am | 4th | Capricorn | Plant potatoes and tubers. Trim to retard growth. |
| Jan 27, 3:37 am–<br>Jan 27, 7:07 pm | 4th | Aquarius | Cultivate. Destroy weeds and pests. Harvest fruits and root crops for food. Trim to retard growth. |

Have you noticed that there are very few blue foods in the world? Only blueberries and blue potatoes occur naturally. This may be why humans do not find blue to be an appetizing color. If you are aiming for weight loss, try buying blue dishes. The color might turn your brain off of whatever you are eating, curbing your appetite.

2016 © Subbotina Anna Image from BigStockPhoto.com

●
*January 27
7:07 pm EST*

JANUARY

| S | M | T | W | T | F | S |
|---|---|---|---|---|---|---|
| 1 | 2 | 3 | 4 | 5 | 6 | 7 |
| 8 | 9 | 10 | 11 | 12 | 13 | 14 |
| 15 | 16 | 17 | 18 | 19 | 20 | 21 |
| 22 | 23 | 24 | 25 | 26 | 27 | 28 |
| 29 | 30 | 31 | | | | |

# ~~~ February
## January 29–February 4

*For what do we live, but to make sport for our neighbors
and laugh at them in our turn?*    ~Jane Austen

| Date | Qtr. | Sign | Activity |
|------|------|------|----------|
| Jan 29, 11:10 am–<br>Jan 31, 4:46 pm | 1st | Pisces | Plant grains, leafy annuals. Fertilize (chemical). Graft or bud plants. Irrigate. Trim to increase growth. |
| Feb 2, 8:50 pm–<br>Feb 3, 11:19 pm | 1st | Taurus | Plant annuals for hardiness. Trim to increase growth. |
| Feb 3, 11:19 pm–<br>Feb 4, 11:44 pm | 2nd | Taurus | Plant annuals for hardiness. Trim to increase growth. |

B oth garden and houseplants love coffee as much as we do. They also like the coffee grounds. You don't even have to compost the grounds, just sprinkle them along a row of plants or in the flowerpots and your plants will get a little "pick-me-up" drink every time they're watered.

_____

_____

_____

_____

◐
*February 3*
*11:19 pm EST*

February

| S | M | T | W | T | F | S |
|---|---|---|---|---|---|---|
|   |   |   | 1 | 2 | 3 | 4 |
| 5 | 6 | 7 | 8 | 9 | 10 | 11 |
| 12 | 13 | 14 | 15 | 16 | 17 | 18 |
| 19 | 20 | 21 | 22 | 23 | 24 | 25 |
| 26 | 27 | 28 |   |   |   |   |

# February 5–February 11  〰

*Only those who will risk going too far can possibly find out
how far one can go.*                                ∼T.S. Eliot

| Date | Qtr. | Sign | Activity |
|------|------|------|----------|
| Feb 7, 2:03 am–Feb 9, 4:41 am | 2nd | Cancer | Plant grains, leafy annuals. Fertilize (chemical). Graft or bud plants. Irrigate. Trim to increase growth. |
| Feb 10, 7:33 pm–Feb 11, 8:52 am | 3rd | Leo | Cultivate. Destroy weeds and pests. Harvest fruits and root crops for food. Trim to retard growth. |
| Feb 11, 8:52 am–Feb 13, 3:43 pm | 3rd | Virgo | Cultivate, especially medicinal plants. Destroy weeds and pests. Trim to retard growth. |

Mint often gets a bad rap for being a nuisance, but it has many uses. Aside from making great teas, mint can be used dried in potpourri or added to homemade soaps for its scent and cleansing properties. Plant it with cabbage and kale to improve flavor and to keep moths and ants at bay. If you're worried about the mint invading your garden, plant it in a buried container to prevent the rhizomes from spreading.

_____

_____

_____

_____

○
*February 10
7:33 pm EST*

**February**

| S | M | T | W | T | F | S |
|---|---|---|---|---|---|---|
|   |   |   | 1 | 2 | 3 | 4 |
| 5 | 6 | 7 | 8 | 9 | 10 | 11 |
| 12 | 13 | 14 | 15 | 16 | 17 | 18 |
| 19 | 20 | 21 | 22 | 23 | 24 | 25 |
| 26 | 27 | 28 |   |   |   |   |

## 〰 February 12–18

*The clearest way into the Universe is through a forest*
*wilderness.*                                                    ~John Muir

| Date | Qtr. | Sign | Activity |
|------|------|------|----------|
| Feb 11, 8:52 am–<br>Feb 13, 3:43 pm | 3rd | Virgo | Cultivate, especially medicinal plants. Destroy weeds and pests. Trim to retard growth. |
| Feb 16, 1:41 am–<br>Feb 18, 1:52 pm | 3rd | Scorpio | Plant biennials, perennials, bulbs, and roots. Prune. Irrigate. Fertilize (organic). |
| Feb 18, 1:52 pm–<br>Feb 18, 2:33 pm | 3rd | Sagittarius | Cultivate. Destroy weeds and pests. Harvest fruits and root crops for food. Trim to retard growth. |
| Feb 18, 2:33 pm–<br>Feb 21, 2:08 am | 4th | Sagittarius | Cultivate. Destroy weeds and pests. Harvest fruits and root crops for food. Trim to retard growth. |

Witch hazel is a product made from the witch-hazel shrub (*Hamamelis virginiana*), which grows in most of America and part of Canada. This clear liquid is used as a face cleanser, itch suppressor, and a skin soother for abrasions. Although some folk remedies involve drinking witch hazel, it is more commonly used topically; any mixture that contains isopropyl alcohol should not be consumed internally.

◗
*February 18*
*2:33 pm EST*

FEBRUARY

| S | M | T | W | T | F | S |
|---|---|---|---|---|---|---|
|   |   |   | 1 | 2 | 3 | 4 |
| 5 | 6 | 7 | 8 | 9 | 10 | 11 |
| 12 | 13 | 14 | 15 | 16 | 17 | 18 |
| 19 | 20 | 21 | 22 | 23 | 24 | 25 |
| 26 | 27 | 28 |   |   |   |   |

2016 © Diana Mower Image from BigStockPhoto.com

## February 19–25

*After climbing a great hill, one only finds that there are many more hills to climb.*

        ~NELSON MANDELA

| Date | Qtr. | Sign | Activity |
|------|------|------|----------|
| Feb 18, 2:33 pm–<br>Feb 21, 2:08 am | 4th | Sagittarius | Cultivate. Destroy weeds and pests. Harvest fruits and root crops for food. Trim to retard growth. |
| Feb 21, 2:08 am–<br>Feb 23, 12:17 pm | 4th | Capricorn | Plant potatoes and tubers. Trim to retard growth. |
| Feb 23, 12:17 pm–<br>Feb 25, 7:24 pm | 4th | Aquarius | Cultivate. Destroy weeds and pests. Harvest fruits and root crops for food. Trim to retard growth. |
| Feb 25, 7:24 pm–<br>Feb 26, 9:58 am | 4th | Pisces | Plant biennials, perennials, bulbs, and roots. Prune. Irrigate. Fertilize (organic). |

Have you heard that the number of bumps on the bottom of a bell pepper can determine if the pepper is better for eating raw (four bumps, female) or cooking (three bumps, male)? Some cooks swear by this trick, but there's no science behind the gender or use of bell peppers, and there aren't male or female peppers. Crunch or cook them however you desire.

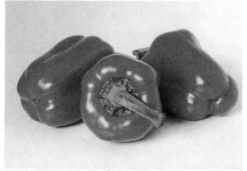

FEBRUARY

| S | M | T | W | T | F | S |
|---|---|---|---|---|---|---|
|   |   |   | 1 | 2 | 3 | 4 |
| 5 | 6 | 7 | 8 | 9 | 10 | 11 |
| 12 | 13 | 14 | 15 | 16 | 17 | 18 |
| 19 | 20 | 21 | 22 | 23 | 24 | 25 |
| 26 | 27 | 28 |   |   |   |   |

# ✄ March
## February 26–March 4

*Folks are usually about as happy as they make their minds up to be.*

*~*ABRAHAM LINCOLN

| Date | Qtr. | Sign | Activity |
|---|---|---|---|
| Feb 25, 7:24 pm–<br>Feb 26, 9:58 am | 4th | Pisces | Plant biennials, perennials, bulbs, and roots. Prune. Irrigate. Fertilize (organic). |
| Feb 26, 9:58 am–<br>Feb 27, 11:52 pm | 1st | Pisces | Plant grains, leafy annuals. Fertilize (chemical). Graft or bud plants. Irrigate. Trim to increase growth. |
| Mar 2, 2:43 am–<br>Mar 4, 5:05 am | 1st | Taurus | Plant annuals for hardiness. Trim to increase growth. |

Grapevines should be pruned in late winter or very early spring, before new growth appears. Many gardeners prune grapes too timidly, which causes too much shade and not enough strong, fruit-bearing canes. Trim off all old wood unless you want it to serve as structure for new canes. If you are leery of spring frosts, leave yourself a "backup cane." When the danger is past, you can prune back that extra cane.

●
*February 26*
*9:58 am EST*

MARCH

| S | M | T | W | T | F | S |
|---|---|---|---|---|---|---|
|   |   |   | 1 | 2 | 3 | 4 |
| 5 | 6 | 7 | 8 | 9 | 10 | 11 |
| 12 | 13 | 14 | 15 | 16 | 17 | 18 |
| 19 | 20 | 21 | 22 | 23 | 24 | 25 |
| 26 | 27 | 28 | 29 | 30 | 31 |   |

# March 5–11 ✷

*May your trails be crooked, winding, lonesome, dangerous,
leading to the most amazing view. May your mountains rise
into and above the clouds.* ~EDWARD ABBEY

| Date | Qtr. | Sign | Activity |
|------|------|------|----------|
| Mar 6, 7:54 am–<br>Mar 8, 11:45 am | 2nd | Cancer | Plant grains, leafy annuals. Fertilize (chemical). Graft or bud plants. Irrigate. Trim to increase growth. |

Invite opportunity into your life with feng shui at the front entryway to your home. Most importantly, clear the clutter. Organize shoes, keys, or any other items that must be stored near the door. Otherwise, move them farther from the entryway. Make sure there's an open, easy path into the house without furnishings blocking the way. Healthy plants, hanging mirrors, crystals, and the colors red and gold can be incorporated to energize this area that invites opportunity and abundance.

_____

_____

_____

_____

2016 © youngnova Image from BigStockPhoto.com

◑
*March 5*
*6:32 am EST*

MARCH

| S | M | T | W | T | F | S |
|---|---|---|---|---|---|---|
|   |   |   | 1 | 2 | 3 | 4 |
| 5 | 6 | 7 | 8 | 9 | 10 | 11 |
| 12 | 13 | 14 | 15 | 16 | 17 | 18 |
| 19 | 20 | 21 | 22 | 23 | 24 | 25 |
| 26 | 27 | 28 | 29 | 30 | 31 |   |

## March 12–18

*We are like butterflies who flutter for a day and think it's forever.*

~CARL SAGAN

| Date | Qtr. | Sign | Activity |
|---|---|---|---|
| Mar 12, 10:54 am–<br>Mar 13, 1:28 am | 3rd | Virgo | Cultivate, especially medicinal plants. Destroy weeds and pests. Trim to retard growth. |
| Mar 15, 11:11 am–<br>Mar 17, 11:00 pm | 3rd | Scorpio | Plant biennials, perennials, bulbs, and roots. Prune. Irrigate. Fertilize (organic). |
| Mar 17, 11:00 pm–<br>Mar 20, 11:31 am | 3rd | Sagittarius | Cultivate. Destroy weeds and pests. Harvest fruits and root crops for food. Trim to retard growth. |

Comfrey (*Symphytum officinale*) is invaluable to the organic gardener. Its deep roots gather many micronutrients from the soil, which are then stored in the leaves. This makes comfrey an excellent addition to the compost pile. Mixing the leaves with hot water can make a fertilizer, which you can use for watering. The sludge left over from the fertilizer can be used for mulch.

_____

_____

_____

*Daylight Saving Time begins*
*March 12, 2:00 am*

O
*March 12, 10:54 am EDT*

MARCH

| S | M | T | W | T | F | S |
|---|---|---|---|---|---|---|
|  |  |  | 1 | 2 | 3 | 4 |
| 5 | 6 | 7 | 8 | 9 | 10 | 11 |
| 12 | 13 | 14 | 15 | 16 | 17 | 18 |
| 19 | 20 | 21 | 22 | 23 | 24 | 25 |
| 26 | 27 | 28 | 29 | 30 | 31 |  |

2016 © H. Brauer Image from BigStockPhoto.com

# March 19–25  ✂

*Happiness and moral duty are inseparably connected.*

~GEORGE WASHINGTON

| Date | Qtr. | Sign | Activity |
|------|------|------|----------|
| Mar 17, 11:00 pm–<br>Mar 20, 11:31 am | 3rd | Sagittarius | Cultivate. Destroy weeds and pests. Harvest fruits and root crops for food. Trim to retard growth. |
| Mar 20, 11:31 am–<br>Mar 20, 11:58 am | 3rd | Capricorn | Plant potatoes and tubers. Trim to retard growth. |
| Mar 20, 11:58 am–<br>Mar 22, 10:28 pm | 4th | Capricorn | Plant potatoes and tubers. Trim to retard growth. |
| Mar 22, 10:28 pm–<br>Mar 25, 6:06 am | 4th | Aquarius | Cultivate. Destroy weeds and pests. Harvest fruits and root crops for food. Trim to retard growth. |
| Mar 25, 6:06 am–<br>Mar 27, 10:11 am | 4th | Pisces | Plant biennials, perennials, bulbs, and roots. Prune. Irrigate. Fertilize (organic). |

The same bugs that attack corn will also attack tomatoes, so don't plant them close to each other. Potatoes and tomatoes belong to the same family and can suffer from the same blight. Basil and borage planted in with the tomatoes will help to improve the flavor, promote strong growth, and deter harmful bugs from getting too close.

2016 © elenathewise Image from BigStockPhoto.com

◑
*March 20*
*11:58 am EDT*

MARCH

| S | M | T | W | T | F | S |
|---|---|---|---|---|---|---|
|   |   |   | 1 | 2 | 3 | 4 |
| 5 | 6 | 7 | 8 | 9 | 10 | 11 |
| 12 | 13 | 14 | 15 | 16 | 17 | 18 |
| 19 | 20 | 21 | 22 | 23 | 24 | 25 |
| 26 | 27 | 28 | 29 | 30 | 31 |   |

# ♈ April
## March 26–April 1

*Between saying and doing, many a pair of shoes is worn out.*

~Italian Proverb

| Date | Qtr. | Sign | Activity |
|------|------|------|----------|
| Mar 27, 10:11 am–<br>Mar 27, 10:57 pm | 4th | Aries | Cultivate. Destroy weeds and pests. Harvest fruits and root crops for food. Trim to retard growth. |
| Mar 29, 11:48 am–<br>Mar 31, 12:40 pm | 1st | Taurus | Plant annuals for hardiness. Trim to increase growth. |

The colorful nasturtium repels cucumber beetles and provides great ground cover and habitat for beneficial and predatory insects, such as spiders. Plant nasturtiums in with cucumbers and squash and let them vine together. Nasturtiums are edible too— young leaves and flower petals make a colorful addition to salads with a mustard flavor. The seeds are edible and delicious when pickled.

⚫

*March 27*
*10:57 pm EDT*

APRIL

| S | M | T | W | T | F | S |
|---|---|---|---|---|---|---|
|   |   |   |   |   |   | 1 |
| 2 | 3 | 4 | 5 | 6 | 7 | 8 |
| 9 | 10 | 11 | 12 | 13 | 14 | 15 |
| 16 | 17 | 18 | 19 | 20 | 21 | 22 |
| 23 | 24 | 25 | 26 | 27 | 28 | 29 |
| 30 |   |   |   |   |   |   |

# April 2–8 ♈

*What is a weed? A plant whose virtues have yet to be
discovered.*
                                    ~RALPH WALDO EMERSON

| Date | Qtr. | Sign | Activity |
|------|------|------|----------|
| Apr 2, 2:27 pm–<br>Apr 3, 2:39 pm | 1st | Cancer | Plant grains, leafy annuals. Fertilize (chemical). Graft or bud plants. Irrigate. Trim to increase growth. |
| Apr 3, 2:39 pm–<br>Apr 4, 6:13 pm | 2nd | Cancer | Plant grains, leafy annuals. Fertilize (chemical). Graft or bud plants. Irrigate. Trim to increase growth. |

Astrology, runes, tarot cards, pendulums, crystal balls, animal totems, dreams, palmreading, and numerology are all symbol systems that display the energies working in our lives. These systems have no biases or fears, no perceptual shortcomings or pride, and no need for vengeance or love. They just show it like it is! This year, consider learning to use one of these systems and add a little pizazz to your life with deep insights.

2016 © ronin69 Image from BigStockPhoto.com

◗
*April 3*
*2:39 pm EDT*

APRIL

| S | M | T | W | T | F | S |
|---|---|---|---|---|---|---|
|   |   |   |   |   |   | 1 |
| 2 | 3 | 4 | 5 | 6 | 7 | 8 |
| 9 | 10 | 11 | 12 | 13 | 14 | 15 |
| 16 | 17 | 18 | 19 | 20 | 21 | 22 |
| 23 | 24 | 25 | 26 | 27 | 28 | 29 |
| 30 |   |   |   |   |   |   |

# ♈ April 9–15

*Falling in love is not at all the most stupid thing that people do—but gravitation cannot be held responsible for it.*

~ALBERT EINSTEIN

| Date | Qtr. | Sign | Activity |
|---|---|---|---|
| Apr 9, 8:34 am–<br>Apr 11, 2:08 am | 2nd | Libra | Plant annuals for fragrance and beauty. Trim to increase growth. |
| Apr 11, 6:42 pm–<br>Apr 14, 6:27 am | 3rd | Scorpio | Plant biennials, perennials, bulbs, and roots. Prune. Irrigate. Fertilize (organic). |
| Apr 14, 6:27 am–<br>Apr 16, 7:05 pm | 3rd | Sagittarius | Cultivate. Destroy weeds and pests. Harvest fruits and root crops for food. Trim to retard growth. |

Grow extra zucchini and squash plants so that you can eat the blossoms as well as the fruits! While most squash blossoms grown for culinary purposes come from zucchini, others squash blossoms can also be used in similar ways. They can be battered and fried, added to quesadillas, or made into soup. My favorite is stuffing them with mushroom pâté and baking them. They're good stuffed with herb cheese and baked, too.

_____

_____

_____

April 11
2:08 am EDT

APRIL

| S | M | T | W | T | F | S |
|---|---|---|---|---|---|---|
|   |   |   |   |   |   | 1 |
| 2 | 3 | 4 | 5 | 6 | 7 | 8 |
| 9 | 10 | 11 | 12 | 13 | 14 | 15 |
| 16 | 17 | 18 | 19 | 20 | 21 | 22 |
| 23 | 24 | 25 | 26 | 27 | 28 | 29 |
| 30 |   |   |   |   |   |   |

# April 16–22 ♈

*When I started counting my blessings, my whole life turned*
*around.*                                    ~WILLIE NELSON

| Date | Qtr. | Sign | Activity |
|------|------|------|----------|
| Apr 14, 6:27 am–<br>Apr 16, 7:05 pm | 3rd | Sagittarius | Cultivate. Destroy weeds and pests. Harvest fruits and root crops for food. Trim to retard growth. |
| Apr 16, 7:05 pm–<br>Apr 19, 5:57 am | 3rd | Capricorn | Plant potatoes and tubers. Trim to retard growth. |
| Apr 19, 5:57 am–<br>Apr 19, 6:52 am | 4th | Capricorn | Plant potatoes and tubers. Trim to retard growth. |
| Apr 19, 6:52 am–<br>Apr 21, 3:43 pm | 4th | Aquarius | Cultivate. Destroy weeds and pests. Harvest fruits and root crops for food. Trim to retard growth. |
| Apr 21, 3:43 pm–<br>Apr 23, 8:32 pm | 4th | Pisces | Plant biennials, perennials, bulbs, and roots. Prune. Irrigate. Fertilize (organic). |

Use an empty contact lens case to carry a small amount of first-aid ointment and itch cream in your purse. Be sure to label which is which, and you'll always be ready for life's little scrapes. When traveling, use contact cases to keep track of small earrings or cuff links.

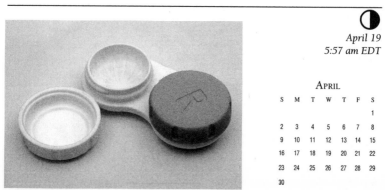

*April 19*
*5:57 am EDT*

APRIL

| S | M | T | W | T | F | S |
|---|---|---|---|---|---|---|
|   |   |   |   |   |   | 1 |
| 2 | 3 | 4 | 5 | 6 | 7 | 8 |
| 9 | 10 | 11 | 12 | 13 | 14 | 15 |
| 16 | 17 | 18 | 19 | 20 | 21 | 22 |
| 23 | 24 | 25 | 26 | 27 | 28 | 29 |
| 30 |   |   |   |   |   |   |

**April 23–29**

*Progress lies not in enhancing what is, but in advancing
toward what will be.* ∼KHALIL GIBRAN

| Date | Qtr. | Sign | Activity |
|---|---|---|---|
| Apr 21, 3:43 pm–<br>Apr 23, 8:32 pm | 4th | Pisces | Plant biennials, perennials, bulbs and roots. Prune. Irrigate. Fertilize (organic). |
| Apr 23, 8:32 pm–<br>Apr 25, 9:56 pm | 4th | Aries | Cultivate. Destroy weeds and pests. Harvest fruits and root crops for food. Trim to retard growth. |
| Apr 25, 9:56 pm–<br>Apr 26, 8:16 am | 4th | Taurus | Plant potatoes and tubers. Trim to retard growth. |
| Apr 26, 8:16 am–<br>Apr 27, 9:39 pm | 1st | Taurus | Plant annuals for hardiness. Trim to increase growth. |
| Apr 29, 9:48 pm–<br>May 2, 12:12 am | 1st | Cancer | Plant grains, leafy annuals. Fertilize (chemical). Graft or bud plants. Irrigate. Trim to increase growth. |

If your solar garden lights are on the fritz, try replacing the batteries with a different brand of rechargeable batteries. Recharge the batteries using a plug-in charger and reinsert them; if the light works, you know the problem is the charging cycle or mechanism, not the light or battery itself.

---

---

---

---

*April 26*
*8:16 am EDT*

APRIL

| S | M | T | W | T | F | S |
|---|---|---|---|---|---|---|
|  |  |  |  |  |  | 1 |
| 2 | 3 | 4 | 5 | 6 | 7 | 8 |
| 9 | 10 | 11 | 12 | 13 | 14 | 15 |
| 16 | 17 | 18 | 19 | 20 | 21 | 22 |
| 23 | 24 | 25 | 26 | 27 | 28 | 29 |
| 30 |  |  |  |  |  |  |

# May
## April 30–May 6

*The busy bee has no time for sorrow.*

~WILLIAM BLAKE

| Date | Qtr. | Sign | Activity |
|------|------|------|----------|
| Apr 29, 9:48 pm–<br>May 2, 12:12 am | 1st | Cancer | Plant grains, leafy annuals. Fertilize (chemical). Graft or bud plants. Irrigate. Trim to increase growth. |
| May 6, 2:20 pm–<br>May 9, 1:01 am | 2nd | Libra | Plant annuals for fragrance and beauty. Trim to increase growth. |

Seed libraries are gaining traction in many parts of the United States. Participants check out a packet of seeds in the spring and plant them. Participants can then save seeds at the end of the season to donate back to the library as a way to pay it forward. Seed libraries aim to promote home gardening by giving a community free access to quality seeds. Could your local library or Little Free Library benefit from such a program?

May 2
10:47 pm EDT

### MAY

| S | M | T | W | T | F | S |
|---|---|---|---|---|---|---|
|   | 1 | 2 | 3 | 4 | 5 | 6 |
| 7 | 8 | 9 | 10 | 11 | 12 | 13 |
| 14 | 15 | 16 | 17 | 18 | 19 | 20 |
| 21 | 22 | 23 | 24 | 25 | 26 | 27 |
| 28 | 29 | 30 | 31 |   |   |   |

2016 © Ansaharju Image from BigStockPhoto.com

**May 7–13**

*Do not anticipate trouble, or worry about what may never happen. Keep in the sunlight.*   ~BENJAMIN FRANKLIN

| Date | Qtr. | Sign | Activity |
|------|------|------|----------|
| May 6, 2:20 pm–<br>May 9, 1:01 am | 2nd | Libra | Plant annuals for fragrance and beauty. Trim to increase growth. |
| May 9, 1:01 am–<br>May 10, 5:42 pm | 2nd | Scorpio | Plant grains, leafy annuals. Fertilize (chemical). Graft or bud plants. Irrigate. Trim to increase growth. |
| May 10, 5:42 pm–<br>May 11, 12:59 pm | 3rd | Scorpio | Plant biennials, perennials, bulbs, and roots. Prune. Irrigate. Fertilize (organic). |
| May 11, 12:59 pm–<br>May 14, 1:37 am | 3rd | Sagittarius | Cultivate. Destroy weeds and pests. Harvest fruits and root crops for food. Trim to retard growth |

I f you live in a city and dream about having a garden, consider finding a community garden. Even smaller cities have a surprising number of community gardens and garden spaces available. You can plant things much closer together by building good soil. If you train plants up a trellis, you can get an astounding amount of food out of a fairly tiny space—and you'll make new friends in the process.

○
*May 10*
*5:42 pm EDT*

MAY

| S | M | T | W | T | F | S |
|---|---|---|---|---|---|---|
|   | 1 | 2 | 3 | 4 | 5 | 6 |
| 7 | 8 | 9 | 10 | 11 | 12 | 13 |
| 14 | 15 | 16 | 17 | 18 | 19 | 20 |
| 21 | 22 | 23 | 24 | 25 | 26 | 27 |
| 28 | 29 | 30 | 31 |   |   |   |

# May 14–20

*Don't judge each day by the harvest you reap, but by the*
*seeds that you plant.*     ~ROBERT LOUIS STEVENSON

| Date | Qtr. | Sign | Activity |
|------|------|------|----------|
| May 11, 12:59 pm–<br>May 14, 1:37 am | 3rd | Sagittarius | Cultivate. Destroy weeds and pests. Harvest fruits and root crops for food. Trim to retard growth. |
| May 14, 1:37 am–<br>May 16, 1:50 pm | 3rd | Capricorn | Plant potatoes and tubers. Trim to retard growth. |
| May 16, 1:50 pm–<br>May 18, 8:33 pm | 3rd | Aquarius | Cultivate. Destroy weeds and pests. Harvest fruits and root crops for food. Trim to retard growth. |
| May 18, 8:33 pm–<br>May 18, 11:52 pm | 4th | Aquarius | Cultivate. Destroy weeds and pests. Harvest fruits and root crops for food. Trim to retard growth. |
| May 18, 11:52 pm–<br>May 21, 6:10 am | 4th | Pisces | Plant biennials, perennials, bulbs, and roots. Prune. Irrigate. Fertilize (organic). |

During warmer months, use your coatrack to display colorful, whimsical, or sentimental items. Favorite holiday ornaments, small stained glass pieces, mala beads, and large necklaces with beautiful stones create visual appeal and positive energy in your entryway or living space when dangled from coatrack arms.

May 18
8:33 pm EDT

### MAY

| S | M | T | W | T | F | S |
|---|---|---|---|---|---|---|
|   |   |   |   |   |   |   |
|   | 1 | 2 | 3 | 4 | 5 | 6 |
| 7 | 8 | 9 | 10 | 11 | 12 | 13 |
| 14 | 15 | 16 | 17 | 18 | 19 | 20 |
| 21 | 22 | 23 | 24 | 25 | 26 | 27 |
| 28 | 29 | 30 | 31 |   |   |   |

2016 © Chris_Elwell Image from BigStockPhoto.com

# ♊ May 21–27

*Jealousy does not wait for reasons.*    ～MAHATMA GANDHI

| Date | Qtr. | Sign | Activity |
|------|------|------|----------|
| May 18, 11:52 pm–<br>May 21, 6:10 am | 4th | Pisces | Plant biennials, perennials, bulbs, and roots. Prune. Irrigate. Fertilize (organic). |
| May 21, 6:10 am–<br>May 23, 8:33 am | 4th | Aries | Cultivate. Destroy weeds and pests. Harvest fruits and root crops for food. Trim to retard growth. |
| May 23, 8:33 am–<br>May 25, 8:15 am | 4th | Taurus | Plant potatoes and tubers. Trim to retard growth. |
| May 25, 8:15 am–<br>May 25, 3:44 pm | 4th | Gemini | Cultivate. Destroy weeds and pests. Harvest fruits and root crops for food. Trim to retard growth. |
| May 27, 7:25 am–<br>May 29, 8:12 am | 1st | Cancer | Plant grains, leafy annuals. Fertilize (chemical). Graft or bud plants. Irrigate. Trim to increase growth. |

Consider putting a beehive in your backyard or garden and learning to be with bees. Plant a variety of bright and beautiful flowers and vegetables around the yard or garden, maybe even a small fruit tree, and watch your bees go to work to feed you. You will be supporting an important aspect of nature, surrounding yourself with beauty, and providing yourself with GMO-free food.

●

*May 25*
*3:44 pm EDT*

MAY

| S | M | T | W | T | F | S |
|---|---|---|---|---|---|---|
|   | 1 | 2 | 3 | 4 | 5 | 6 |
| 7 | 8 | 9 | 10 | 11 | 12 | 13 |
| 14 | 15 | 16 | 17 | 18 | 19 | 20 |
| 21 | 22 | 23 | 24 | 25 | 26 | 27 |
| 28 | 29 | 30 | 31 |   |   |   |

# June
## May 28–June 3

𝕀𝕀

*The right time is any time that one is still so lucky as to have.*

~HENRY JAMES

| Date | Qtr. | Sign | Activity |
|------|------|------|----------|
| May 27, 7:25 am–<br>May 29, 8:12 am | 1st | Cancer | Plant grains, leafy annuals. Fertilize (chemical). Graft or bud plants. Irrigate. Trim to increase growth. |
| Jun 2, 8:04 pm–<br>Jun 5, 6:46 am | 2nd | Libra | Plant annuals for fragrance and beauty. Trim to increase growth. |

When it's too warm or time-consuming to bake, offer treats that do not require heat. Get creative with canned pumpkin, granola, nut butters, honey, and dried fruits! Roll approximately two parts dry ingredients with one part smooth, like organic peanut butter or pumpkin with a bit of honey or agave syrup. From a cookie batter consistency, form one-inch balls and sprinkle with cinnamon, coconut, or chopped nuts, and then refrigerate.

◐

*June 1*
*8:42 am EDT*

JUNE

| S | M | T | W | T | F | S |
|---|---|---|---|---|---|---|
|   |   |   |   | 1 | 2 | 3 |
| 4 | 5 | 6 | 7 | 8 | 9 | 10 |
| 11 | 12 | 13 | 14 | 15 | 16 | 17 |
| 18 | 19 | 20 | 21 | 22 | 23 | 24 |
| 25 | 26 | 27 | 28 | 29 | 30 |   |

# ♊ June 4–June 10

*When we are planning for posterity, we ought to remember
that virtue is not hereditary.* ~THOMAS PAINE

| Date | Qtr. | Sign | Activity |
|---|---|---|---|
| Jun 2, 8:04 pm–<br>Jun 5, 6:46 am | 2nd | Libra | Plant annuals for fragrance and beauty. Trim to increase growth. |
| Jun 5, 6:46 am–<br>Jun 7, 6:59 pm | 2nd | Scorpio | Plant grains, leafy annuals. Fertilize (chemical). Graft or bud plants. Irrigate. Trim to increase growth. |
| Jun 9, 9:10 am–<br>Jun 10, 7:36 am | 3rd | Sagittarius | Cultivate. Destroy weeds and pests. Harvest fruits and root crops for food. Trim to retard growth. |
| Jun 10, 7:36 am–<br>Jun 12, 7:45 pm | 3rd | Capricorn | Plant potatoes and tubers. Trim to retard growth. |

Turmeric is good for your skin. The ground turmeric you use for Mediterranean or Indian dishes can also be added to lotions and facial masks as an anti-inflammatory substitute. Turmeric and water mixed to a pasty consistency helps clot blood and prevent infection when applied to cuts and shallow wounds. Drink milk with tumeric and honey to soothe from the inside out.

_____

_____

_____

_____

○
*June 9*
*9:10 am EDT*

JUNE

| S | M | T | W | T | F | S |
|---|---|---|---|---|---|---|
|  |  |  |  | 1 | 2 | 3 |
| 4 | 5 | 6 | 7 | 8 | 9 | 10 |
| 11 | 12 | 13 | 14 | 15 | 16 | 17 |
| 18 | 19 | 20 | 21 | 22 | 23 | 24 |
| 25 | 26 | 27 | 28 | 29 | 30 |  |

# June 11–17 ♊

*If you can see things out of whack, then you can see how*
*things can be in whack.*                    ～ Dr. Seuss

| Date | Qtr. | Sign | Activity |
|------|------|------|----------|
| Jun 10, 7:36 am–<br>Jun 12, 7:45 pm | 3rd | Capricorn | Plant potatoes and tubers. Trim to retard growth. |
| Jun 12, 7:45 pm–<br>Jun 15, 6:17 am | 3rd | Aquarius | Cultivate. Destroy weeds and pests. Harvest fruits and root crops for food. Trim to retard growth. |
| Jun 15, 6:17 am–<br>Jun 17, 7:33 am | 3rd | Pisces | Plant biennials, perennials, bulbs, and roots. Prune. Irrigate. Fertilize (organic). |
| Jun 17, 7:33 am–<br>Jun 17, 1:55 pm | 4th | Pisces | Plant biennials, perennials, bulbs, and roots. Prune. Irrigate. Fertilize (organic). |
| Jun 17, 1:55 pm–<br>Jun 19, 5:53 pm | 4th | Aries | Cultivate. Destroy weeds and pests. Harvest fruits and root crops for food. Trim to retard growth. |

Don't chase pigweed away from your corn! It can bring valuable nutrients up to the surface for corn's shallow root system to absorb. Corn also makes a great support system for beans and squash—in fact, corn, beans, and squash were grown together and called "the Three Sisters" by Native Americans.

2016 © Hcommunications Image from BigStockPhoto.com

◐

*June 17*
*7:33 am EDT*

JUNE

| S | M | T | W | T | F | S |
|---|---|---|---|---|---|---|
|   |   |   |   | 1 | 2 | 3 |
| 4 | 5 | 6 | 7 | 8 | 9 | 10 |
| 11 | 12 | 13 | 14 | 15 | 16 | 17 |
| 18 | 19 | 20 | 21 | 22 | 23 | 24 |
| 25 | 26 | 27 | 28 | 29 | 30 |  |

# June 18–24

*The bulk of the world's knowledge is an imaginary construction.*
                                          ~HELEN KELLER

| Date | Qtr. | Sign | Activity |
|------|------|------|----------|
| Jun 17, 1:55 pm–<br>Jun 19, 5:53 pm | 4th | Aries | Cultivate. Destroy weeds and pests. Harvest fruits and root crops for food. Trim to retard growth. |
| Jun 19, 5:53 pm–<br>Jun 21, 6:44 pm | 4th | Taurus | Plant potatoes and tubers. Trim to retard growth. |
| Jun 21, 6:44 pm–<br>Jun 23, 6:07 pm | 4th | Gemini | Cultivate. Destroy weeds and pests. Harvest fruits and root crops for food. Trim to retard growth. |
| Jun 23, 6:07 pm–<br>Jun 23, 10:31 pm | 4th | Cancer | Plant biennials, perennials, bulbs, and roots. Prune. Irrigate. Fertilize (organic). |
| Jun 23, 10:31 pm–<br>Jun 25, 6:06 pm | 1st | Cancer | Plant grains, leafy annuals. Fertilize (chemical). Graft or bud plants. Irrigate. Trim to increase growth. |

Experiment with making a "living masque" from what you grow and putting it on your skin. Try mixing cucumber, flaxseed oil, raw egg, and cream and patting it on your face, chest, leg, or wherever your skin needs healing. Add a little oatmeal or rice bran to thicken if needed. You could also start with carrots or strawberries—go online to find all sorts of recipes. Food is wonderful medicine.

*June 23*
*10:31 pm EDT*

JUNE

| S | M | T | W | T | F | S |
|---|---|---|---|---|---|---|
|   |   |   |   | 1 | 2 | 3 |
| 4 | 5 | 6 | 7 | 8 | 9 | 10 |
| 11 | 12 | 13 | 14 | 15 | 16 | 17 |
| 18 | 19 | 20 | 21 | 22 | 23 | 24 |
| 25 | 26 | 27 | 28 | 29 | 30 |   |

2016 © Kalcutta Image from BigStockPhoto.com

# July ♋

**June 25–July 1**

*We must live it, now, a day at a time and be very careful not to hurt each other.*
          ~ERNEST HEMINGWAY

| Date | Qtr. | Sign | Activity |
|------|------|------|----------|
| Jun 23, 10:31 pm–<br>Jun 25, 6:06 pm | 1st | Cancer | Plant grains, leafy annuals. Fertilize (chemical). Graft or bud plants. Irrigate. Trim to increase growth. |
| Jun 30, 3:02 am–<br>Jun 30, 8:51 pm | 1st | Libra | Plant annuals for fragrance and beauty. Trim to increase growth. |
| Jun 30, 8:51 pm–<br>Jul 2, 12:59 pm | 2nd | Libra | Plant annuals for fragrance and beauty. Trim to increase growth. |

Call 811 a few days before you start ANY project that involves digging in your yard. What if it's just a foot? Still call. Better safe than sorry when it comes to utilities like power, water, sewer, and cable. Buried electrical cables that run into a home are usually only 18 to 24 inches below the surface. The line-marking service is free and easy to use. Visit call811.com for more information.

_____

_____

_____

_____

2016 © omphoto Image from BigStockPhoto.com

◗

*June 30*
*8:51 pm EDT*

JULY

| S | M | T | W | T | F | S |
|---|---|---|---|---|---|---|
|  |  |  |  |  |  | 1 |
| 2 | 3 | 4 | 5 | 6 | 7 | 8 |
| 9 | 10 | 11 | 12 | 13 | 14 | 15 |
| 16 | 17 | 18 | 19 | 20 | 21 | 22 |
| 23 | 24 | 25 | 26 | 27 | 28 | 29 |
| 30 | 31 |  |  |  |  |  |

# ♋ July 2–July 8

*Find something you're passionate about and keep*
*tremendously interested in it.*    ~JULIA CHILD

| Date | Qtr. | Sign | Activity |
|------|------|------|----------|
| Jun 30, 8:51 pm–<br>Jul 2, 12:59 pm | 2nd | Libra | Plant annuals for fragrance and beauty. Trim to increase growth. |
| Jul 2, 12:59 pm–<br>Jul 5, 1:08 am | 2nd | Scorpio | Plant grains, leafy annuals. Fertilize (chemical). Graft or bud plants. Irrigate. Trim to increase growth. |
| Jul 7, 1:45 pm–<br>Jul 9, 12:07 am | 2nd | Capricorn | Graft or bud plants. Trim to increase growth. |

Sangria is a popular summer drink that's easy to make at home. Start with a basic recipe: Combine 1 bottle of red or white wine with 2 cups of club soda or ginger ale, 1 shot of liquor (rum, brandy, or triple sec are popular), about 2 tablespoons sugar, 1 sliced lemon, and 1 sliced orange. Add your favorite summer fruits. As with most recipes, there's no right or wrong way, so choose the wine, liquor, and fruit YOU prefer. For a more cohesive drink, combine all but the soda or ginger ale at least 8 hours before drinking.

JULY

| S | M | T | W | T | F | S |
|---|---|---|---|---|---|---|
|  |  |  |  |  |  | 1 |
| 2 | 3 | 4 | 5 | 6 | 7 | 8 |
| 9 | 10 | 11 | 12 | 13 | 14 | 15 |
| 16 | 17 | 18 | 19 | 20 | 21 | 22 |
| 23 | 24 | 25 | 26 | 27 | 28 | 29 |
| 30 | 31 |  |  |  |  |  |

2016 © margouillat photo Image from BigStockPhoto.com

# July 9–15 ♋

*A good book is the precious lifeblood of a master spirit.*

~JOHN MILTON

| Date | Qtr. | Sign | Activity |
|------|------|------|----------|
| Jul 7, 1:45 pm–<br>Jul 9, 12:07 am | 2nd | Capricorn | Graft or bud plants. Trim to increase growth. |
| Jul 9, 12:07 am–<br>Jul 10, 1:35 am | 3rd | Capricorn | Plant potatoes and tubers. Trim to retard growth. |
| Jul 10, 1:35 am–<br>Jul 12, 11:51 am | 3rd | Aquarius | Cultivate. Destroy weeds and pests. Harvest fruits and root crops for food. Trim to retard growth. |
| Jul 12, 11:51 am–<br>Jul 14, 7:52 pm | 3rd | Pisces | Plant biennials, perennials, bulbs, and roots. Prune. Irrigate. Fertilize (organic). |
| Jul 14, 7:52 pm–<br>Jul 16, 3:26 pm | 3rd | Aries | Cultivate. Destroy weeds and pests. Harvest fruits and root crops for food. Trim to retard growth. |

I f your clothespins took an unintentional shower in the rain or you are hoping to use old pins for crafts, they might need cleaning. Soak them in warm bleach water, diluted one part bleach to ten parts water. After ten minutes, scrub them with a medium-bristle cleaning brush and let them air dry. Especially grimy pins may need to be taken apart, cleaned, and then put back together.

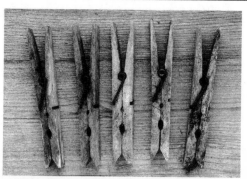

○
*July 9*
*12:07 am EDT*

JULY

| S | M | T | W | T | F | S |
|---|---|---|---|---|---|---|
|   |   |   |   |   |   | 1 |
| 2 | 3 | 4 | 5 | 6 | 7 | 8 |
| 9 | 10 | 11 | 12 | 13 | 14 | 15 |
| 16 | 17 | 18 | 19 | 20 | 21 | 22 |
| 23 | 24 | 25 | 26 | 27 | 28 | 29 |
| 30 | 31 |   |   |   |   |   |

# ♋ July 16–22

*A scholar's ink lasts longer than a martyr's blood.*

~IRISH PROVERB

| Date | Qtr. | Sign | Activity |
|------|------|------|----------|
| Jul 14, 7:52 pm–<br>Jul 16, 3:26 pm | 3rd | Aries | Cultivate. Destroy weeds and pests. Harvest fruits and root crops for food. Trim to retard growth. |
| Jul 16, 3:26 pm–<br>Jul 17, 1:04 am | 4th | Aries | Cultivate. Destroy weeds and pests. Harvest fruits and root crops for food. Trim to retard growth. |
| Jul 17, 1:04 am–<br>Jul 19, 3:31 am | 4th | Taurus | Plant potatoes and tubers. Trim to retard growth. |
| Jul 19, 3:31 am–<br>Jul 21, 4:09 am | 4th | Gemini | Cultivate. Destroy weeds and pests. Harvest fruits and root crops for food. Trim to retard growth. |
| Jul 21, 4:09 am–<br>Jul 23, 4:34 am | 4th | Cancer | Plant biennials, perennials, bulbs, and roots. Prune. Irrigate. Fertilize (organic). |

Lemonade is everywhere, but limeade is just as refreshing. Boil 1 cup of water in a saucepan and add ½ cup sugar or honey, stirring until dissolved. Pour this into a pitcher with 4 cups of water and ½ cup lime juice (5 to 7 limes). Stir until blended and chill for one hour. Garnish your glasses with lime slices and enjoy.

_____

_____

_____

◐
*July 16*
*3:26 pm EDT*

JULY

| S | M | T | W | T | F | S |
|---|---|---|---|---|---|---|
|   |   |   |   |   |   | 1 |
| 2 | 3 | 4 | 5 | 6 | 7 | 8 |
| 9 | 10 | 11 | 12 | 13 | 14 | 15 |
| 16 | 17 | 18 | 19 | 20 | 21 | 22 |
| 23 | 24 | 25 | 26 | 27 | 28 | 29 |
| 30 | 31 |   |   |   |   |   |

2016 © bhofack22 Image from BigStockPhoto.com

# July 23–29 ♌

*By the time a person has achieved years adequate for choosing a direction, the die is cast and the moment has long since passed which determined the future.*    ~ZELDA FITZGERALD

| Date | Qtr. | Sign | Activity |
|------|------|------|----------|
| Jul 21, 4:09 am–<br>Jul 23, 4:34 am | 4th | Cancer | Plant biennials, perennials, bulbs, and roots. Prune. Irrigate. Fertilize (organic). |
| Jul 23, 4:34 am–<br>Jul 23, 5:46 am | 4th | Leo | Cultivate. Destroy weeds and pests. Harvest fruits and root crops for food. Trim to retard growth. |
| Jul 27, 11:37 am–<br>Jul 29, 8:23 pm | 1st | Libra | Plant annuals for fragrance and beauty. Trim to increase growth. |
| Jul 29, 8:23 pm–<br>Jul 30, 11:23 am | 1st | Scorpio | Plant grains, leafy annuals. Fertilize (chemical). Graft or bud plants. Irrigate. Trim to increase growth. |

Pepper heat can be measured on the Scoville scale, developed by pharmacist Wilbur Scoville in the early twentieth century. Capsaicin provides the heat in peppers, but the scale has no fixed measurement for the amount of capsaicin in foods. A more scientific test known as HPLC, which weighs the components that produce heat, was developed in the 1980s.

*July 23*
*5:46 am EDT*

JULY

| S | M | T | W | T | F | S |
|---|---|---|---|---|---|---|
|   |   |   |   |   |   | 1 |
| 2 | 3 | 4 | 5 | 6 | 7 | 8 |
| 9 | 10 | 11 | 12 | 13 | 14 | 15 |
| 16 | 17 | 18 | 19 | 20 | 21 | 22 |
| 23 | 24 | 25 | 26 | 27 | 28 | 29 |
| 30 | 31 |   |   |   |   |   |

# ♏ August
## July 30–August 5

*Look deep into nature, and then you will understand*
*everything better.*                    ∽ALBERT EINSTEIN

| Date | Qtr. | Sign | Activity |
|------|------|------|----------|
| Jul 29, 8:23 pm–<br>Jul 30, 11:23 am | 1st | Scorpio | Plant grains, leafy annuals. Fertilize (chemical). Graft or bud plants. Irrigate. Trim to increase growth. |
| Jul 30, 11:23 am–<br>Aug 1, 8:01 am | 2nd | Scorpio | Plant grains, leafy annuals. Fertilize (chemical). Graft or bud plants. Irrigate. Trim to increase growth. |
| Aug 3, 8:37 pm–<br>Aug 6, 8:15 am | 2nd | Capricorn | Graft or bud plants. Trim to increase growth. |

National Night Out is the first Tuesday in August (October in Texas and Florida). The event started in 1984 to build community ties, foster goodwill with police departments, and deter neighborhood crime. Typical National Night Out parties are divided by block and may include a potluck dinner, visits from local police or fire department personnel, and games for kids.

_____

_____

_____

_____

◑
*July 30*
*11:23 am EDT*

AUGUST

| S | M | T | W | T | F | S |
|---|---|---|---|---|---|---|
|   |   | 1 | 2 | 3 | 4 | 5 |
| 6 | 7 | 8 | 9 | 10 | 11 | 12 |
| 13 | 14 | 15 | 16 | 17 | 18 | 19 |
| 20 | 21 | 22 | 23 | 24 | 25 | 26 |
| 27 | 28 | 29 | 30 | 31 |   |   |

2016 © monkeybusinessimages Image from BigStockPhoto.com

# August 6–12 ♌

*In any city with lots of skyscrapers, lots of skyline, the moon seems bigger than it is. It's called the moon illusion.*

~NEIL DEGRASSE TYSON

| Date | Qtr. | Sign | Activity |
|---|---|---|---|
| Aug 3, 8:37 pm–<br>Aug 6, 8:15 am | 2nd | Capricorn | Graft or bud plants. Trim to increase growth. |
| Aug 7, 2:11 pm–<br>Aug 8, 5:56 pm | 3rd | Aquarius | Cultivate. Destroy weeds and pests. Harvest fruits and root crops for food. Trim to retard growth. |
| Aug 8, 5:56 pm–<br>Aug 11, 1:22 am | 3rd | Pisces | Plant biennials, perennials, bulbs, and roots. Prune. Irrigate. Fertilize (organic). |
| Aug 11, 1:22 am–<br>Aug 13, 6:40 am | 3rd | Aries | Cultivate. Destroy weeds and pests. Harvest fruits and root crops for food. Trim to retard growth. |

If cutting back on energy bills seems to be a constant uphill-battle, keep this trick in your back pocket for the right time. For hot summer days when the comfort of air conditioning clashes with the guilt of energy use, consider hanging a damp sheet in an open window—the evaporating water cools the incoming breeze.

2016 © MarkHowland Image from BigStockPhoto.com

○
*August 7*
*2:11 pm EDT*

AUGUST

| S | M | T | W | T | F | S |
|---|---|---|---|---|---|---|
| | | 1 | 2 | 3 | 4 | 5 |
| 6 | 7 | 8 | 9 | 10 | 11 | 12 |
| 13 | 14 | 15 | 16 | 17 | 18 | 19 |
| 20 | 21 | 22 | 23 | 24 | 25 | 26 |
| 27 | 28 | 29 | 30 | 31 | | |

# ♌ August 13–19

*Friendship is far more tragic than love. It lasts longer.*

~Oscar Wilde

| Date | Qtr. | Sign | Activity |
|------|------|------|----------|
| Aug 11, 1:22 am–Aug 13, 6:40 am | 3rd | Aries | Cultivate. Destroy weeds and pests. Harvest fruits and root crops for food. Trim to retard growth. |
| Aug 13, 6:40 am–Aug 14, 9:15 pm | 3rd | Taurus | Plant potatoes and tubers. Trim to retard growth. |
| Aug 14, 9:15 pm–Aug 15, 10:06 am | 4th | Taurus | Plant potatoes and tubers. Trim to retard growth. |
| Aug 15, 10:06 am–Aug 17, 12:13 pm | 4th | Gemini | Cultivate. Destroy weeds and pests. Harvest fruits and root crops for food. Trim to retard growth. |
| Aug 17, 12:13 pm–Aug 19, 1:55 pm | 4th | Cancer | Plant biennials, perennials, bulbs, and roots. Prune. Irrigate. Fertilize (organic). |
| Aug 19, 1:55 pm–Aug 21, 2:30 pm | 4th | Leo | Cultivate. Destroy weeds and pests. Harvest fruits and root crops for food. Trim to retard growth. |

Bee balm (*Monarda didyma, Monarda fistulosa*) is not only beautiful in the garden, but it has a myriad of uses. It attracts pollinators such as bees, butterflies, and hummingbirds. The leaves and flowers are edible and make an aromatic tea that is used to aid digestion and reduce fevers. A poultice of the leaves placed on the skin is said to reduce inflammation and draw out infection.

◗
*August 14*
*9:15 pm EDT*

### August

| S | M | T | W | T | F | S |
|---|---|---|---|---|---|---|
|   |   | 1 | 2 | 3 | 4 | 5 |
| 6 | 7 | 8 | 9 | 10 | 11 | 12 |
| 13 | 14 | 15 | 16 | 17 | 18 | 19 |
| 20 | 21 | 22 | 23 | 24 | 25 | 26 |
| 27 | 28 | 29 | 30 | 31 |   |   |

2016 © ArrantPariah Image from BigStockPhoto.com

# August 20–26 ♌

*Everybody needs beauty as well as bread, places to play
in and pray in, where nature may heal and cheer and give
strength to body and soul.*

~John Muir

| Date | Qtr. | Sign | Activity |
|------|------|------|----------|
| Aug 19, 1:55 pm–<br>Aug 21, 2:30 pm | 4th | Leo | Cultivate. Destroy weeds and pests. Harvest fruits and root crops for food. Trim to retard growth. |
| Aug 23, 9:05 pm–<br>Aug 26, 4:53 am | 1st | Libra | Plant annuals for fragrance and beauty. Trim to increase growth. |
| Aug 26, 4:53 am–<br>Aug 28, 3:48 pm | 1st | Scorpio | Plant grains, leafy annuals. Fertilize (chemical). Graft or bud plants. Irrigate. Trim to increase growth. |

Some foods are known by different names depending on where you are in the world. Cilantro is also called Chinese parsley and is known as coriander in the United Kingdom. Rutabagas are known as swedes in the UK but as turnips in Scotland. Celery root is also called celeriac, and eggplant is known by the French name *aubergine* in most of the UK and as *brinjal* in parts of Asia and Africa.

_____

_____

_____

_____

2016 © Yastremska Image from BigStockPhoto.com

●

*August 21
2:30 pm EDT*

August

| S | M | T | W | T | F | S |
|---|---|---|---|---|---|---|
|   |   | 1 | 2 | 3 | 4 | 5 |
| 6 | 7 | 8 | 9 | 10 | 11 | 12 |
| 13 | 14 | 15 | 16 | 17 | 18 | 19 |
| 20 | 21 | 22 | 23 | 24 | 25 | 26 |
| 27 | 28 | 29 | 30 | 31 |   |   |

# ♍ September

## August 27–September 2

*Art washes away from the soul the dust of everyday life.*

~PABLO PICASSO

| Date | Qtr. | Sign | Activity |
|------|------|------|----------|
| Aug 26, 4:53 am–<br>Aug 28, 3:48 pm | 1st | Scorpio | Plant grains, leafy annuals. Fertilize (chemical). Graft or bud plants. Irrigate. Trim to increase growth. |
| Aug 31, 4:18 am–<br>Sep 2, 4:06 pm | 2nd | Capricorn | Graft or bud plants. Trim to increase growth. |

Use a length of strap and a parachute buckle, both available at craft stores, to inexpensively and easily kid-proof those two-door lower cabinets. Thread the strap around the doors between the hinges, then adjust the buckles until the doors barely open. Kids will quickly realize they can't get in and move on to more interesting things. This method is great for doors without knobs, or for temporary kid-proofing when friends or family visit.

_____

_____

_____

_____

◑

*August 29*
*4:13 am EDT*

SEPTEMBER

| S | M | T | W | T | F | S |
|---|---|---|---|---|---|---|
|   |   |   |   |   | 1 | 2 |
| 3 | 4 | 5 | 6 | 7 | 8 | 9 |
| 10 | 11 | 12 | 13 | 14 | 15 | 16 |
| 17 | 18 | 19 | 20 | 21 | 22 | 23 |
| 24 | 25 | 26 | 27 | 28 | 29 | 30 |

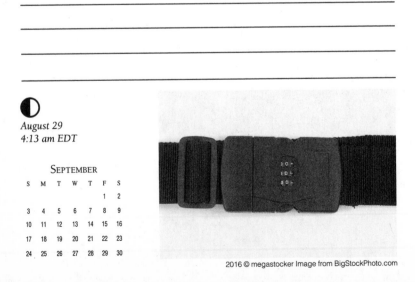

# September 3–9 ♍

*Give me the liberty to know, to utter, and to argue freely*
*according to my conscience, above all liberties.*

~JOHN MILTON

| Date | Qtr. | Sign | Activity |
|------|------|------|----------|
| Sep 5, 1:28 am–<br>Sep 6, 3:03 am | 2nd | Pisces | Plant grains, leafy annuals. Fertilize (chemical). Graft or bud plants. Irrigate. Trim to increase growth. |
| Sep 6, 3:03 am–<br>Sep 7, 8:01 am | 3rd | Pisces | Plant biennials, perennials, bulbs, and roots. Prune. Irrigate. Fertilize (organic). |
| Sep 7, 8:01 am–<br>Sep 9, 12:23 pm | 3rd | Aries | Cultivate. Destroy weeds and pests. Harvest fruits and root crops for food. Trim to retard growth. |
| Sep 9, 12:23 pm–<br>Sep 11, 3:29 pm | 3rd | Taurus | Plant potatoes and tubers. Trim to retard growth. |

If you can't bear to part with a collection of T-shirts, you can try making them into a T-shirt quilt. These are great for sports shirts, shirts from races or concerts, or even shirts that your child loved growing up. Cut your largest design first, then cut all the other T-shirt fronts that same size. Use iron-on interfacing to stiffen the shirts and lessen the stretch in your quilt squares.

○
*September 6*
*3:03 am EDT*

SEPTEMBER

| S | M | T | W | T | F | S |
|---|---|---|---|---|---|---|
| | | | | | 1 | 2 |
| 3 | 4 | 5 | 6 | 7 | 8 | 9 |
| 10 | 11 | 12 | 13 | 14 | 15 | 16 |
| 17 | 18 | 19 | 20 | 21 | 22 | 23 |
| 24 | 25 | 26 | 27 | 28 | 29 | 30 |

# ♍ September 10–16

*An unattended mind is the breeding ground of self defeat.*

~GUY FINLEY

| Date | Qtr. | Sign | Activity |
|------|------|------|----------|
| Sep 11, 3:29 pm–<br>Sep 13, 2:25 am | 3rd | Gemini | Cultivate. Destroy weeds and pests. Harvest fruits and root crops for food. Trim to retard growth. |
| Sep 13, 2:25 am–<br>Sep 13, 6:12 pm | 4th | Gemini | Cultivate. Destroy weeds and pests. Harvest fruits and root crops for food. Trim to retard growth. |
| Sep 13, 6:12 pm–<br>Sep 15, 9:09 pm | 4th | Cancer | Plant biennials, perennials, bulbs, and roots. Prune. Irrigate. Fertilize (organic). |
| Sep 15, 9:09 pm–<br>Sep 18, 12:52 am | 4th | Leo | Cultivate. Destroy weeds and pests. Harvest fruits and root crops for food. Trim to retard growth. |

Take up the study of something that will enhance your understanding of the earth and mother nature. You might devote a season to studying permaculture, square foot gardening, or biodynamics. While learning all the new information and techniques, you will discover a new love of the whole world of plants, insects, and animals while gaining a grasp of your place in the order of things.

◗

*September 13*
*2:25 am EDT*

SEPTEMBER

| S | M | T | W | T | F | S |
|---|---|---|---|---|---|---|
|   |   |   |   |   | 1 | 2 |
| 3 | 4 | 5 | 6 | 7 | 8 | 9 |
| 10 | 11 | 12 | 13 | 14 | 15 | 16 |
| 17 | 18 | 19 | 20 | 21 | 22 | 23 |
| 24 | 25 | 26 | 27 | 28 | 29 | 30 |

2016 © stefanolunardi Image from BigStockPhoto.com

# September 17–23 ♍

*If we crave some cosmic purpose, then let us find ourselves a*
*worthy goal.*
　　　　　　　　　　　　　　　　　　　　　　~CARL SAGAN

| Date | Qtr. | Sign | Activity |
|---|---|---|---|
| Sep 15, 9:09 pm–<br>Sep 18, 12:52 am | 4th | Leo | Cultivate. Destroy weeds and pests. Harvest fruits and root crops for food. Trim to retard growth. |
| Sep 18, 12:52 am–<br>Sep 20, 1:30 am | 4th | Virgo | Cultivate, especially medicinal plants. Destroy weeds and pests. Trim to retard growth. |
| Sep 20, 6:06 am–<br>Sep 22, 1:40 pm | 1st | Libra | Plant annuals for fragrance and beauty. Trim to increase growth. |
| Sep 22, 1:40 pm–<br>Sep 25, 12:01 am | 1st | Scorpio | Plant grains, leafy annuals. Fertilize (chemical). Graft or bud plants. Irrigate. Trim to increase growth. |

This fall, commit yourself to a year of renewal. Your main focus will be to rebuild your body, renew your mind, and recover a sense of youthful freedom and movement. Include a good diet based on whole foods rather than factory foods, regular exercise at least 4 to 5 days per week, plenty of water, willingness to add necessary supplements, and commit to getting enough sleep every night. You owe it to yourself to take responsibility for yourself.

2016 © Romario Ien Image from BigStockPhoto.com

*September 20*
*1:30 am EDT*

## SEPTEMBER

| S | M | T | W | T | F | S |
|---|---|---|---|---|---|---|
|   |   |   |   |   | 1 | 2 |
| 3 | 4 | 5 | 6 | 7 | 8 | 9 |
| 10 | 11 | 12 | 13 | 14 | 15 | 16 |
| 17 | 18 | 19 | 20 | 21 | 22 | 23 |
| 24 | 25 | 26 | 27 | 28 | 29 | 30 |

## ♎ September 24–30

*Success is like reaching an important birthday and finding you're exactly the same.*    ～AUDREY HEPBURN

| Date | Qtr. | Sign | Activity |
|------|------|------|----------|
| Sep 22, 1:40 pm–<br>Sep 25, 12:01 am | 1st | Scorpio | Plant grains, leafy annuals. Fertilize (chemical). Graft or bud plants. Irrigate. Trim to increase growth. |
| Sep 27, 12:24 pm–<br>Sep 27, 10:54 pm | 1st | Capricorn | Graft or bud plants. Trim to increase growth. |
| Sep 27, 10:54 pm–<br>Sep 30, 12:40 am | 2nd | Capricorn | Graft or bud plants. Trim to increase growth. |

Add a new flavor to your jam routine this year with cinnamon rhubarb jam. You can search the Internet for recipes that are suitable for fresh use, freezer storage, or water bath canning. Like most rhubarb foods, this isn't a low-sugar option, but it does have a wonderful flavor that brings to mind summer and fall.

_____

_____

_____

◑

*September 27*
*10:54 pm EDT*

SEPTEMBER

| S | M | T | W | T | F | S |
|---|---|---|---|---|---|---|
|   |   |   |   |   | 1 | 2 |
| 3 | 4 | 5 | 6 | 7 | 8 | 9 |
| 10 | 11 | 12 | 13 | 14 | 15 | 16 |
| 17 | 18 | 19 | 20 | 21 | 22 | 23 |
| 24 | 25 | 26 | 27 | 28 | 29 | 30 |

# October ⚊

## October 1–7

*No accident ever comes late; it always arrives precisely on
time.*
~MARK TWAIN

| Date | Qtr. | Sign | Activity |
|------|------|------|----------|
| Oct 2, 10:26 am–<br>Oct 4, 4:40 pm | 2nd | Pisces | Plant grains, leafy annuals. Fertilize (chemical). Graft or bud plants. Irrigate. Trim to increase growth. |
| Oct 5, 2:40 pm–<br>Oct 6, 7:56 pm | 3rd | Aries | Cultivate. Destroy weeds and pests. Harvest fruits and root crops for food. Trim to retard growth. |
| Oct 6, 7:56 pm–<br>Oct 8, 9:44 pm | 3rd | Taurus | Plant potatoes and tubers. Trim to retard growth. |

There's always dog food right in your kitchen cupboards. Substitute or supplement your dog's food with canned tuna or sardines and fresh or previously frozen vegetables. Make instant oatmeal and offer a half a cup with two hard-boiled eggs. Before feeding these foods as a complete meal, introduce one at a time in small portions with your pet's usual food. When traveling, scrambled eggs and plain yogurt are available at convenience stores and diners for feeding on the go.

○
*October 5*
*2:40 pm EDT*

OCTOBER

| S | M | T | W | T | F | S |
|---|---|---|---|---|---|---|
| 1 | 2 | 3 | 4 | 5 | 6 | 7 |
| 8 | 9 | 10 | 11 | 12 | 13 | 14 |
| 15 | 16 | 17 | 18 | 19 | 20 | 21 |
| 22 | 23 | 24 | 25 | 26 | 27 | 28 |
| 29 | 30 | 31 | | | | |

# ♎ October 8–14

*Eggs and oaths are easily broken.*      ~DANISH PROVERB

| Date | Qtr. | Sign | Activity |
|---|---|---|---|
| Oct 6, 7:56 pm–<br>Oct 8, 9:44 pm | 3rd | Taurus | Plant potatoes and tubers. Trim to retard growth. |
| Oct 8, 9:44 pm–<br>Oct 10, 11:38 pm | 3rd | Gemini | Cultivate. Destroy weeds and pests. Harvest fruits and root crops for food. Trim to retard growth. |
| Oct 10, 11:38 pm–<br>Oct 12, 8:25 am | 3rd | Cancer | Plant biennials, perennials, bulbs, and roots. Prune. Irrigate. Fertilize (organic). |
| Oct 12, 8:25 am–<br>Oct 13, 2:41 am | 4th | Cancer | Plant biennials, perennials, bulbs, and roots. Prune. Irrigate. Fertilize (organic). |
| Oct 13, 2:41 am–<br>Oct 15, 7:19 am | 4th | Leo | Cultivate. Destroy weeds and pests. Harvest fruits and root crops for food. Trim to retard growth. |

Shitali breath has a cool quality that helps balance the over-heated body or mind. Shape your tongue like a taco shell and inhale over the tongue. Count to six as each smooth breath flows in like liquid through a straw. Relax the tongue and exhale slowly through your nose. As the inhale is like water, the exhale is like vapor. Take several cycles of breath to cool down physically or emotionally.

_____

_____

_____

◑
*October 12*
*8:25 am EDT*

OCTOBER

| S | M | T | W | T | F | S |
|---|---|---|---|---|---|---|
| 1 | 2 | 3 | 4 | 5 | 6 | 7 |
| 8 | 9 | 10 | 11 | 12 | 13 | 14 |
| 15 | 16 | 17 | 18 | 19 | 20 | 21 |
| 22 | 23 | 24 | 25 | 26 | 27 | 28 |
| 29 | 30 | 31 | | | | |

# October 15–21 ♎

*Life is much too important a thing ever to talk seriously about it.*

                              ~OSCAR WILDE

| Date | Qtr. | Sign | Activity |
|------|------|------|----------|
| Oct 13, 2:41 am–<br>Oct 15, 7:19 am | 4th | Leo | Cultivate. Destroy weeds and pests. Harvest fruits and root crops for food. Trim to retard growth. |
| Oct 15, 7:19 am–<br>Oct 17, 1:35 pm | 4th | Virgo | Cultivate, especially medicinal plants. Destroy weeds and pests. Trim to retard growth. |
| Oct 19, 3:12 pm–<br>Oct 19, 9:41 pm | 1st | Libra | Plant annuals for fragrance and beauty. Trim to increase growth. |
| Oct 19, 9:41 pm–<br>Oct 22, 7:57 am | 1st | Scorpio | Plant grains, leafy annuals. Fertilize (chemical). Graft or bud plants. Irrigate. Trim to increase growth. |

Use sound vibrations to clear and heal your living or work space. Along with playing music you love, have chimes, bells, tambourines, a xylophone, or tuning forks available for easy attunements throughout the day. Explore the healing vibrations of *solfreggio* tuning forks and any recorded music available online. Let sound resonate in your space after intense interactions, since sound helps break up any residue from emotional events.

October 19
3:12 pm EDT

OCTOBER

| S | M | T | W | T | F | S |
|---|---|---|---|---|---|---|
| 1 | 2 | 3 | 4 | 5 | 6 | 7 |
| 8 | 9 | 10 | 11 | 12 | 13 | 14 |
| 15 | 16 | 17 | 18 | 19 | 20 | 21 |
| 22 | 23 | 24 | 25 | 26 | 27 | 28 |
| 29 | 30 | 31 | | | | |

# ♎ October 22–28

*Imagination is the beginning of creation. You imagine what you desire, you will what you imagine; and at last you create what you will.*    ～ GEORGE BERNARD SHAW

| Date | Qtr. | Sign | Activity |
|---|---|---|---|
| Oct 19, 9:41 pm–<br>Oct 22, 7:57 am | 1st | Scorpio | Plant grains, leafy annuals. Fertilize (chemical). Graft or bud plants. Irrigate. Trim to increase growth. |
| Oct 24, 8:12 pm–<br>Oct 27, 8:59 am | 1st | Capricorn | Graft or bud plants. Trim to increase growth. |

Wild roses offer both blooms and fruit. *Rosa rugosa*, which grows in shades of pink and white, blooms effortlessly in areas where other roses may be temperamental. Its vigorous growth habit makes impenetrable hedges, filled with color year-round. Flowers are prolific in spring and summer, and the hips add color in the colder months. Both of these are edible and valued by the home-brewer as well as canners and bakers.

_____

_____

_____

_____

◗

*October 27*
*6:22 pm EDT*

OCTOBER

| S | M | T | W | T | F | S |
|---|---|---|---|---|---|---|
|  | 1 | 2 | 3 | 4 | 5 | 6 | 7 |
| 8 | 9 | 10 | 11 | 12 | 13 | 14 |
| 15 | 16 | 17 | 18 | 19 | 20 | 21 |
| 22 | 23 | 24 | 25 | 26 | 27 | 28 |
| 29 | 30 | 31 |  |  |  |  |

# November ♏

## October 29–November 4

*For poems are like rainbows; they escape you quickly.*

~ LANGSTON HUGHES

| Date | Qtr. | Sign | Activity |
|------|------|------|----------|
| Oct 29, 7:46 pm–<br>Nov 1, 2:43 am | 2nd | Pisces | Plant grains, leafy annuals. Fertilize (chemical). Graft or bud plants. Irrigate. Trim to increase growth. |
| Nov 3, 5:46 am–<br>Nov 4, 1:23 am | 2nd | Taurus | Plant annuals for hardiness. Trim to increase growth. |
| Nov 4, 1:23 am–<br>Nov 5, 5:26 am | 3rd | Taurus | Plant potatoes and tubers. Trim to retard growth. |

Canners, rejoice! The maker of Ball and Kerr canning lids no longer recommends heating jar lids prior to processing. Years ago, lids were made using latex, which did need to be heated in order to soften and seal correctly, but this is no longer the case. If your recipe calls for processing longer than 10 minutes, you can also skip the step of boiling jars to sterilize them before filling.

○
*November 4*
*1:23 am EDT*

NOVEMBER

| S | M | T | W | T | F | S |
|---|---|---|---|---|---|---|
|   |   |   | 1 | 2 | 3 | 4 |
| 5 | 6 | 7 | 8 | 9 | 10 | 11 |
| 12 | 13 | 14 | 15 | 16 | 17 | 18 |
| 19 | 20 | 21 | 22 | 23 | 24 | 25 |
| 26 | 27 | 28 | 29 | 30 |   |   |

# ♏ November 5–11

*A writer is somebody for whom writing is more difficult than*
*it is for other people.*                              ~THOMAS MANN

| Date | Qtr. | Sign | Activity |
|------|------|------|----------|
| Nov 4, 1:23 am–<br>Nov 5, 5:26 am | 3rd | Taurus | Plant potatoes and tubers. Trim to retard growth. |
| Nov 5, 5:26 am–<br>Nov 7, 5:45 am | 3rd | Gemini | Cultivate. Destroy weeds and pests. Harvest fruits and root crops for food. Trim to retard growth. |
| Nov 7, 5:45 am–<br>Nov 9, 7:29 am | 3rd | Cancer | Plant biennials, perennials, bulbs, and roots. Prune. Irrigate. Fertilize (organic). |
| Nov 9, 7:29 am–<br>Nov 10, 3:36 pm | 3rd | Leo | Cultivate. Destroy weeds and pests. Harvest fruits and root crops for food. Trim to retard growth. |
| Nov 10, 3:36 pm–<br>Nov 11, 11:41 am | 4th | Leo | Cultivate. Destroy weeds and pests. Harvest fruits and root crops for food. Trim to retard growth. |
| Nov 11, 11:41 am–<br>Nov 13, 6:26 pm | 4th | Virgo | Cultivate, especially medicinal plants. Destroy weeds and pests. Trim to retard growth. |

Remember that wrapping tissue that is perfectly intact but still ends up in the trash after a birthday or holiday? Save that wrinkled tissue paper for wrapping up knickknacks or as cushioning in boxes when the time comes to move or transport those belongings.

*Daylight Saving Time*
*ends November 5, 2:00 am*

◖

*November 10, 3:36 pm EST*

### NOVEMBER

| S | M | T | W | T | F | S |
|---|---|---|---|---|---|---|
|   |   |   | 1 | 2 | 3 | 4 |
| 5 | 6 | 7 | 8 | 9 | 10 | 11 |
| 12 | 13 | 14 | 15 | 16 | 17 | 18 |
| 19 | 20 | 21 | 22 | 23 | 24 | 25 |
| 26 | 27 | 28 | 29 | 30 |   |   |

2016 © marilyna Image from BigStockPhoto.com

# November 12–18 ♏

*We live on this speck called Earth—think about what you might do, today or tomorrow—and make the most of it.*

~Neil deGrasse Tyson

| Date | Qtr. | Sign | Activity |
|------|------|------|----------|
| Nov 11, 11:41 am–<br>Nov 13, 6:26 pm | 4th | Virgo | Cultivate, especially medicinal plants. Destroy weeds and pests. Trim to retard growth. |
| Nov 16, 3:19 am–<br>Nov 18, 6:42 am | 4th | Scorpio | Plant biennials, perennials, bulbs, and roots. Prune. Irrigate. Fertilize (organic). |
| Nov 18, 6:42 am–<br>Nov 18, 1:59 pm | 1st | Scorpio | Plant grains, leafy annuals. Fertilize (chemical). Graft or bud plants. Irrigate. Trim to increase growth. |

Color is important to the mood created in the bedroom for both intimacy and sleep. Avoid too much heat, such as orange or red, since hot colors seep in and disrupt sleep patterns, even in the dark. To attract love into your life, add pink, Venus's color for romance and relationship. Green also resonates with fertility, abundance, and the heart. Both colors are calming and encourage restful sleep.

2016 © Kasia Bialasiewicz Image from BigStockPhoto.com

●

*November 18*
*6:42 am EST*

### November

| S | M | T | W | T | F | S |
|---|---|---|---|---|---|---|
|   |   |   | 1 | 2 | 3 | 4 |
| 5 | 6 | 7 | 8 | 9 | 10 | 11 |
| 12 | 13 | 14 | 15 | 16 | 17 | 18 |
| 19 | 20 | 21 | 22 | 23 | 24 | 25 |
| 26 | 27 | 28 | 29 | 30 |   |   |

# ♏ November 19–25

*We choose our joys and sorrows long before we experience them.*                    ~KHALIL GIBRAN

| Date | Qtr. | Sign | Activity |
|------|------|------|----------|
| Nov 21, 2:14 am–<br>Nov 23, 3:14 pm | 1st | Capricorn | Graft or bud plants. Trim to increase growth. |

Try growing a few culinary herbs in your garden and discover the magic they create in everything from salads and smoothies to roast chicken or steamed vegetables. If you can't grow from seed, purchase young plants such as parsley, marjoram, thyme, and basil from your local nursery and plant them among flowers or vegetables. Dry them on screens in a warm place in front of a small fan, in an oven on the lowest setting and with the door open, or in a simple dehydrator. Crumble the leaves into a glass jar and cover tightly. Sprinkle on your favorite dishes and enjoy!

_____

_____

_____

_____

### NOVEMBER

| S | M | T | W | T | F | S |
|---|---|---|---|---|---|---|
|   |   |   | 1 | 2 | 3 | 4 |
| 5 | 6 | 7 | 8 | 9 | 10 | 11 |
| 12 | 13 | 14 | 15 | 16 | 17 | 18 |
| 19 | 20 | 21 | 22 | 23 | 24 | 25 |
| 26 | 27 | 28 | 29 | 30 |   |   |

2016 © Geo-grafika Image from BigStockPhoto.com

# December
## November 26–December 2

*Anything can make me stop and look and wonder, and*
*sometimes learn.*  ~KURT VONNEGUT

| Date | Qtr. | Sign | Activity |
|---|---|---|---|
| Nov 26, 3:04 am–<br>Nov 26, 12:03 pm | 1st | Pisces | Plant grains, leafy annuals. Fertilize (chemical). Graft or bud plants. Irrigate. Trim to increase growth. |
| Nov 26, 12:03 pm–<br>Nov 28, 11:30 am | 2nd | Pisces | Plant grains, leafy annuals. Fertilize (chemical). Graft or bud plants. Irrigate. Trim to increase growth. |
| Nov 30, 3:38 pm–<br>Dec 2, 4:21 pm | 2nd | Taurus | Plant annuals for hardiness. Trim to increase growth. |

The humble onion isn't just for culinary delights! An onion cut in half and placed under sink drains can help to collect negativity. Remember to change it every couple of weeks—the New and the Full Moons are a timely reminder! Half an onion rubbed on the skin is said to help to draw out illness, while ritual blades passed over half an onion will be purified.

*November 26*
*12:03 pm EST*

DECEMBER

| S | M | T | W | T | F | S |
|---|---|---|---|---|---|---|
| | | | | | 1 | 2 |
| 3 | 4 | 5 | 6 | 7 | 8 | 9 |
| 10 | 11 | 12 | 13 | 14 | 15 | 16 |
| 17 | 18 | 19 | 20 | 21 | 22 | 23 |
| 24 | 25 | 26 | 27 | 28 | 29 | 30 |
| 31 | | | | | | |

2016 © Odua Images Image from BigStockPhoto.com

# December 3–9

*How very little can be done under the spirit of fear.*

~FLORENCE NIGHTINGALE

| Date | Qtr. | Sign | Activity |
|------|------|------|----------|
| Dec 3, 10:47 am–<br>Dec 4, 3:37 pm | 3rd | Gemini | Cultivate. Destroy weeds and pests. Harvest fruits and root crops for food. Trim to retard growth. |
| Dec 4, 3:37 pm–<br>Dec 6, 3:37 pm | 3rd | Cancer | Plant biennials, perennials, bulbs, and roots. Prune. Irrigate. Fertilize (organic). |
| Dec 6, 3:37 pm–<br>Dec 8, 6:09 pm | 3rd | Leo | Cultivate. Destroy weeds and pests. Harvest fruits and root crops for food. Trim to retard growth. |
| Dec 8, 6:09 pm–<br>Dec 10, 2:51 am | 3rd | Virgo | Cultivate, especially medicinal plants. Destroy weeds and pests. Trim to retard growth. |

To stay hydrated longer, add chia seeds to your water or cool tea. These tiny seeds expand in liquid and take on a gelatinous consistency that may take time to adjust to. The benefits outweigh the texture since chia prolongs hydration and helps prevent muscle cramping during exercise in the heat and humidity. Chia seeds are also considered safe for kids and pregnant women.

_____

_____

_____

○
*December 3*
*10:47 am EST*

DECEMBER

| S | M | T | W | T | F | S |
|---|---|---|---|---|---|---|
|   |   |   |   |   | 1 | 2 |
| 3 | 4 | 5 | 6 | 7 | 8 | 9 |
| 10 | 11 | 12 | 13 | 14 | 15 | 16 |
| 17 | 18 | 19 | 20 | 21 | 22 | 23 |
| 24 | 25 | 26 | 27 | 28 | 29 | 30 |
| 31 |   |   |   |   |   |   |

2016 © Ildi Papp Image from BigStockPhoto.com

# December 10–16 ↗

*Honesty is the first chapter in the book of wisdom.*

~THOMAS JEFFERSON

| Date | Qtr. | Sign | Activity |
|------|------|------|----------|
| Dec 8, 6:09 pm–<br>Dec 10, 2:51 am | 3rd | Virgo | Cultivate, especially medicinal plants. Destroy weeds and pests. Trim to retard growth. |
| Dec 10, 2:51 am–<br>Dec 11, 12:01 am | 4th | Virgo | Cultivate, especially medicinal plants. Destroy weeds and pests. Trim to retard growth. |
| Dec 13, 8:59 am–<br>Dec 15, 8:07 pm | 4th | Scorpio | Plant biennials, perennials, bulbs, and roots. Prune. Irrigate. Fertilize (organic). |
| Dec 15, 8:07 pm–<br>Dec 18, 1:30 am | 4th | Sagittarius | Cultivate. Destroy weeds and pests. Harvest fruits and root crops for food. Trim to retard growth |

Plant garlic in with fruit trees, roses, cabbage, and tomatoes. It will help to deter beetles and aphids. Garlic can also be applied topically in a spray. Crush an entire bulb of garlic and soak it in half a gallon of water overnight. Add a teaspoon of environmentally friendly dishwashing liquid (to help it stick), and spray onto plants to deter beetles, moths, and aphids. Repeat twice a week and after it rains.

2016 © Ovidiu David Image from BigStockPhoto.com

◐

*December 10*
*2:51 am EST*

DECEMBER

| S | M | T | W | T | F | S |
|---|---|---|---|---|---|---|
|   |   |   |   |   | 1 | 2 |
| 3 | 4 | 5 | 6 | 7 | 8 | 9 |
| 10 | 11 | 12 | 13 | 14 | 15 | 16 |
| 17 | 18 | 19 | 20 | 21 | 22 | 23 |
| 24 | 25 | 26 | 27 | 28 | 29 | 30 |
| 31 |   |   |   |   |   |   |

## December 17–23

*I would rather dance as a ballerina, though faultily, than as a flawless clown.*
                                              ~Margaret Atwood

| Date | Qtr. | Sign | Activity |
|------|------|------|----------|
| Dec 15, 8:07 pm–<br>Dec 18, 1:30 am | 4th | Sagittarius | Cultivate. Destroy weeds and pests. Harvest fruits and root crops for food. Trim to retard growth. |
| Dec 18, 8:33 am–<br>Dec 20, 9:29 pm | 1st | Capricorn | Graft or bud plants. Trim to increase growth. |
| Dec 23, 9:42 am–<br>Dec 25, 7:27 pm | 1st | Pisces | Plant grains, leafy annuals. Fertilize (chemical). Graft or bud plants. Irrigate. Trim to increase growth. |

Decluttering can give you a fresh feeling even in the darkest days of winter. Bring one paper grocery bag to your dresser or closet. Pick out items that are in good condition but no longer suit your taste or flatter your figure, not to mention items where you have multiples. Once you've filled your bag, stop! If you are still in a purging mood tomorrow, do another bag. Starting slowly means you're less likely to burn out and quit before you've even gotten to your excess kitchen items.

December 18
1:30 am EST

### DECEMBER

| S | M | T | W | T | F | S |
|---|---|---|---|---|---|---|
|   |   |   |   |   | 1 | 2 |
| 3 | 4 | 5 | 6 | 7 | 8 | 9 |
| 10 | 11 | 12 | 13 | 14 | 15 | 16 |
| 17 | 18 | 19 | 20 | 21 | 22 | 23 |
| 24 | 25 | 26 | 27 | 28 | 29 | 30 |
| 31 |   |   |   |   |   |   |

# December 24–30 ♑

*A mill cannot grind with water that is past.*

~Proverb

| Date | Qtr. | Sign | Activity |
|------|------|------|----------|
| Dec 23, 9:42 am– Dec 25, 7:27 pm | 1st | Pisces | Plant grains, leafy annuals. Fertilize (chemical). Graft or bud plants. Irrigate. Trim to increase growth. |
| Dec 28, 1:23 am– Dec 30, 3:31 am | 2nd | Taurus | Plant annuals for hardiness. Trim to increase growth. |

During the holidays, fill your home with good smells—but not the kind that lead to overeating and weight gain. Buy candles that give off a lavender or apple-cinnamon smell, potpourri that has been infused with Nag Champa or evergreen scents, or incense sticks that fill your space with sandalwood. You could also buy an infuser and then choose from a number of essential oils that heal and soothe and add wonderful aromas.

◖

*December 26*
*4:20 am EST*

DECEMBER

| S | M | T | W | T | F | S |
|---|---|---|---|---|---|---|
|   |   |   |   |   | 1 | 2 |
| 3 | 4 | 5 | 6 | 7 | 8 | 9 |
| 10 | 11 | 12 | 13 | 14 | 15 | 16 |
| 17 | 18 | 19 | 20 | 21 | 22 | 23 |
| 24 | 25 | 26 | 27 | 28 | 29 | 30 |
| 31 |   |   |   |   |   |   |

2016 © pyansetia2008 Image from BigStockPhoto.com

# ♑ December 31–January 6, 2018

*You gain strength, courage and confidence by every*
*experience in which you really stop to look fear in the face.*

~ELEANOR ROOSEVELT

| Date | Qtr. | Sign | Activity |
|------|------|------|----------|
| Jan 1, 9:24 pm–<br>Jan 3, 2:23 am | 3rd | Cancer | Plant biennials, perennials, bulbs, and roots. Prune. Irrigate. Fertilize (organic). |
| Jan 3, 2:23 am–<br>Jan 5, 3:12 am | 3rd | Leo | Cultivate. Destroy weeds and pests. Harvest fruits and root crops for food. Trim to retard growth. |
| Jan 5, 3:12 am–<br>Jan 7, 7:15 am | 3rd | Virgo | Cultivate, especially medicinal plants. Destroy weeds and pests. Trim to retard growth. |

If you live in a climate where snow falls regularly during the winter, shoveling heavy snow can become a big problem. Instead of investing in a fancy shovel, consider using an old broom laying around in the garage to clear off snow from porches or decks. This method even works well for clearing off the windshields and roofs of cars, saving time and energy. The motion of sweeping can replace the strain from repeated shoveling of snow.

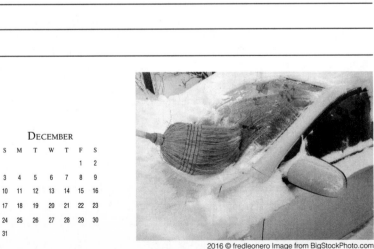

DECEMBER

| S | M | T | W | T | F | S |
|---|---|---|---|---|---|---|
|   |   |   |   |   | 1 | 2 |
| 3 | 4 | 5 | 6 | 7 | 8 | 9 |
| 10 | 11 | 12 | 13 | 14 | 15 | 16 |
| 17 | 18 | 19 | 20 | 21 | 22 | 23 |
| 24 | 25 | 26 | 27 | 28 | 29 | 30 |
| 31 |   |   |   |   |   |   |

2016 © fredleonero Image from BigStockPhoto.com

# Gardening by the Moon

Today, people often reject the notion of gardening according to the Moon's phase and sign. The usual nonbeliever is not a scientist but the city dweller who has never had any real contact with nature and little experience of natural rhythms.

Camille Flammarion, the French astronomer, testifies to the success of Moon planting, though:

"Cucumbers increase at Full Moon, as well as radishes, turnips, leeks, lilies, horseradish, and saffron; onions, on the contrary, are much larger and better nourished during the decline and old age of the Moon than at its increase, during its youth and fullness, which is the reason the Egyptians abstained from onions, on account of their antipathy to the Moon. Herbs gathered while the Moon increases are of great efficiency. If the vines are trimmed at night when the Moon is in the sign of the Lion, Sagittarius, the Scorpion, or the Bull, it will save them from field rats, moles, snails, flies, and other animals."

Dr. Clark Timmins is one of the few modern scientists to have conducted tests in Moon planting. Following is a summary of his experiments:

**Beets:** When sown with the Moon in Scorpio, the germination rate was 71 percent; when sown in Sagittarius, the germination rate was 58 percent.

**Scotch marigold:** When sown with the Moon in Cancer, the germination rate was 90 percent; when sown in Leo, the rate was 32 percent.

**Carrots:** When sown with the Moon in Scorpio, the germination rate was 64 percent; when sown with the Moon in Sagittarius, the germination rate was 47 percent.

**Tomatoes:** When sown with the Moon in Cancer, the germination rate was 90 percent; but when sown with the Moon in Leo, the germination rate was 58 percent.

Two things should be emphasized. First, remember that this is only a summary of the results of the experiments; the experiments themselves were conducted in a scientific manner to eliminate any variation in soil, temperature, moisture, and so on, so that only the Moon sign is varied. Second, note that these astonishing results were obtained without regard to the phase of the Moon—the other factor we use in Moon planting, and which presumably would have increased the differential in germination rates.

Dr. Timmins also tried transplanting Cancer- and Leo-planted tomato seedlings while the Cancer Moon was waxing. The result was 100 percent survival. When transplanting was done with the waning Sagittarius Moon, there was 0 percent survival. Dr. Timmins's tests show that the Cancer-planted tomatoes had blossoms twelve days earlier than those planted under Leo; the Cancer-planted tomatoes had an average height of twenty inches at that time compared to fifteen inches for the Leo-planted; the first ripe tomatoes were gathered from the Cancer plantings eleven days ahead of the Leo plantings; and a count of the hanging fruit and its size and weight shows an advantage to the Cancer plants over the Leo plants of 45 percent.

Dr. Timmins also observed that there have been similar tests that did not indicate results favorable to the Moon planting theory. As a scientist, he asked why one set of experiments indicated a positive verification of Moon planting, and others did not. He checked these other tests and found that the experimenters had not followed the geocentric system for determining the Moon sign positions, but the heliocentric. When the times used in these other tests were converted to the geocentric system, the dates chosen often were found to be in barren, rather than fertile, signs. Without going into a technical explanation, it is sufficient to point out that geocentric and heliocentric positions often vary by as much as four days. This is a large enough differential to place the Moon in Cancer, for example, in the heliocentric system, and at the same time in Leo by the geocentric system.

Most almanacs and calendars show the Moon's signs heliocentrically—and thus incorrectly for Moon planting—while the *Moon Sign Book* is calculated correctly for planting purposes, using the geocentric system. Some readers are confused because the *Moon Sign Book* talks about first, second, third, and fourth quarters, while other almanacs refer to these same divisions as New Moon, first quarter, Full Moon, and fourth quarter. Thus the almanacs say first quarter when the *Moon Sign Book* says second quarter.

There is nothing complicated about using astrology in agriculture and horticulture in order to increase both pleasure and profit, but there is one very important rule that is often neglected—use common sense! Of course this is one rule that should be remembered in every activity we undertake, but in the case of gardening and farming by the Moon, if it is not possible to use the best dates for planting or harvesting, we must select the next best and just try to do the best we can.

This brings up the matter of the other factors to consider in your gardening work. The dates we give as best for a certain activity apply to the entire country (with slight time correction), but in your section of the country you may be buried under three feet of snow on a date we say is good to plant your flowers. So we have factors of weather, season, temperature, and moisture variations, soil conditions, your own available time and opportunity, and so forth. Some astrologers like to think it is all a matter of science, but gardening is also an art. In art, you develop an instinctive identification with your work and influence it with your feelings and wishes.

The *Moon Sign Book* gives you the place of the Moon for every day of the year so that you can select the best times once you have become familiar with the rules and practices of lunar agriculture. We give you specific, easy-to-follow directions so that you can get right down to work.

We give you the best dates for planting, and also for various related activities, including cultivation, fertilizing, harvesting, irrigation, and getting rid of weeds and pests. But we cannot tell you exactly when it's good to plant. Many of these rules were learned by observation and experience; as the body of experience grew, we could see various patterns emerging that allowed us to make judgments about new things. That's what you should do, too. After you have worked with lunar agriculture for a while and have gained a working knowledge, you will probably begin to try new things—and we hope you will share your experiments and findings with us. That's how the science grows.

Here's an example of what we mean. Years ago Llewellyn George suggested we try to combine our bits of knowledge about what to expect in planting under each of the Moon signs in order to benefit from several lunar factors in one plant. From this came our rule for developing "thoroughbred seed." To develop thoroughbred seed, save the seed for three successive years from plants grown by the correct Moon sign and phase. You can plant in the first quarter phase and in the sign of Cancer for fruitfulness; the second year, plant seeds from the first year plants in Libra for beauty; and in the third year, plant the seeds from the second year plants in Taurus to produce hardiness. In a similar manner you can combine the fruitfulness of Cancer, the good root growth of Pisces, and the sturdiness and good vine growth of Scorpio. And don't forget the characteristics of Capricorn: hardy like Taurus, but drier and perhaps more resistant to drought and disease.

Unlike common almanacs, we consider both the Moon's phase and the Moon's sign in making our calculations for the proper timing of our work. It is perhaps a little easier to understand this if we remind you that we are all living in the center of a vast electromagnetic field that is Earth and its environment in space. Everything that occurs within this electromagnetic field has an effect on everything else within the field. The Moon and the Sun are the most important of the factors affecting the life of Earth, and it is their relative positions to Earth that we project for each day of the year.

Many people claim that not only do they achieve larger crops gardening by the Moon, but that their fruits and vegetables are much tastier. A number of organic gardeners have also become lunar gardeners using the natural rhythm of life forces that we experience through the relative movements of the Sun and Moon. We provide a few basic rules and then give you day-by-day guidance for your gardening work. You will be able to choose the best dates to meet your own needs and opportunities.

## Planting by the Moon's Phases

During the increasing or waxing light—from New Moon to Full Moon—plant annuals that produce their yield above the ground. An annual is a plant that completes its entire life cycle within one growing season and has to be seeded each year. During the decreasing or waning light—from Full Moon to New Moon—plant biennials, perennials, and bulb and root plants. Biennials include crops that are planted one season to winter over and produce crops the next, such as winter wheat. Perennials and bulb and root plants include all plants that grow from the same root each year.

A simpler, less-accurate rule is to plant crops that produce above the ground during the waxing Moon, and to plant crops that produce below the ground during the waning Moon. Thus the old adage, "Plant potatoes during the dark of the Moon." Llewellyn George's system divided the lunar month into quarters. The first two from New Moon to Full Moon are the first and second quarters, and the last two from Full Moon to New Moon the third and fourth quarters. Using these divisions, we can increase our accuracy in timing our efforts to coincide with natural forces.

## First Quarter

Plant annuals producing their yield above the ground, which are generally of the leafy kind that produce their seed outside the fruit. Some examples are asparagus, broccoli, brussels sprouts, cabbage, cauliflower, celery, cress, endive, kohlrabi, lettuce, parsley, and spinach. Cucumbers are an exception, as they do best in the first quarter rather than the second, even though the seeds are inside the fruit. Also plant cereals and grains.

## Second Quarter

Plant annuals producing their yield above the ground, which are generally of the viney kind that produce their seed inside the fruit. Some examples include beans, eggplant, melons, peas, peppers, pumpkins, squash, tomatoes, etc. These are not hard-and-fast divisions. If you can't plant during the first quarter, plant during the second, and vice versa. There are many plants that seem to do equally well planted in either quarter, such as watermelon, hay, and cereals and grains.

## Third Quarter

Plant biennials, perennials, bulbs, root plants, trees, shrubs, berries, grapes, strawberries, beets, carrots, onions, parsnips, rutabagas, potatoes, radishes, peanuts, rhubarb, turnips, winter wheat, etc.

## Fourth Quarter

This is the best time to cultivate, turn sod, pull weeds, and destroy pests of all kinds, especially when the Moon is in Aries, Leo, Virgo, Gemini, Aquarius, and Sagittarius.

## The Moon in the Signs

### *Moon in Aries*

Barren, dry, fiery, and masculine. Use for destroying noxious weeds.

### *Moon in Taurus*

Productive, moist, earthy, and feminine. Use for planting many crops when hardiness is important, particularly root crops. Also used for lettuce, cabbage, and similar leafy vegetables.

### *Moon in Gemini*

Barren and dry, airy and masculine. Use for destroying noxious growths, weeds, and pests, and for cultivation.

### *Moon in Cancer*

Fruitful, moist, feminine. Use for planting and irrigation.

### *Moon in Leo*

Barren, dry, fiery, masculine. Use for killing weeds or cultivation.

### *Moon in Virgo*

Barren, dry, earthy, and feminine. Use for cultivation and destroying weeds and pests.

## Moon in Libra

Semi-fruitful, moist, and airy. Use for planting crops that need good pulp growth. A very good sign for flowers and vines. Also used for seeding hay, corn fodder, and the like.

## Moon in Scorpio

Very fruitful and moist, watery and feminine. Nearly as productive as Cancer; use for the same purposes. Especially good for vine growth and sturdiness.

## Moon in Sagittarius

Barren and dry, fiery and masculine. Use for planting onions, seeding hay, and for cultivation.

## Moon in Capricorn

Productive and dry, earthy and feminine. Use for planting potatoes and other tubers.

## Moon in Aquarius

Barren, dry, airy, and masculine. Use for cultivation and destroying noxious growths and pests.

## Moon in Pisces

Very fruitful, moist, watery, and feminine. Especially good for root growth.

# A Guide to Planting

| Plant | Quarter | Sign |
|-------|---------|------|
| Annuals | 1st or 2nd | |
| Apple tree | 2nd or 3rd | Cancer, Pisces, Virgo |
| Artichoke | 1st | Cancer, Pisces |
| Asparagus | 1st | Cancer, Scorpio, Pisces |
| Aster | 1st or 2nd | Virgo, Libra |
| Barley | 1st or 2nd | Cancer, Pisces, Libra, Capricorn, Virgo |
| Beans (bush & pole) | 2nd | Cancer, Taurus, Pisces, Libra |
| Beans (kidney, white & navy) | 1st or 2nd | Cancer, Pisces |
| Beech tree | 2nd or 3rd | Virgo, Taurus |
| Beets | 3rd | Cancer, Capricorn, Pisces, Libra |
| Biennials | 3rd or 4th | |
| Broccoli | 1st | Cancer, Scorpio, Pisces, Libra |
| Brussels sprouts | 1st | Cancer, Scorpio, Pisces, Libra |
| Buckwheat | 1st or 2nd | Capricorn |
| Bulbs | 3rd | Cancer, Scorpio, Pisces |
| Bulbs for seed | 2nd or 3rd | |
| Cabbage | 1st | Cancer, Scorpio, Pisces, Taurus, Libra |
| Canes (raspberry, blackberry & gooseberry) | 2nd | Cancer, Scorpio, Pisces |
| Cantaloupe | 1st or 2nd | Cancer, Scorpio, Pisces, Taurus, Libra |
| Carrots | 3rd | Cancer, Scorpio, Pisces, Taurus, Libra |
| Cauliflower | 1st | Cancer, Scorpio, Pisces, Libra |
| Celeriac | 3rd | Cancer, Scorpio, Pisces |
| Celery | 1st | Cancer, Scorpio, Pisces |
| Cereals | 1st or 2nd | Cancer, Scorpio, Pisces, Libra |
| Chard | 1st or 2nd | Cancer, Scorpio, Pisces |
| Chicory | 2nd or 3rd | Cancer, Scorpio, Pisces |
| Chrysanthemum | 1st or 2nd | Virgo |
| Clover | 1st or 2nd | Cancer, Scorpio, Pisces |

| Plant | Quarter | Sign |
|-------|---------|------|
| Coreopsis | 2nd or 3rd | Libra |
| Corn | 1st | Cancer, Scorpio, Pisces |
| Corn for fodder | 1st or 2nd | Libra |
| Cosmos | 2nd or 3rd | Libra |
| Cress | 1st | Cancer, Scorpio, Pisces |
| Crocus | 1st or 2nd | Virgo |
| Cucumber | 1st | Cancer, Scorpio, Pisces |
| Daffodil | 1st or 2nd | Libra, Virgo |
| Dahlia | 1st or 2nd | Libra, Virgo |
| Deciduous trees | 2nd or 3rd | Cancer, Scorpio, Pisces, Virgo, Libra |
| Eggplant | 2nd | Cancer, Scorpio, Pisces, Libra |
| Endive | 1st | Cancer, Scorpio, Pisces, Libra |
| Flowers | 1st | Cancer, Scorpio, Pisces, Libra, Taurus, Virgo |
| Garlic | 3rd | Libra, Taurus, Pisces |
| Gladiola | 1st or 2nd | Libra, Virgo |
| Gourds | 1st or 2nd | Cancer, Scorpio, Pisces, Libra |
| Grapes | 2nd or 3rd | Cancer, Scorpio, Pisces, Virgo |
| Hay | 1st or 2nd | Cancer, Scorpio, Pisces, Libra, Taurus |
| Herbs | 1st or 2nd | Cancer, Scorpio, Pisces |
| Honeysuckle | 1st or 2nd | Scorpio, Virgo |
| Hops | 1st or 2nd | Scorpio, Libra |
| Horseradish | 1st or 2nd | Cancer, Scorpio, Pisces |
| Houseplants | 1st | Cancer, Scorpio, Pisces, Libra |
| Hyacinth | 3rd | Cancer, Scorpio, Pisces |
| Iris | 1st or 2nd | Cancer, Virgo |
| Kohlrabi | 1st or 2nd | Cancer, Scorpio, Pisces, Libra |
| Leek | 2nd or 3rd | Sagittarius |
| Lettuce | 1st | Cancer, Scorpio, Pisces, Libra, Taurus |
| Lily | 1st or 2nd | Cancer, Scorpio, Pisces |
| Maple tree | 2nd or 3rd | Taurus, Virgo, Cancer, Pisces |
| Melon | 2nd | Cancer, Scorpio, Pisces |
| Moon vine | 1st or 2nd | Virgo |

| Plant | Quarter | Sign |
|---|---|---|
| Morning glory | 1st or 2nd | Cancer, Scorpio, Pisces, Virgo |
| Oak tree | 2nd or 3rd | Taurus, Virgo, Cancer, Pisces |
| Oats | 1st or 2nd | Cancer, Scorpio, Pisces, Libra |
| Okra | 1st or 2nd | Cancer, Scorpio, Pisces, Libra |
| Onion seed | 2nd | Cancer, Scorpio, Sagittarius |
| Onion set | 3rd or 4th | Cancer, Pisces, Taurus, Libra |
| Pansies | 1st or 2nd | Cancer, Scorpio, Pisces |
| Parsley | 1st | Cancer, Scorpio, Pisces, Libra |
| Parsnip | 3rd | Cancer, Scorpio, Taurus, Capricorn |
| Peach tree | 2nd or 3rd | Cancer, Taurus, Virgo, Libra |
| Peanuts | 3rd | Cancer, Scorpio, Pisces |
| Pear tree | 2nd or 3rd | Cancer, Scorpio, Pisces, Libra |
| Peas | 2nd | Cancer, Scorpio, Pisces, Libra |
| Peony | 1st or 2nd | Virgo |
| Peppers | 2nd | Cancer, Scorpio, Pisces |
| Perennials | 3rd | |
| Petunia | 1st or 2nd | Libra, Virgo |
| Plum tree | 2nd or 3rd | Cancer, Pisces, Taurus, Virgo |
| Poppies | 1st or 2nd | Virgo |
| Portulaca | 1st or 2nd | Virgo |
| Potatoes | 3rd | Cancer, Scorpio, Libra, Taurus, Capricorn |
| Privet | 1st or 2nd | Taurus, Libra |
| Pumpkin | 2nd | Cancer, Scorpio, Pisces, Libra |
| Quince | 1st or 2nd | Capricorn |
| Radishes | 3rd | Cancer, Scorpio, Pisces, Libra, Capricorn |
| Rhubarb | 3rd | Cancer, Pisces |
| Rice | 1st or 2nd | Scorpio |
| Roses | 1st or 2nd | Cancer, Virgo |
| Rutabaga | 3rd | Cancer, Scorpio, Pisces, Taurus |
| Saffron | 1st or 2nd | Cancer, Scorpio, Pisces |
| Sage | 3rd | Cancer, Scorpio, Pisces |

| Plant | Quarter | Sign |
|-------|---------|------|
| Salsify | 1st | Cancer, Scorpio, Pisces |
| Shallot | 2nd | Scorpio |
| Spinach | 1st | Cancer, Scorpio, Pisces |
| Squash | 2nd | Cancer, Scorpio, Pisces, Libra |
| Strawberries | 3rd | Cancer, Scorpio, Pisces |
| String beans | 1st or 2nd | Taurus |
| Sunflowers | 1st or 2nd | Libra, Cancer |
| Sweet peas | 1st or 2nd | Any |
| Tomatoes | 2nd | Cancer, Scorpio, Pisces, Capricorn |
| Trees, shade | 3rd | Taurus, Capricorn |
| Trees, ornamental | 2nd | Libra, Taurus |
| Trumpet vine | 1st or 2nd | Cancer, Scorpio, Pisces |
| Tubers for seed | 3rd | Cancer, Scorpio, Pisces, Libra |
| Tulips | 1st or 2nd | Libra, Virgo |
| Turnips | 3rd | Cancer, Scorpio, Pisces, Taurus, Capricorn, Libra |
| Valerian | 1st or 2nd | Virgo, Gemini |
| Watermelon | 1st or 2nd | Cancer, Scorpio, Pisces, Libra |
| Wheat | 1st or 2nd | Cancer, Scorpio, Pisces, Libra |

# Companion Planting Guide

| Plant | Companions | Hindered by |
|---|---|---|
| Asparagus | Tomatoes, parsley, basil | None known |
| Beans | Tomatoes, carrots, cucumbers, garlic, cabbage, beets, corn | Onions, gladiolas |
| Beets | Onions, cabbage, lettuce, mint, catnip | Pole beans |
| Broccoli | Beans, celery, potatoes, onions | Tomatoes |
| Cabbage | Peppermint, sage, thyme, tomatoes | Strawberries, grapes |
| Carrots | Peas, lettuce, chives, radishes, leeks, onions, sage | Dill, anise |
| Citrus trees | Guava, live oak, rubber trees, peppers | None known |
| Corn | Potatoes, beans, peas, melon, squash, pumpkin, sunflowers, soybeans | Quack grass, wheat, straw, mulch |
| Cucumbers | Beans, cabbage, radishes, sunflowers, lettuce, broccoli, squash | Aromatic herbs |
| Eggplant | Green beans, lettuce, kale | None known |
| Grapes | Peas, beans, blackberries | Cabbage, radishes |
| Melons | Corn, peas | Potatoes, gourds |
| Onions, leeks | Beets, chamomile, carrots, lettuce | Peas, beans, sage |
| Parsnip | Peas | None known |
| Peas | Radishes, carrots, corn, cucumbers, beans, tomatoes, spinach, turnips | Onion, garlic |
| Potatoes | Beans, corn, peas, cabbage, hemp, cucumbers, eggplant, catnip | Raspberries, pumpkins, tomatoes, sunflowers |
| Radishes | Peas, lettuce, nasturtiums, cucumbers | Hyssop |
| Spinach | Strawberries | None known |
| Squash/Pumpkin | Nasturtiums, corn, mint, catnip | Potatoes |
| Tomatoes | Asparagus, parsley, chives, onions, carrots, marigolds, nasturtiums, dill | Black walnut roots, fennel, potatoes |
| Turnips | Peas, beans, brussels sprouts | Potatoes |

| Plant | Companions | Uses |
|---|---|---|
| Anise | Coriander | Flavor candy, pastry, cheeses, cookies |
| Basil | Tomatoes | Dislikes rue; repels flies and mosquitoes |
| Borage | Tomatoes, squash | Use in teas |
| Buttercup | Clover | Hinders delphinium, peonies, monkshood, columbine |
| Catnip | | Repels flea beetles |
| Chamomile | Peppermint, wheat, onions, cabbage | Roman chamomile may control damping-off disease; use in herbal sprays |
| Chervil | Radishes | Good in soups and other dishes |
| Chives | Carrots | Use in spray to deter black spot on roses |
| Coriander | Plant anywhere | Hinders seed formation in fennel |
| Cosmos | | Repels corn earworms |
| Dill | Cabbage | Hinders carrots and tomatoes |
| Fennel | Plant in borders | Disliked by all garden plants |
| Horseradish | | Repels potato bugs |
| Horsetail | | Makes fungicide spray |
| Hyssop | | Attracts cabbage flies; harmful to radishes |
| Lavender | Plant anywhere | Use in spray to control insects on cotton, repels clothes moths |
| Lovage | | Lures horn worms away from tomatoes |
| Marigolds | | Pest repellent; use against Mexican bean beetles and nematodes |
| Mint | Cabbage, tomatoes | Repels ants, flea beetles, cabbage worm butterflies |
| Morning glory | Corn | Helps melon germination |
| Nasturtium | Cabbage, cucumbers | Deters aphids, squash bugs, pumpkin beetles |
| Okra | Eggplant | Attracts leafhopper (lure insects from other plants) |
| Parsley | Tomatoes, asparagus | Freeze chopped-up leaves to flavor foods |
| Purslane | | Good ground cover |
| Rosemary | | Repels cabbage moths, bean beetles, carrot flies |
| Savory | | Plant with onions for added sweetness |
| Tansy | | Deters Japanese beetles, striped cucumber beetles, squash bugs |
| Thyme | | Repels cabbage worms |
| Yarrow | | Increases essential oils of neighbors |

# Moon Void-of-Course

*By Kim Rogers-Gallagher*

The Moon circles the Earth in about twenty-eight days, moving through each zodiac sign in two-and-a-half days. As she passes through the thirty degrees of each sign, she "visits" with the planets in numerical order, forming aspects with them. Because she moves one degree in just two to two and a half hours, her influence on each planet lasts only a few hours. She eventually reaches the planet that's in the highest degree of any sign and forms what will be her final aspect before leaving the sign. From this point until she enters the next sign, she is referred to as void-of-course.

Think of it this way: the Moon is the emotional "tone" of the day, carrying feelings with her particular to the sign she's "wearing" at the moment. After she has contacted each of the planets, she symbolically "rests" before changing her costume, so her instinct is temporarily on hold. It's during this time that many people feel "fuzzy" or "vague." Plans or decisions made now often do not pan out. Without the instinctual "knowing" the Moon provides as she touches each planet, we tend to be unrealistic or exercise poor judgment. The traditional definition of the void Moon is that "nothing will come of this." Actions initiated under a void Moon are often wasted, irrelevant, or incorrect—usually because information is hidden, missing, or has been overlooked.

Although it's not a good time to initiate plans, routine tasks seem to go along just fine. This period is ideal for reflection. On the lighter side, remember there are good uses for the void Moon. It is the period when the universe seems to be most open to loopholes. It's a great time to make plans you don't want to fulfill or schedule things you don't want to do. See the tables on pages 76–81 for a schedule of the Moon's void-of-course times.

**Last Aspect**                    **Moon Enters New Sign**

|  |  | January |  |  |
|---|---|---|---|---|
| 2 | 2:59 am | 2 | Pisces | 4:57 am |
| 4 | 11:14 am | 4 | Aries | 11:20 am |
| 6 | 1:41 pm | 6 | Taurus | 3:18 pm |
| 7 | 9:23 pm | 8 | Gemini | 5:06 pm |
| 10 | 4:38 pm | 10 | Cancer | 5:49 pm |
| 12 | 6:34 am | 12 | Leo | 7:08 pm |
| 14 | 10:17 am | 14 | Virgo | 10:52 pm |
| 17 | 1:09 am | 17 | Libra | 6:16 am |
| 19 | 3:55 am | 19 | Scorpio | 5:09 pm |
| 21 | 8:24 pm | 22 | Sagittarius | 5:45 am |
| 24 | 12:33 pm | 24 | Capricorn | 5:43 pm |
| 27 | 2:18 am | 27 | Aquarius | 3:37 am |
| 29 | 12:52 am | 29 | Pisces | 11:10 am |
| 31 | 12:36 pm | 31 | Aries | 4:46 pm |
|  |  | February |  |  |
| 2 | 11:50 am | 2 | Taurus | 8:50 pm |
| 4 | 5:42 pm | 4 | Gemini | 11:44 pm |
| 6 | 5:53 pm | 7 | Cancer | 2:03 am |
| 8 | 5:00 pm | 9 | Leo | 4:41 am |
| 11 | 12:52 am | 11 | Virgo | 8:52 am |
| 13 | 7:36 am | 13 | Libra | 3:43 pm |
| 15 | 8:54 pm | 16 | Scorpio | 1:41 am |
| 17 | 2:38 pm | 18 | Sagittarius | 1:52 pm |
| 20 | 6:37 pm | 21 | Capricorn | 2:08 am |
| 22 | 10:24 pm | 23 | Aquarius | 12:17 pm |
| 25 | 1:11 pm | 25 | Pisces | 7:24 pm |
| 27 | 6:08 pm | 27 | Aries | 11:52 pm |

## Last Aspect                    Moon Enters New Sign

|  |  | March |  |  |
|---|---|---|---|---|
| 1 | 9:18 pm | 2 | Taurus | 2:43 am |
| 3 | 10:20 am | 4 | Gemini | 5:05 am |
| 6 | 3:22 am | 6 | Cancer | 7:54 am |
| 8 | 9:59 am | 8 | Leo | 11:45 am |
| 10 | 12:06 pm | 10 | Virgo | 5:07 pm |
| 12 | 10:36 pm | 13 | Libra | 1:28 am |
| 15 | 6:05 am | 15 | Scorpio | 11:11 am |
| 17 | 5:56 pm | 17 | Sagittarius | 11:00 pm |
| 20 | 6:37 am | 20 | Capricorn | 11:31 am |
| 22 | 9:20 am | 22 | Aquarius | 10:28 pm |
| 25 | 1:56 am | 25 | Pisces | 6:06 am |
| 27 | 6:19 am | 27 | Aries | 10:11 am |
| 29 | 8:07 am | 29 | Taurus | 11:48 am |
| 30 | 7:12 pm | 31 | Gemini | 12:40 pm |
|  |  | April |  |  |
| 2 | 10:43 am | 2 | Cancer | 2:27 pm |
| 4 | 4:45 pm | 4 | Leo | 6:13 pm |
| 6 | 8:16 pm | 7 | Virgo | 12:20 am |
| 9 | 4:21 am | 9 | Libra | 8:34 am |
| 11 | 2:19 pm | 11 | Scorpio | 6:42 pm |
| 14 | 12:18 am | 14 | Sagittarius | 6:27 am |
| 16 | 2:26 pm | 16 | Capricorn | 7:05 pm |
| 19 | 5:57 am | 19 | Aquarius | 6:52 am |
| 21 | 2:23 pm | 21 | Pisces | 3:43 pm |
| 23 | 5:34 pm | 23 | Aries | 8:32 pm |
| 25 | 5:53 pm | 25 | Taurus | 9:56 pm |
| 27 | 9:18 pm | 27 | Gemini | 9:39 pm |
| 29 | 5:28 pm | 29 | Cancer | 9:48 pm |

## Last Aspect    Moon Enters New Sign

| | | | May | | |
|---|---|---|---|---|---|
| 1 | 4:23 pm | 2 | | Leo | 12:12 am |
| 4 | 12:35 am | 4 | | Virgo | 5:47 am |
| 6 | 8:42 am | 6 | | Libra | 2:20 pm |
| 8 | 6:59 pm | 9 | | Scorpio | 1:01 am |
| 10 | 5:42 pm | 11 | | Sagittarius | 12:59 pm |
| 13 | 10:14 pm | 14 | | Capricorn | 1:37 am |
| 16 | 6:22 am | 16 | | Aquarius | 1:50 pm |
| 18 | 8:33 pm | 18 | | Pisces | 11:52 pm |
| 20 | 11:39 pm | 21 | | Aries | 6:10 am |
| 23 | 2:59 am | 23 | | Taurus | 8:33 am |
| 24 | 3:08 pm | 25 | | Gemini | 8:15 am |
| 27 | 2:18 am | 27 | | Cancer | 7:25 am |
| 29 | 2:59 am | 29 | | Leo | 8:12 am |
| 31 | 7:14 am | 31 | | Virgo | 12:16 pm |
| | | | June | | |
| 2 | 5:48 pm | 2 | | Libra | 8:04 pm |
| 5 | 4:57 am | 5 | | Scorpio | 6:46 am |
| 6 | 8:35 pm | 7 | | Sagittarius | 6:59 pm |
| 10 | 2:20 am | 10 | | Capricorn | 7:36 am |
| 12 | 2:45 pm | 12 | | Aquarius | 7:45 pm |
| 15 | 1:40 am | 15 | | Pisces | 6:17 am |
| 17 | 7:33 am | 17 | | Aries | 1:55 pm |
| 19 | 3:42 pm | 19 | | Taurus | 5:53 pm |
| 21 | 12:26 am | 21 | | Gemini | 6:44 pm |
| 23 | 2:45 pm | 23 | | Cancer | 6:07 pm |
| 25 | 2:44 pm | 25 | | Leo | 6:06 pm |
| 27 | 5:12 pm | 27 | | Virgo | 8:41 pm |
| 29 | 4:35 pm | 30 | | Libra | 3:02 am |

## Last Aspect                    Moon Enters New Sign

| | | | July | | |
|---|---|---|---|---|---|
| 2 | 9:16 am | 2 | | Scorpio | 12:59 pm |
| 4 | 9:34 pm | 5 | | Sagittarius | 1:08 am |
| 7 | 10:12 am | 7 | | Capricorn | 1:45 pm |
| 9 | 10:12 pm | 10 | | Aquarius | 1:35 am |
| 12 | 8:40 am | 12 | | Pisces | 11:51 am |
| 14 | 1:00 pm | 14 | | Aries | 7:52 pm |
| 16 | 10:19 pm | 17 | | Taurus | 1:04 am |
| 19 | 2:11 am | 19 | | Gemini | 3:31 am |
| 21 | 1:41 am | 21 | | Cancer | 4:09 am |
| 23 | 2:05 am | 23 | | Leo | 4:34 am |
| 25 | 5:22 am | 25 | | Virgo | 6:32 am |
| 27 | 2:31 am | 27 | | Libra | 11:37 am |
| 29 | 5:30 pm | 29 | | Scorpio | 8:23 pm |
| 31 | 7:10 am | 8/1 | | Sagittarius | 8:01 am |
| | | | August | | |
| 3 | 5:38 pm | 3 | | Capricorn | 8:37 pm |
| 6 | 5:22 am | 6 | | Aquarius | 8:15 am |
| 8 | 3:07 pm | 8 | | Pisces | 5:56 pm |
| 10 | 9:38 am | 11 | | Aries | 1:22 am |
| 13 | 4:01 am | 13 | | Taurus | 6:40 am |
| 14 | 9:15 pm | 15 | | Gemini | 10:06 am |
| 17 | 9:38 am | 17 | | Cancer | 12:13 pm |
| 19 | 11:17 am | 19 | | Leo | 1:55 pm |
| 21 | 2:30 pm | 21 | | Virgo | 4:25 pm |
| 23 | 4:02 pm | 23 | | Libra | 9:05 pm |
| 26 | 1:39 am | 26 | | Scorpio | 4:53 am |
| 28 | 5:38 am | 28 | | Sagittarius | 3:48 pm |
| 31 | 12:42 am | 31 | | Capricorn | 4:18 am |

**Last Aspect**　　　　**Moon Enters New Sign**

| | | | | | |
|---|---|---|---|---|---|
| | | **September** | | | |
| 2 | 12:30 pm | 2 | | Aquarius | 4:06 pm |
| 5 | 1:15 am | 5 | | Pisces | 1:28 am |
| 6 | 4:29 pm | 7 | | Aries | 8:01 am |
| 9 | 11:52 am | 9 | | Taurus | 12:23 pm |
| 10 | 8:54 pm | 11 | | Gemini | 3:29 pm |
| 13 | 2:35 pm | 13 | | Cancer | 6:12 pm |
| 15 | 5:23 pm | 15 | | Leo | 9:09 pm |
| 17 | 8:55 pm | 18 | | Virgo | 12:52 am |
| 20 | 1:30 am | 20 | | Libra | 6:06 am |
| 22 | 9:04 am | 22 | | Scorpio | 1:40 pm |
| 24 | 3:33 am | 25 | | Sagittarius | 12:01 am |
| 27 | 7:08 am | 27 | | Capricorn | 12:24 pm |
| 29 | 8:14 pm | 30 | | Aquarius | 12:40 am |
| | | **October** | | | |
| 2 | 7:13 am | 2 | | Pisces | 10:26 am |
| 4 | 3:19 am | 4 | | Aries | 4:40 pm |
| 6 | 6:38 pm | 6 | | Taurus | 7:56 pm |
| 8 | 9:45 am | 8 | | Gemini | 9:44 pm |
| 10 | 6:25 pm | 10 | | Cancer | 11:38 pm |
| 13 | 12:00 am | 13 | | Leo | 2:41 am |
| 15 | 1:28 am | 15 | | Virgo | 7:19 am |
| 17 | 7:27 am | 17 | | Libra | 1:35 pm |
| 19 | 3:12 pm | 19 | | Scorpio | 9:41 pm |
| 22 | 7:35 am | 22 | | Sagittarius | 7:57 am |
| 24 | 12:44 pm | 24 | | Capricorn | 8:12 pm |
| 27 | 1:22 am | 27 | | Aquarius | 8:59 am |
| 29 | 12:22 pm | 29 | | Pisces | 7:46 pm |
| 31 | 5:08 pm | 11/1 | | Aries | 2:43 am |

## Last Aspect                    Moon Enters New Sign

| | | | | |
|---|---|---|---|---|
| | | **November** | | |
| 2 | 11:03 pm | 3 | Taurus | 5:46 am |
| 5 | 4:29 am | 5 | Gemini | 5:26 am |
| 7 | 5:40 am | 7 | Cancer | 5:45 am |
| 9 | 12:14 am | 9 | Leo | 7:29 am |
| 11 | 3:55 am | 11 | Virgo | 11:41 am |
| 13 | 10:45 am | 13 | Libra | 6:26 pm |
| 15 | 7:50 pm | 16 | Scorpio | 3:19 am |
| 18 | 6:42 am | 18 | Sagittarius | 1:59 pm |
| 20 | 7:26 pm | 21 | Capricorn | 2:14 am |
| 23 | 5:33 am | 23 | Aquarius | 3:14 pm |
| 25 | 9:37 pm | 26 | Pisces | 3:04 am |
| 28 | 7:09 am | 28 | Aries | 11:30 am |
| 30 | 1:37 pm | 30 | Taurus | 3:38 pm |
| | | **December** | | |
| 1 | 8:53 pm | 2 | Gemini | 4:21 pm |
| 4 | 2:13 pm | 4 | Cancer | 3:37 pm |
| 6 | 12:56 pm | 6 | Leo | 3:37 pm |
| 8 | 5:40 pm | 8 | Virgo | 6:09 pm |
| 10 | 10:02 pm | 11 | Libra | 12:01 am |
| 13 | 7:27 am | 13 | Scorpio | 8:59 am |
| 14 | 8:42 pm | 15 | Sagittarius | 8:07 pm |
| 18 | 8:10 am | 18 | Capricorn | 8:33 am |
| 20 | 10:37 am | 20 | Aquarius | 9:29 am |
| 23 | 5:13 am | 23 | Pisces | 9:42 am |
| 24 | 9:48 pm | 25 | Aries | 7:27 pm |
| 27 | 3:57 pm | 28 | Taurus | 1:23 am |
| 29 | 9:01 am | 30 | Gemini | 3:31 am |

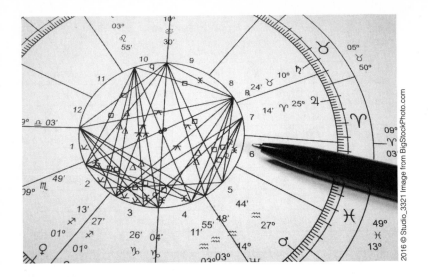

# The Moon's Rhythm

The Moon journeys around Earth in an elliptical orbit that takes about 27.33 days, which is known as a sidereal month (period of revolution of one body about another). She can move up to 15 degrees or as few as 11 degrees in a day, with the fastest motion occurring when the Moon is at perigee (closest approach to Earth). The Moon is never retrograde, but when her motion is slow, the effect is similar to a retrograde period.

Astrologers have observed that people born on a day when the Moon is fast will process information differently from those who are born when the Moon is slow in motion. People born when the Moon is fast process information quickly and tend to react quickly, while those born during a slow Moon will be more deliberate.

The time from New Moon to New Moon is called the synodic month (involving a conjunction), and the average time span between this Sun-Moon alignment is 29.53 days. Since 29.53

won't divide into 365 evenly, we can have a month with two Full Moons or two New Moons.

## Moon Aspects

The aspects the Moon will make during the times you are considering are also important. A trine or sextile, and sometimes a conjunction, are considered favorable aspects. A trine or sextile between the Sun and Moon is an excellent foundation for success. Whether or not a conjunction is considered favorable depends upon the planet the Moon is making a conjunction to. If it's joining the Sun, Venus, Mercury, Jupiter, or even Saturn, the aspect is favorable. If the Moon joins Pluto or Mars, however, that would not be considered favorable. There may be exceptions, but it would depend on what you are electing to do. For example, a trine to Pluto might hasten the end of a relationship you want to be free of.

It is important to avoid times when the Moon makes an aspect to or is conjoining any retrograde planet, unless, of course, you want the thing started to end in failure.

After the Moon has completed an aspect to a planet, that planetary energy has passed. For example, if the Moon squares Saturn at 10:00 am, you can disregard Saturn's influence on your activity if it will occur after that time. You should always look ahead at aspects the Moon will make on the day in question, though, because if the Moon opposes Mars at 11:30 pm on that day, you can expect events that stretch into the evening to be affected by the Moon-Mars aspect. A testy conversation might lead to an argument, or more.

## Moon Signs

Much agricultural work is ruled by earth signs—Virgo, Capricorn, and Taurus. The air signs—Gemini, Aquarius, and Libra—rule flying and intellectual pursuits.

Each planet has one or two signs in which its characteristics are enhanced or "dignified," and the planet is said to "rule" that sign. The Sun rules Leo and the Moon rules Cancer, for example. The ruling planet for each sign is listed below. These should not be considered complete lists. We recommend that you purchase a book of planetary rulerships for more complete information.

### Aries Moon

The energy of an Aries Moon is masculine, dry, barren, and fiery. Aries provides great start-up energy, but things started at this time may be the result of impulsive action that lacks research or necessary support. Aries lacks staying power.

Use this assertive, outgoing Moon sign to initiate change, but have a plan in place for someone to pick up the reins when you're impatient to move on to the next thing. Work that requires skillful but not necessarily patient use of tools—cutting down trees, hammering, etc.—is appropriate in Aries. Expect things to occur rapidly but to also quickly pass. If you are prone to injury or accidents, exercise caution and good judgment in Aries-related activities.

RULER: Mars

IMPULSE: Action

RULES: Head and face

### Taurus Moon

A Taurus Moon's energy is feminine, semi-fruitful, and earthy. The Moon is exalted—very strong—in Taurus. Taurus is known as the farmer's sign because of its associations with farmland and precipitation that is the typical day-long "soaker" variety. Taurus energy is good to incorporate into your plans when patience, practicality, and perseverance are needed. Be aware, though, that you may also experience stubbornness in this sign.

Things started in Taurus tend to be long lasting and to increase in value. This can be very supportive energy in a marriage election. On the downside, the fixed energy of this sign resists change or the letting go of even the most difficult situations. A divorce following a marriage that occurred during a Taurus Moon may be difficult and costly to end. Things begun now tend to become habitual and hard to alter. If you want to make changes in something you started, it would be better to wait for Gemini. This is a good time to get a loan, but expect the people in charge of money to be cautious and slow to make decisions.

RULER: Venus

IMPULSE: Stability

RULES: Neck, throat, and voice

## Gemini Moon

A Gemini Moon's energy is masculine, dry, barren, and airy. People are more changeable than usual and may prefer to follow intellectual pursuits and play mental games rather than apply themselves to practical concerns.

This sign is not favored for agricultural matters, but it is an excellent time to prepare for activities, to run errands, and write letters. Plan to use a Gemini Moon to exchange ideas, meet people, go on vacations that include walking or biking, or be in situations that require versatility and quick thinking on your feet.

RULER: Mercury

IMPULSE: Versatility

RULES: Shoulders, hands, arms, lungs, and nervous system

## Cancer Moon

A Cancer Moon's energy is feminine, fruitful, moist, and very strong. Use this sign when you want to grow things—flowers, fruits, vegetables, commodities, stocks, or collections—for example. This sensitive sign stimulates rapport between people. Considered the most fertile of the signs, it is often associated with mothering. You can use this moontime to build personal friendships that support mutual growth.

Cancer is associated with emotions and feelings. Prominent Cancer energy promotes growth, but it can also turn people pouty and prone to withdrawing into their shells.

RULER: The Moon

IMPULSE: Tenacity

RULES: Chest area, breasts, and stomach

## Leo Moon

A Leo Moon's energy is masculine, hot, dry, fiery, and barren. Use it whenever you need to put on a show, make a presentation, or entertain colleagues or guests. This is a proud yet playful energy that exudes self-confidence and is often associated with romance.

This is an excellent time for fundraisers and ceremonies or to be straightforward, frank, and honest about something. It is advisable not to put yourself in a position of needing public approval or where you might have to cope with underhandedness, as trouble in these areas can bring out the worst Leo traits. There is a tendency in this sign to become arrogant or self-centered.

RULER: The Sun

IMPULSE: I am

RULES: Heart and upper back

## Virgo Moon

A Virgo Moon is feminine, dry, barren, earthy energy. It is favorable for anything that needs painstaking attention—especially those things where exactness rather than innovation is preferred.

Use this sign for activities when you must analyze information or when you must determine the value of something. Virgo is the sign of bargain hunting. It's friendly toward agricultural matters with an emphasis on animals and harvesting vegetables. It is an excellent time to care for animals, especially training them and veterinary work.

This sign is most beneficial when decisions have already been made and now need to be carried out. The inclination here is to see details rather than the bigger picture.

There is a tendency in this sign to overdo. Precautions should be taken to avoid becoming too dull from all work and no play. Build a little relaxation and pleasure into your routine from the beginning.

RULER: Mercury

IMPULSE: Discriminating

RULES: Abdomen and intestines

### Libra Moon

A Libra Moon's energy is masculine, semi-fruitful, and airy. This energy will benefit any attempt to bring beauty to a place or thing. Libra is considered good energy for starting things of an intellectual nature. Libra is the sign of partnership and unions, which makes it an excellent time to form partnerships of any kind, to make agreements, and to negotiate. Even though this sign is good for initiating things, it is crucial to work with a partner who will provide incentive and encouragement, however. A Libra Moon accentuates teamwork (particularly teams of two) and artistic work (especially work that involves color). Make use of this sign when you are decorating your home or shopping for better-quality clothing.

RULER: Venus

IMPULSE: Balance

RULES: Lower back, kidneys, and buttocks

### Scorpio Moon

The Scorpio Moon is feminine, fruitful, cold, and moist. It is useful when intensity (that sometimes borders on obsession) is needed. Scorpio is considered a very psychic sign. Use this Moon sign when you must back up something you strongly believe in, such as union or employer relations. There is strong group loyalty here, but a Scorpio Moon is also a good time to end connections thoroughly. This is also a good time to conduct research.

The desire nature is so strong here that there is a tendency to manipulate situations to get what one wants or to not see one's responsibility in an act.

RULER: Pluto, Mars (traditional)

IMPULSE: Transformation

RULES: Reproductive organs, genitals, groin, and pelvis

## Sagittarius Moon

The Moon's energy is masculine, dry, barren, and fiery in Sagittarius, encouraging flights of imagination and confidence in the flow of life. Sagittarius is the most philosophical sign. Candor and honesty are enhanced when the Moon is here. This is an excellent time to "get things off your chest" and to deal with institutions of higher learning, publishing companies, and the law. It's also a good time for sport and adventure.

Sagittarians are the crusaders of this world. This is a good time to tackle things that need improvement, but don't try to be the diplomat while influenced by this energy. Opinions can run strong, and the tendency to proselytize is increased.

RULER: Jupiter

IMPULSE: Expansion

RULES: Thighs and hips

## Capricorn Moon

In Capricorn the Moon's energy is feminine, semi-fruitful, and earthy. Because Cancer and Capricorn are polar opposites, the Moon's energy is thought to be weakened here. This energy encourages the need for structure, discipline, and organization. This is a good time to set goals and plan for the future, tend to family business, and to take care of details requiring patience or a businesslike manner. Institutional activities are favored. This sign should be avoided if you're seeking favors, as those in authority can be insensitive under this influence.

RULER: Saturn

IMPULSE: Ambitious

RULES: Bones, skin, and knees

### Aquarius Moon

An Aquarius Moon's energy is masculine, barren, dry, and airy. Activities that are unique, individualistic, concerned with humanitarian issues, society as a whole, and making improvements are favored under this Moon. It is this quality of making improvements that has caused this sign to be associated with inventors and new inventions.

An Aquarius Moon promotes the gathering of social groups for friendly exchanges. People tend to react and speak from an intellectual rather than emotional viewpoint when the Moon is in this sign.

RULER: Uranus and Saturn

IMPULSE: Reformer

RULES: Calves and ankles

### Pisces Moon

A Pisces Moon is feminine, fruitful, cool, and moist. This is an excellent time to retreat, meditate, sleep, pray, or make that dreamed-of escape into a fantasy vacation. However, things are not always what they seem to be with the Moon in Pisces. Personal boundaries tend to be fuzzy, and you may not be seeing things clearly. People tend to be idealistic under this sign, which can prevent them from seeing reality.

There is a live-and-let-live philosophy attached to this sign, which in the idealistic world may work well enough, but chaos is frequently the result. That's why this sign is also associated with alcohol and drug abuse, drug trafficking, and counterfeiting. On the lighter side, many musicians and artists are ruled by Pisces. It's only when they move too far away from reality that the dark side of substance abuse, suicide, or crime takes away life.

RULER: Jupiter and Neptune

IMPULSE: Empathetic

RULES: Feet

## More About Zodiac Signs

### Element (Triplicity)

Each of the zodiac signs is classified as belonging to an element; these are the four basic elements:

**Fire Signs**

Aries, Sagittarius, and Leo are action-oriented, outgoing, energetic, and spontaneous.

**Earth Signs**

Taurus, Capricorn, and Virgo are stable, conservative, practical, and oriented to the physical and material realm.

**Air Signs**

Gemini, Aquarius, and Libra are sociable and critical, and they tend to represent intellectual responses rather than feelings.

**Water Signs**

Cancer, Scorpio, and Pisces are emotional, receptive, intuitive, and can be very sensitive.

### Quality (Quadruplicity)

Each zodiac sign is further classified as being cardinal, mutable, or fixed. There are four signs in each quadruplicity, one sign from each element.

**Cardinal Signs**

Aries, Cancer, Libra, and Capricorn represent beginnings and newly initiated action. They initiate each new season in the cycle of the year.

## Fixed Signs

Taurus, Leo, Scorpio, and Aquarius want to maintain the status quo through stubbornness and persistence; they represent that "between" time. For example, Leo is the month when summer really feels like summer.

## Mutable Signs

Pisces, Gemini, Virgo, and Sagittarius adapt to change and tolerate situations. They represent the last month of each season, when things are changing in preparation for the coming season.

## *Nature and Fertility*

In addition to a sign's element and quality, each sign is further classified as either fruitful, semi-fruitful, or barren. This classification is the most important for readers who use the gardening information in the *Moon Sign Book* because the timing of most events depends on the fertility of the sign occupied by the Moon. The water signs of Cancer, Scorpio, and Pisces are the most fruitful. The semi-fruitful signs are the earth signs Taurus and Capricorn, and the air sign Libra. The barren signs correspond to fire-signs Aries, Leo, and Sagittarius; air-signs Gemini and Aquarius; and earth-sign Virgo.

# Good Timing

*By Sharon Leah*

Electional astrology is the art of electing times to begin any undertaking. Say, for example, you want to start a business. That business will experience ups and downs, as well as reach its potential, according to the promise held in the universe at the time the business was started—its birth time. The horoscope (birth chart) set for the date, time, and place that a business starts would indicate the outcome—its potential to succeed.

So, you might ask yourself the question: If the horoscope for a business start can show success or failure, why not begin at a time that is more favorable to the venture? Well, you can.

While no time is perfect, there are better times and better days to undertake specific activities. There are thousands of examples that prove electional astrology is not only practical, but that it can make a difference in our lives. There are rules for electing times to begin various activities—even shopping. You'll find detailed instructions about how to make elections beginning on page 107.

## Personalizing Elections

The election rules in this almanac are based upon the planetary positions at the time for which the election is made. They do not depend on any type of birth chart. However, a birth chart based upon the time, date, and birthplace of an event has advantages. No election is effective for every person. For example, you may leave home to begin a trip at the same time as a friend, but each of you will have a different experience according to whether or not your birth chart favors the trip.

Not all elections require a birth chart, but the timing of very important events—business starts, marriages, etc.—would benefit from the additional accuracy a birth chart provides. To order a birth chart for yourself or a planned event, visit our Web site at www .llewellyn.com.

### Some Things to Consider

You've probably experienced good timing in your life. Maybe you were at the right place at the right time to meet a friend whom you hadn't seen in years. Frequently, when something like that happens, it is the result of following an intuitive impulse—that "gut instinct." Consider for a moment that you were actually responding to planetary energies. Electional astrology is a tool that can help you to align with energies, present and future, that are available to us through planetary placements.

### Significators

Decide upon the important significators (planet, sign, and house ruling the matter) for which the election is being made. The Moon is the most important significator in any election, so the Moon should always be fortified (strong by sign and making favorable aspects to other planets). The Moon's aspects to other planets are more important than the sign the Moon is in.

Other important considerations are the significators of the Ascendant and Midheaven—the house ruling the election matter and the ruler of the sign on that house cusp. Finally, any planet or sign that has a general rulership over the matter in question should be taken into consideration.

### Nature and Fertility

Determine the general nature of the sign that is appropriate for your election. For example, much agricultural work is ruled by the earth signs of Virgo, Capricorn, and Taurus; while the air signs—Gemini, Aquarius, and Libra—rule intellectual pursuits.

### One Final Comment

Use common sense. If you must do something, like plant your garden or take an airplane trip on a day that doesn't have the best aspects, proceed anyway, but try to minimize problems. For example, leave early for the airport to avoid being left behind due to delays in the security lanes. When you have no other choice, do the best that you can under the circumstances at the time.

If you want to personalize your elections, please turn to page 107 for more information. If you want a quick and easy answer, you can refer to Llewellyn's Astro Almanac on the following pages.

## Llewellyn's Astro Almanac

The Astro Almanac tables, beginning on the next page, can help you find the dates best suited to particular activities. The dates provided are determined from the Moon's sign, phase, and aspects to other planets. Please note that the Astro Almanac does not take personal factors, such as your Sun and Moon sign, into account. The dates are general, and they will apply for everyone. Some activities will not have ideal dates during a particular month.

| Activity | January |
|---|---|
| Animals (Neuter or spay) | 2–4, 22, 23, 25–27, 30 |
| Animals (Sell or buy) | 1, 6, 10, 11, 28 |
| Automobile (Buy) | 10, 15, 25 |
| Brewing | 20, 21 |
| Build (Start foundation) | 1, 29 |
| Business (Conducting for self and others) | 3, 7, 17, 22 |
| Business (Start new) | no ideal dates |
| Can Fruits and Vegetables | 20, 21 |
| Can Preserves | 20, 21 |
| Concrete (Pour) | 13, 14 |
| Construction (Begin new) | 1, 7, 10, 14, 17, 22, 24, 28 |
| Consultants (Begin work with) | 1, 2, 6, 10, 14, 15, 19, 20, 24, 25, 28, 30 |
| Contracts (Bid on) | 1, 2, 6, 10, 28, 30 |
| Cultivate | no ideal dates |
| Decorating | 1, 2, 8–10, 27–29 |
| Demolition | 12, 13, 22, 23 |
| Electronics (Buy) | 1, 10, 28 |
| Entertain Guests | 11 |
| Floor Covering (Laying new) | 13–19 |
| Habits (Break) | 25 |
| Hair (Cut to increase growth) | 3, 6–9, 30 |
| Hair (Cut to decrease growth) | 22–26 |
| Harvest (Grain for storage) | 13, 14 |
| Harvest (Root crops) | 12–14, 22–24 |
| Investments (New) | 7, 17 |
| Loan (Ask for) | 6–8 |
| Massage (Relaxing) | 2, 6, 11 |
| Mow Lawn (Decrease growth) | 13–26 |
| Mow Lawn (Increase growth) | 1–11, 28–31 |
| Mushrooms (Pick) | 11–13 |
| Negotiate (Business for the elderly) | 1, 14 |
| Prune for Better Fruit | 19–23 |
| Prune to Promote Healing | 25–27 |
| Wean Children | 1, 2, 22–29 |
| Wood Floors (Installing) | 25–27 |
| Write Letters or Contracts | 1, 10, 14, 23, 25, 28 |

| Activity | February |
|---|---|
| Animals (Neuter or spay) | 18–21, 25–27 |
| Animals (Sell or buy) | 5, 6, 9 |
| Automobile (Buy) | 6 |
| Brewing | 16–18 |
| Build (Start foundation) | no ideal dates |
| Business (Conducting for self and others) | 1, 6, 15, 21 |
| Business (Start new) | no ideal dates |
| Can Fruits and Vegetables | 16, 17, 26 |
| Can Preserves | 16, 17 |
| Concrete (Pour) | 24, 25 |
| Construction (Begin new) | 1, 6, 10, 15, 20, 21, 25 |
| Consultants (Begin work with) | 4, 6, 10, 14, 15, 20, 25 |
| Contracts (Bid on) | 4, 6, 10 |
| Cultivate | 24, 25 |
| Decorating | 5–7 |
| Demolition | 10, 18–20 |
| Electronics (Buy) | 6, 14, 25 |
| Entertain Guests | 5, 9 |
| Floor Covering (Laying new) | 11–15, 23, 24 |
| Habits (Break) | 21, 23–25 |
| Hair (Cut to increase growth) | 2–7, 9, 26 |
| Hair (Cut to decrease growth) | 18–22 |
| Harvest (Grain for storage) | 11, 18 |
| Harvest (Root crops) | 18–20, 23–25 |
| Investments (New) | 6, 15 |
| Loan (Ask for) | 2–4, 9 |
| Massage (Relaxing) | 9, 24 |
| Mow Lawn (Decrease growth) | 11–25 |
| Mow Lawn (Increase growth) | 1–9, 27, 28 |
| Mushrooms (Pick) | 9–11 |
| Negotiate (Business for the elderly) | 2, 15, 25 |
| Prune for Better Fruit | 16–18, 20 |
| Prune to Promote Healing | 21, 22 |
| Wean Children | 19–25 |
| Wood Floors (Installing) | 21, 22 |
| Write Letters or Contracts | 6, 10, 20, 25 |

| Activity | March |
|---|---|
| Animals (Neuter or spay) | 20–22, 25–27 |
| Animals (Sell or buy) | 9, 10, 31 |
| Automobile (Buy) | 5 |
| Brewing | 16, 17, 26 |
| Build (Start foundation) | no ideal dates |
| Business (Conducting for self and others) | 3, 7, 17, 23 |
| Business (Start new) | no ideal dates |
| Can Fruits and Vegetables | 16, 17, 26 |
| Can Preserves | 16, 17 |
| Concrete (Pour) | 23, 24 |
| Construction (Begin new) | 3, 5, 7, 10, 19, 23, 24 |
| Consultants (Begin work with) | 2, 5, 7, 10, 14, 18, 19, 24, 29 |
| Contracts (Bid on) | 2, 5, 7, 10, 29 |
| Cultivate | 18–20, 23–25 |
| Decorating | 4–6, 31 |
| Demolition | 18, 19, 27 |
| Electronics (Buy) | 5, 24 |
| Entertain Guests | 5, 9, 31 |
| Floor Covering (Laying new) | 13–15, 23, 24 |
| Habits (Break) | 21, 24, 25 |
| Hair (Cut to increase growth) | 2–5, 8, 29–31 |
| Hair (Cut to decrease growth) | 18–21, 26 |
| Harvest (Grain for storage) | 17–19 |
| Harvest (Root crops) | 18, 19, 23, 24 |
| Investments (New) | 7, 17 |
| Loan (Ask for) | 2, 3, 8–10, 30, 31 |
| Massage (Relaxing) | 9, 23 |
| Mow Lawn (Decrease growth) | 13–26 |
| Mow Lawn (Increase growth) | 1–11, 28–31 |
| Mushrooms (Pick) | 11–13 |
| Negotiate (Business for the elderly) | 1, 10, 29 |
| Prune for Better Fruit | 15–19 |
| Prune to Promote Healing | 20–22 |
| Wean Children | 18–25 |
| Wood Floors (Installing) | 20–22 |
| Write Letters or Contracts | 10, 19, 24, 29 |

| Activity | April |
|---|---|
| Animals (Neuter or spay) | 19, 22, 23 |
| Animals (Sell or buy) | 1, 4, 27 |
| Automobile (Buy) | 2, 7, 16, 29 |
| Brewing | 12, 13, 22, 23 |
| Build (Start foundation) | no ideal dates |
| Business (Conducting for self and others) | 1, 5, 16, 21, 30 |
| Business (Start new) | no ideal dates |
| Can Fruits and Vegetables | 12, 13, 22, 23 |
| Can Preserves | 12, 13 |
| Concrete (Pour) | 20, 21 |
| Construction (Begin new) | 1, 5, 6, 15, 16, 20, 28, 30 |
| Consultants (Begin work with) | 1, 2, 6, 7, 10, 15, 16, 20, 21, 25, 28, 29 |
| Contracts (Bid on) | 1, 2, 6, 7, 10, 28, 29, |
| Cultivate | 14–16, 19–21, 24, 25 |
| Decorating | 1, 2, 9, 10, 27–29 |
| Demolition | 14, 15, 23, 24 |
| Electronics (Buy) | 2, 21, 29 |
| Entertain Guests | 4, 27 |
| Floor Covering (Laying new) | 11, 19, 20 |
| Habits (Break) | 20, 23, 25 |
| Hair (Cut to increase growth) | 1, 4, 26–28 |
| Hair (Cut to decrease growth) | 14–18, 22, 25 |
| Harvest (Grain for storage) | 14–16 |
| Harvest (Root crops) | 14–16, 19–21, 23–25 |
| Investments (New) | 5, 16 |
| Loan (Ask for) | 4–6, 26, 27 |
| Massage (Relaxing) | 4, 27 |
| Mow Lawn (Decrease growth) | 12–25 |
| Mow Lawn (Increase growth) | 1–9, 27–30 |
| Mushrooms (Pick) | 10–12 |
| Negotiate (Business for the elderly) | 6, 11, 21, 25 |
| Prune for Better Fruit | 12–16 |
| Prune to Promote Healing | 17–19 |
| Wean Children | 14–21 |
| Wood Floors (Installing) | 16–19 |
| Write Letters or Contracts | 2, 6, 16, 21, 25, 29 |

| Activity | May |
|---|---|
| Animals (Neuter or spay) | 19, 21 |
| Animals (Sell or buy) | 3, 30, 31 |
| Automobile (Buy) | 27 |
| Brewing | 11, 19, 20 |
| Build (Start foundation) | 31 |
| Business (Conducting for self and others) | 5, 16, 21, 29 |
| Business (Start new) | no ideal dates |
| Can Fruits and Vegetables | 19, 20 |
| Can Preserves | 24 |
| Concrete (Pour) | 17, 18, 24 |
| Construction (Begin new) | 3, 5, 12, 16, 17, 21, 26, 29, 30 |
| Consultants (Begin work with) | 3, 7, 12, 13, 17, 19, 23, 26, 28, 30 |
| Contracts (Bid on) | 3, 7, 26, 28, 30 |
| Cultivate | 12, 13, 18, 21–23 |
| Decorating | 6–8, 25–27 |
| Demolition | 11–13, 21, 22 |
| Electronics (Buy) | 18, 27 |
| Entertain Guests | 2, 26, 31 |
| Floor Covering (Laying new) | 16–18, 23–25 |
| Habits (Break) | 21, 23 |
| Hair (Cut to increase growth) | 26, 29 |
| Hair (Cut to decrease growth) | 11–15, 19, 20, 23–25 |
| Harvest (Grain for storage) | 11–13, 16–18 |
| Harvest (Root crops) | 11–13, 16–18, 21, 22 |
| Investments (New) | 5, 16 |
| Loan (Ask for) | 2–4, 29–31 |
| Massage (Relaxing) | 17, 31 |
| Mow Lawn (Decrease growth) | 11–24 |
| Mow Lawn (Increase growth) | 1–9, 26–31 |
| Mushrooms (Pick) | 9–11 |
| Negotiate (Business for the elderly) | 8, 18 |
| Prune for Better Fruit | 10–13 |
| Prune to Promote Healing | 14–16 |
| Wean Children | 12–18 |
| Wood Floors (Installing) | 14–16 |
| Write Letters or Contracts | 3, 13, 18, 23, 27, 31 |

| Activity | June |
|---|---|
| Animals (Neuter or spay) | 17 |
| Animals (Sell or buy) | 8, 25, 26, 29 |
| Automobile (Buy) | 2, 23, 29 |
| Brewing | 16, 17 |
| Build (Start foundation) | 27 |
| Business (Conducting for self and others) | 3, 14, 19, 28 |
| Business (Start new) | no ideal dates |
| Can Fruits and Vegetables | 16 |
| Can Preserves | 20, 21 |
| Concrete (Pour) | 13, 14, 20, 21 |
| Construction (Begin new) | 3, 8, 13, 14, 19, 22, 26, 28 |
| Consultants (Begin work with) | 2, 3, 8, 13, 19, 22, 24, 26, 29 |
| Contracts (Bid on) | 2, 3, 8, 24, 26, 29 |
| Cultivate | 9, 10, 18, 19, 22, 23 |
| Decorating | 3–5, 30 |
| Demolition | 9, 18 |
| Electronics (Buy) | 13, 15, 23 |
| Entertain Guests | 20, 25 |
| Floor Covering (Laying new) | 13, 14, 20–23 |
| Habits (Break) | 19, 22 |
| Hair (Cut to increase growth) | 7, 8, 25 |
| Hair (Cut to decrease growth) | 10, 11, 16, 19–22 |
| Harvest (Grain for storage) | 10, 12–14 |
| Harvest (Root crops) | 9, 13, 14, 18, 19, 22 |
| Investments (New) | 3, 14 |
| Loan (Ask for) | 25–27 |
| Massage (Relaxing) | 20, 25 |
| Mow Lawn (Decrease growth) | 10–22 |
| Mow Lawn (Increase growth) | 1–8, 24–30 |
| Mushrooms (Pick) | 8–10 |
| Negotiate (Business for the elderly) | 4, 14, 19, 27 |
| Prune for Better Fruit | 9 |
| Prune to Promote Healing | 10–12 |
| Wean Children | 8–15 |
| Wood Floors (Installing) | 10–12 |
| Write Letters or Contracts | 10, 15, 23, 24, 27 |

| Activity | July |
|---|---|
| Animals (Neuter or spay) | no ideal dates |
| Animals (Sell or buy) | 6, 24, 29 |
| Automobile (Buy) | 20, 21, |
| Brewing | 13, 14, 22 |
| Build (Start foundation) | 24 |
| Business (Conducting for self and others) | 3, 14, 18, 27 |
| Business (Start new) | 8 |
| Can Fruits and Vegetables | 13, 14, 22 |
| Can Preserves | 17, 18, 22 |
| Concrete (Pour) | 10, 11, 17, 18 |
| Construction (Begin new) | 6, 11, 18, 20, 24, 27 |
| Consultants (Begin work with) | 1, 4, 6, 11, 16, 20, 24, 25, 28, 30 |
| Contracts (Bid on) | 1, 4, 6, 24, 25, 28, 30 |
| Cultivate | 16, 19–21 |
| Decorating | 1, 2, 27–29 |
| Demolition | 14–16 |
| Electronics (Buy) | 12, 20, 21 |
| Entertain Guests | 20, 24, 29 |
| Floor Covering (Laying new) | 10, 11, 17–20 |
| Habits (Break) | 19–21 |
| Hair (Cut to increase growth) | 5–7, 23 |
| Hair (Cut to decrease growth) | 10, 13, 17–20 |
| Harvest (Grain for storage) | 10, 11, 14, 15 |
| Harvest (Root crops) | 10, 11, 14–16, 19, 20 |
| Investments (New) | 3, 14 |
| Loan (Ask for) | 23–25 |
| Massage (Relaxing) | 10, 24, 29 |
| Mow Lawn (Decrease growth) | 10–22 |
| Mow Lawn (Increase growth) | 1–7, 24–31 |
| Mushrooms (Pick) | 8–10 |
| Negotiate (Business for the elderly) | 1, 11, 16, 24 |
| Prune for Better Fruit | no ideal dates |
| Prune to Promote Healing | 9, 10 |
| Wean Children | 5–12 |
| Wood Floors (Installing) | 9, 10 |
| Write Letters or Contracts | 7, 12, 21, 25 |

| Activity | August |
|---|---|
| Animals (Neuter or spay) | 29 |
| Animals (Sell or buy) | 2, 23, 30 |
| Automobile (Buy) | 4, 17, 22, 31 |
| Brewing | 9, 18, 19 |
| Build (Start foundation) | no ideal dates |
| Business (Conducting for self and others) | 2, 12, 17, 26, 31 |
| Business (Start new) | 5 |
| Can Fruits and Vegetables | 9, 18 |
| Can Preserves | 14, 18 |
| Concrete (Pour) | 8, 14, 20 |
| Construction (Begin new) | 2, 7, 12, 16, 17, 20, 30, 31 |
| Consultants (Begin work with) | 2, 4, 7, 14, 16, 18, 20, 22, 25, 26, 30, 31 |
| Contracts (Bid on) | 2, 4, 7, 22, 25, 26, 30, 31 |
| Cultivate | 16, 17, 20, 21 |
| Decorating | 6, 7, 24–26 |
| Demolition | 11, 12, 20 |
| Electronics (Buy) | 8, 17 |
| Entertain Guests | 19 |
| Floor Covering (Laying new) | 13–17, 20, 21 |
| Habits (Break) | 15–17, 20 |
| Hair (Cut to increase growth) | 1–5, 28–31 |
| Hair (Cut to decrease growth) | 9, 10, 13–16, 19 |
| Harvest (Grain for storage) | 8, 11, 12 |
| Harvest (Root crops) | 7, 8, 11, 12, 15–17, 20 |
| Investments (New) | 2, 12, 31 |
| Loan (Ask for) | no ideal dates |
| Massage (Relaxing) | 14, 19 |
| Mow Lawn (Decrease growth) | 8–20 |
| Mow Lawn (Increase growth) | 1–6, 22–31 |
| Mushrooms (Pick) | 6–8 |
| Negotiate (Business for the elderly) | 12, 25 |
| Prune for Better Fruit | no ideal dates |
| Prune to Promote Healing | no ideal dates |
| Wean Children | 2–8, 29–31 |
| Wood Floors (Installing) | no ideal dates |
| Write Letters or Contracts | 3, 8, 17, 21, 22, 31 |

| Activity | September |
|---|---|
| Animals (Neuter or spay) | 25, 27 |
| Animals (Sell or buy) | 22, 28 |
| Automobile (Buy) | 13, 18 |
| Brewing | 14, 15 |
| Build (Start foundation) | no ideal dates |
| Business (Conducting for self and others) | 10, 15, 25, 30 |
| Business (Start new) | 2, 29 |
| Can Fruits and Vegetables | 6, 14, 15 |
| Can Preserves | 10, 11, 14, 15 |
| Concrete (Pour) | 10, 11, 16 |
| Construction (Begin new) | 4, 10, 13, 15, 17, 25, 27, 30 |
| Consultants (Begin work with) | 4, 9, 13, 14, 17, 18, 22, 24, 27, 30 |
| Contracts (Bid on) | 4, 22, 24, 27, 30 |
| Cultivate | 13, 16–19 |
| Decorating | 3–5, 21, 22, 30 |
| Demolition | 7, 8, 16, 17 |
| Electronics (Buy) | 4, 13, 30 |
| Entertain Guests | 13, 17, 22 |
| Floor Covering (Laying new) | 9–13, 16–19 |
| Habits (Break) | 13, 16, 17 |
| Hair (Cut to increase growth) | 1, 5, 25–29 |
| Hair (Cut to decrease growth) | 9–12, 15 |
| Harvest (Grain for storage) | 7, 8, 11, 12 |
| Harvest (Root crops) | 7–9, 11–13, 16, 17 |
| Investments (New) | 10, 30 |
| Loan (Ask for) | no ideal dates |
| Massage (Relaxing) | 17 |
| Mow Lawn (Decrease growth) | 7–18 |
| Mow Lawn (Increase growth) | 1–5, 21–30 |
| Mushrooms (Pick) | 5–7 |
| Negotiate (Business for the elderly) | 4, 8, 17, 21 |
| Prune for Better Fruit | no ideal dates |
| Prune to Promote Healing | no ideal dates |
| Wean Children | 1–5, 25–30 |
| Wood Floors (Installing) | no ideal dates |
| Write Letters or Contracts | 4, 13, 17, 18 |

| Activity | October |
|---|---|
| Animals (Neuter or spay) | 23, 25–27 |
| Animals (Sell or buy) | 2, 23, 25, 28, 30 |
| Automobile (Buy) | 10, 26 |
| Brewing | 11 |
| Build (Start foundation) | no ideal dates |
| Business (Conducting for self and others) | 10, 14, 25, 30 |
| Business (Start new) | 25 |
| Can Fruits and Vegetables | 11 |
| Can Preserves | 7, 8, 11 |
| Concrete (Pour) | 7, 8, 13, 14 |
| Construction (Begin new) | 2, 10, 14, 15, 25 |
| Consultants (Begin work with) | 2, 10, 15, 20, 25, 26, 30, 31 |
| Contracts (Bid on) | 2, 20, 25, 26, 30, 31 |
| Cultivate | 13–17 |
| Decorating | 1, 2, 19, 27–29 |
| Demolition | 5, 13, 14 |
| Electronics (Buy) | 2, 10, 29 |
| Entertain Guests | 13, 17 |
| Floor Covering (Laying new) | 6–9, 13–19 |
| Habits (Break) | 14, 15 |
| Hair (Cut to increase growth) | 3, 23–26, 30, 31 |
| Hair (Cut to decrease growth) | 6–9 |
| Harvest (Grain for storage) | 6, 8–10 |
| Harvest (Root crops) | 5, 6, 8–10, 13, 14 |
| Investments (New) | 10, 30 |
| Loan (Ask for) | no ideal dates |
| Massage (Relaxing) | 8, 13, 17, 28 |
| Mow Lawn (Decrease growth) | 6–18 |
| Mow Lawn (Increase growth) | 1–4, 20–31 |
| Mushrooms (Pick) | 4–6 |
| Negotiate (Business for the elderly) | 1, 14, 19, 29 |
| Prune for Better Fruit | no ideal dates |
| Prune to Promote Healing | no ideal dates |
| Wean Children | 1, 2, 23–29 |
| Wood Floors (Installing) | no ideal dates |
| Write Letters or Contracts | 2, 10, 15, 20, 24, 29 |

| Activity | November |
|---|---|
| Animals (Neuter or spay) | 19–21, 23 |
| Animals (Sell or buy) | 21, 28 |
| Automobile (Buy) | 6 |
| Brewing | 8, 16, 17 |
| Build (Start foundation) | 25 |
| Business (Conducting for self and others) | 8, 13, 23, 29 |
| Business (Start new) | 3, 21 |
| Can Fruits and Vegetables | 8, 16, 17 |
| Can Preserves | 4, 8, 16, 17 |
| Concrete (Pour) | 4, 10 |
| Construction (Begin new) | 7, 8, 12, 13, 21, 23, 29 |
| Consultants (Begin work with) | 7, 9, 12, 14, 16, 20, 21, 25, 26, 30 |
| Contracts (Bid on) | 20, 21, 25, 26, 30 |
| Cultivate | 10–13 |
| Decorating | 23–25 |
| Demolition | 9, 10 |
| Electronics (Buy) | 6, 14, 25 |
| Entertain Guests | no ideal dates |
| Floor Covering (Laying new) | 4–6, 9–15 |
| Habits (Break) | 11 |
| Hair (Cut to increase growth) | 19–22, 27, 30 |
| Hair (Cut to decrease growth) | 5, 6, 9 |
| Harvest (Grain for storage) | 6, 9, 10 |
| Harvest (Root crops) | 6, 9, 10 |
| Investments (New) | 8, 29 |
| Loan (Ask for) | 30 |
| Massage (Relaxing) | no ideal dates |
| Mow Lawn (Decrease growth) | 5–17 |
| Mow Lawn (Increase growth) | 1, 2, 19–30 |
| Mushrooms (Pick) | 3–5 |
| Negotiate (Business for the elderly) | 2, 15, 25, 30 |
| Prune for Better Fruit | 16–18 |
| Prune to Promote Healing | no ideal dates |
| Wean Children | 19–25 |
| Wood Floors (Installing) | no ideal dates |
| Write Letters or Contracts | 6, 11, 20, 25 |

| Activity | December |
|---|---|
| Animals (Neuter or spay) | 16–20, 23–25 |
| Animals (Sell or buy) | 19, 23, 24 |
| Automobile (Buy) | 4, 31 |
| Brewing | 5, 6, 14, 15 |
| Build (Start foundation) | 23 |
| Business (Conducting for self and others) | 7, 12, 23, 28 |
| Business (Start new) | 1, 19, 28, 29 |
| Can Fruits and Vegetables | 5, 6, 14, 15 |
| Can Preserves | 5, 6, 14, 15 |
| Concrete (Pour) | 7, 8 |
| Construction (Begin new) | 5, 7, 9, 12, 19, 28 |
| Consultants (Begin work with) | 5, 8, 9, 12, 14, 17, 19, 21, 24, 26 |
| Contracts (Bid on) | 19, 21, 24, 26 |
| Cultivate | 10 |
| Decorating | 2, 3, 21–23, 30, 31 |
| Demolition | 7, 16, 17 |
| Electronics (Buy) | 4, 12, 21, 22, 31 |
| Entertain Guests | 12 |
| Floor Covering (Laying new) | 7–13 |
| Habits (Break) | no ideal dates |
| Hair (Cut to increase growth) | 1, 2, 18, 19, 23, 24, 28–31 |
| Hair (Cut to decrease growth) | 6, 16, 17 |
| Harvest (Grain for storage) | 4, 6–8 |
| Harvest (Root crops) | 3, 4, 7, 8, 16 |
| Investments (New) | 7, 28 |
| Loan (Ask for) | 1, 2, 28, 29 |
| Massage (Relaxing) | 7, 12, 23, 28 |
| Mow Lawn (Decrease growth) | 4–16 |
| Mow Lawn (Increase growth) | 1, 2, 19–31 |
| Mushrooms (Pick) | 2–4 |
| Negotiate (Business for the elderly) | 8, 23 |
| Prune for Better Fruit | 13–17 |
| Prune to Promote Healing | no ideal dates |
| Wean Children | 16–23 |
| Wood Floors (Installing) | no ideal dates |
| Write Letters or Contracts | 4, 8, 17, 22, 31 |

# Choose the Best Time for Your Activities

When rules for elections refer to "favorable" and "unfavorable" aspects to your Sun or other planets, please refer to the Favorable and Unfavorable Days Tables and Lunar Aspectarian for more information. You'll find instructions beginning on page 129 and the tables beginning on page 136.

The material in this section came from several sources including: *The New A to Z Horoscope Maker and Delineator* by Llewellyn George (Llewellyn, 1999), *Moon Sign Book* (Llewellyn, 1945), and *Electional Astrology* by Vivian Robson (Slingshot Publishing, 2000). Robson's book was originally published in 1937.

## Advertise (Internet)

The Moon should be conjunct, sextile, or trine Mercury or Uranus and in the sign of Gemini, Capricorn, or Aquarius.

## Advertise (Print)

Write ads on a day favorable to your Sun. The Moon should be conjunct, sextile, or trine Mercury or Venus. Avoid hard aspects to Mars and Saturn. Ad campaigns produce the best results when the Moon is well aspected in Gemini (to enhance communication) or Capricorn (to build business).

## Animals

Take home new pets when the day is favorable to your Sun, or when the Moon is trine, sextile, or conjunct Mercury, Jupiter or Venus, or in the sign of Virgo or Pisces. However, avoid days when the Moon is either square or opposing the Sun, Mars, Saturn, Uranus, Neptune, or Pluto. When selecting a pet, have the Moon well aspected by the planet that rules the animal. Cats are ruled by the Sun, dogs by Mercury, birds by Venus, horses by Jupiter, and fish by Neptune. Buy large animals when the Moon is in Sagittarius or Pisces and making favorable aspects to Jupiter or Mercury. Buy animals smaller than sheep when the Moon is in Virgo with favorable aspects to Mercury or Venus.

## Animals (Breed)

Animals are easiest to handle when the Moon is in Taurus, Cancer, Libra, or Pisces, but try to avoid the Full Moon. To encourage healthy births, animals should be mated so births occur when the Moon is increasing in Taurus, Cancer, Pisces, or Libra. Those born during a semi-fruitful sign (Taurus and Capricorn) will produce leaner meat. Libra yields beautiful animals for showing and racing.

## Animals (Declaw)

Declaw cats for medical purposes in the dark of the Moon. Avoid the week before and after the Full Moon and the sign of Pisces.

## Animals (Neuter or Spay)

Have livestock and pets neutered or spayed when the Moon is in Sagittarius, Capricorn, or Pisces, after it has passed through Scorpio, the sign that rules reproductive organs. Avoid the week before and after the Full Moon.

## Animals (Sell or Buy)

In either buying or selling, it is important to keep the Moon and Mercury free from any aspect to Mars. Aspects to Mars will create discord and increase the likelihood of wrangling over price and quality. The Moon should be passing from the first quarter to full and sextile or trine Venus or Jupiter. When buying racehorses, let the Moon be in an air sign. The Moon should be in air signs when you buy birds. If the birds are to be pets, let the Moon be in good aspect to Venus.

## Animals (Train)

Train pets when the Moon is in Virgo or trine to Mercury.

## Animals (Train Dogs to Hunt)

Let the Moon be in Aries in conjunction with Mars, which makes them courageous and quick to learn. But let Jupiter also be in aspect to preserve them from danger in hunting.

## Automobiles

When buying an automobile, select a time when the Moon is conjunct, sextile, or trine to Mercury, Saturn, or Uranus and in the sign of Gemini or Capricorn. Avoid times when Mercury is in retrograde motion.

## Baking Cakes

Your cakes will have a lighter texture if you see that the Moon is in Gemini, Libra, or Aquarius and in good aspect to Venus or Mercury. If you are decorating a cake or confections are being made, have the Moon placed in Libra.

## Beauty Treatments (Massage, etc.)

See that the Moon is in Taurus, Cancer, Leo, Libra, or Aquarius and in favorable aspect to Venus. In the case of plastic surgery, aspects to Mars should be avoided, and the Moon should not be in the sign ruling the part to be operated on.

## Borrow (Money or Goods)

See that the Moon is not placed between 15 degrees Libra and 15 degrees Scorpio. Let the Moon be waning and in Leo, Scorpio (16 to 30 degrees), Sagittarius, or Pisces. Venus should be in good aspect to the Moon, and the Moon should not be square, opposing, or conjunct either Saturn or Mars.

## Brewing

Start brewing during the third or fourth quarter, when the Moon is in Cancer, Scorpio, or Pisces.

## Build (Start Foundation)

Turning the first sod for the foundation marks the beginning of the building. For best results, excavate the site when the Moon is in the first quarter of a fixed sign and making favorable aspects to Saturn.

## Business (Start New)

When starting a business, have the Moon be in Taurus, Virgo, or Capricorn and increasing. The Moon should be sextile or trine Jupiter or Saturn, but avoid oppositions or squares. The planet ruling the business should be well aspected, too.

## Buy Goods

Buy during the third quarter, when the Moon is in Taurus for quality or in a mutable sign (Gemini, Sagittarius, Virgo, or Pisces) for savings. Good aspects to Venus or the Sun are desirable. If you are buying for yourself, it is good if the day is favorable for your Sun sign. You may also apply rules for buying specific items.

# Canning

Can fruits and vegetables when the Moon is in either the third or fourth quarter and in the water sign Cancer or Pisces. Preserves and jellies use the same quarters and the signs Cancer, Pisces, or Taurus.

# Clothing

Buy clothing on a day that is favorable for your Sun sign and when Venus or Mercury is well aspected. Avoid aspects to Mars and Saturn. Buy your clothing when the Moon is in Taurus if you want to remain satisfied. Do not buy clothing or jewelry when the Moon is in Scorpio or Aries. See that the Moon is sextile or trine the Sun during the first or second quarters.

# Collections

Try to make collections on days when your natal Sun is well aspected. Avoid days when the Moon is opposing or square Mars or Saturn. If possible, the Moon should be in a cardinal sign (Aries, Cancer, Libra, or Capricorn). It is more difficult to collect when the Moon is in Taurus or Scorpio.

# Concrete

Pour concrete when the Moon is in the third quarter of the fixed sign Taurus, Leo, or Aquarius.

# Construction (Begin New)

The Moon should be sextile or trine Jupiter. According to Hermes, no building should be begun when the Moon is in Scorpio or Pisces. The best time to begin building is when the Moon is in Aquarius.

# Consultants (Work with)

The Moon should be conjunct, sextile, or trine Mercury or Jupiter.

## Contracts (Bid On)

The Moon should be in Gemini or Capricorn and either the Moon or Mercury should be conjunct, sextile, or trine Jupiter.

## Copyrights/Patents

The Moon should be conjunct, trine, or sextile either Mercury or Jupiter.

## Coronations and Installations

Let the Moon be in Leo and in favorable aspect to Venus, Jupiter, or Mercury. The Moon should be applying to these planets.

## Cultivate

Cultivate when the Moon is in a barren sign and waning, ideally the fourth quarter in Aries, Gemini, Leo, Virgo, or Aquarius. The third quarter in the sign of Sagittarius will also work.

## Cut Timber

Timber cut during the waning Moon does not become worm-eaten; it will season well and not warp, decay, or snap during burning. Cut when the Moon is in Taurus, Gemini, Virgo, or

Capricorn—especially in August. Avoid the water signs. Look for favorable aspects to Mars.

## Decorating or Home Repairs

Have the Moon waxing and in the sign of Libra, Gemini, or Aquarius. Avoid squares or oppositions to either Mars or Saturn. Venus in good aspect to Mars or Saturn is beneficial.

## Demolition

Let the waning Moon be in Leo, Sagittarius, or Aries.

## Dental and Dentists

Visit the dentist when the Moon is in Virgo, or pick a day marked favorable for your Sun sign. Mars should be marked sextile, conjunct, or trine; avoid squares or oppositions to Saturn, Uranus, or Jupiter.

Teeth are best removed when the Moon is in Gemini, Virgo, Sagittarius, or Pisces and during the first or second quarter. Avoid the Full Moon! The day should be favorable for your lunar cycle, and Mars and Saturn should be marked conjunct, trine, or sextile. Fillings should be done in the third or fourth quarters in the sign of Taurus, Leo, Scorpio, or Pisces. The same applies for dentures.

## Dressmaking

William Lilly wrote in 1676: "Make no new clothes, or first put them on when the Moon is in Scorpio or afflicted by Mars, for they will be apt to be torn and quickly worn out." Design, repair, and sew clothes in the first and second quarters of Taurus, Leo, or Libra on a day marked favorable for your Sun sign. Venus, Jupiter, and Mercury should be favorably aspected, but avoid hard aspects to Mars or Saturn.

## Egg-Setting (see p. 161)

Eggs should be set so chicks will hatch during fruitful signs. To set eggs, subtract the number of days given for incubation or gestation from the fruitful dates. Chickens incubate in twenty-one days, turkeys and geese in twenty-eight days.

A freshly laid egg loses quality rapidly if it is not handled properly. Use plenty of clean litter in the nests to reduce the number of dirty or cracked eggs. Gather eggs daily in mild weather and at least two times daily in hot or cold weather. The eggs should be placed in a cooler immediately after gathering and stored at 50 to 55°F. Do not store eggs with foods or products that give off pungent odors since eggs may absorb the odors.

Eggs saved for hatching purposes should not be washed. Only clean and slightly soiled eggs should be saved for hatching. Dirty eggs should not be incubated. Eggs should be stored in a cool place with the large ends up. It is not advisable to store the eggs longer than one week before setting them in an incubator.

## Electricity and Gas (Install)

The Moon should be in a fire sign, and there should be no squares, oppositions, or conjunctions with Uranus (ruler of electricity), Neptune (ruler of gas), Saturn, or Mars. Hard aspects to Mars can cause fires.

## Electronics (Buying)

Choose a day when the Moon is in an air sign (Gemini, Libra, Aquarius) and well aspected by Mercury and/or Uranus when buying electronics.

## Electronics (Repair)

The Moon should be sextile or trine Mars or Uranus and in a fixed sign (Taurus, Leo, Scorpio, Aquarius).

## Entertain Friends

Let the Moon be in Leo or Libra and making good aspects to Venus. Avoid squares or oppositions to either Mars or Saturn by the Moon or Venus.

## Eyes and Eyeglasses

Have your eyes tested and glasses fitted on a day marked favorable for your Sun sign, and on a day that falls during your favorable lunar cycle. Mars should not be in aspect with the Moon. The same applies for any treatment of the eyes, which should also be started during the Moon's first or second quarter.

## Fence Posts

Set posts when the Moon is in the third or fourth quarter of the fixed sign Taurus or Leo.

## Fertilize and Compost

Fertilize when the Moon is in a fruitful sign (Cancer, Scorpio, Pisces). Organic fertilizers are best when the Moon is waning. Use chemical fertilizers when the Moon is waxing. Start compost when the Moon is in the fourth quarter in a water sign.

## Find Hidden Treasure

Let the Moon be in good aspect to Jupiter or Venus. If you erect a horoscope for this election, place the Moon in the Fourth House.

## Find Lost Articles

Search for lost articles during the first quarter and when your Sun sign is marked favorable. Also check to see that the planet ruling the lost item is trine, sextile, or conjunct the Moon. The Moon rules household utensils; Mercury rules letters and books; and Venus rules clothing, jewelry, and money.

# Fishing

During the summer months, the best time of the day to fish is from sunrise to three hours after and from two hours before sunset until one hour after. Fish do not bite in cooler months until the air is warm, from noon to three pm. Warm, cloudy days are good. The most favorable winds are from the south and southwest. Easterly winds are unfavorable. The best days of the month for fishing are when the Moon changes quarters, especially if the change occurs on a day when the Moon is in a water sign (Cancer, Scorpio, Pisces). The best period in any month is the day after the Full Moon.

# Friendship

The need for friendship is greater when the Moon is in Aquarius or when Uranus aspects the Moon. Friendship prospers when Venus or Uranus is trine, sextile, or conjunct the Moon. The Moon in Gemini facilitates the chance meeting of acquaintances and friends.

# Grafting or Budding

Grafting is the process of introducing new varieties of fruit on less desirable trees. For this process you should use the increasing phase of the Moon in fruitful signs such as Cancer, Scorpio, or Pisces. Capricorn may be used, too. Cut your grafts while trees are dormant, from December to March. Keep them in a cool, dark place, not too dry or too damp. Do the grafting before the sap starts to flow and while the Moon is waxing, preferably while it is in Cancer, Scorpio, or Pisces. The type of plant should determine both cutting and planting times.

# Habit (Breaking)

To end an undesirable habit, and this applies to ending everything from a bad relationship to smoking, start on a day when the Moon is in the fourth quarter and in the barren sign of Gemini, Leo, or

Aquarius. Aries, Virgo, and Capricorn may be suitable as well, depending on the habit you want to be rid of. Make sure that your lunar cycle is favorable. Avoid lunar aspects to Mars or Jupiter. However, favorable aspects to Pluto are helpful.

## Haircuts

Cut hair when the Moon is in Gemini, Sagittarius, Pisces, Taurus, or Capricorn, but not in Virgo. Look for favorable aspects to Venus. For faster growth, cut hair when the Moon is increasing in Cancer or Pisces. To make hair grow thicker, cut when the Moon is full in the signs of Taurus, Cancer, or Leo. If you want your hair to grow more slowly, have the Moon be decreasing in Aries, Gemini, or Virgo, and have the Moon square or opposing Saturn.

Permanents, straightening, and hair coloring will take well if the Moon is in Taurus or Leo and trine or sextile Venus. Avoid hair treatments if Mars is marked as square or in opposition, especially if heat is to be used. For permanents, a trine to Jupiter is helpful. The Moon also should be in the first quarter. Check the lunar cycle for a favorable day in relation to your Sun sign.

## Harvest Crops

Harvest root crops when the Moon is in a dry sign (Aries, Leo, Sagittarius, Gemini, Aquarius) and waning. Harvest grain for storage just after the Full Moon, avoiding Cancer, Scorpio, or Pisces. Harvest in the third and fourth quarters in dry signs. Dry crops in the third quarter in fire signs.

## Health

A diagnosis is more likely to be successful when the Moon is in Aries, Cancer, Libra, or Capricorn and less so when in Gemini, Sagittarius, Pisces, or Virgo. Begin a recuperation program or enter a hospital when the Moon is in a cardinal or fixed sign and the day is favorable to your Sun sign. For surgery, see "Surgical Procedures." Buy medicines when the Moon is in Virgo or Scorpio.

## Home (Buy new)

If you desire a permanent home, buy when the New Moon is in a fixed sign—Taurus or Leo, for example. Each sign will affect your decision in a different way. A house bought when the Moon is in Taurus is likely to be more practical and have a country look—right down to the split-rail fence. A house purchased when the Moon is in Leo will more likely be a real showplace.

If you're buying for speculation and a quick turnover, be certain that the Moon is in a cardinal sign (Aries, Cancer, Libra, Capricorn). Avoid buying when the Moon is in a fixed sign (Leo, Scorpio, Aquarius, Taurus).

## Home (Make Repairs)

In all repairs, avoid squares, oppositions, or conjunctions to the planet ruling the place or thing to be repaired. For example, bathrooms are ruled by Scorpio and Cancer. You would not want to start a project in those rooms when the Moon or Pluto is receiving hard aspects. The front entrance, hall, dining room, and porch are ruled by the Sun. So you would want to avoid times when Saturn or Mars are square, opposing, or conjunct the Sun. Also, let the Moon be waxing.

## Home (Sell)

Make a strong effort to list your property for sale when the Sun is marked favorable in your sign and in good aspect to Jupiter. Avoid adverse aspects to as many planets as possible.

## Home Furnishings (Buy New)

Saturn days (Saturday) are good for buying, and Jupiter days (Thursday) are good for selling. Items bought on days when Saturn is well aspected tend to wear longer and purchases tend to be more conservative.

## Job (Start New)

Jupiter and Venus should be sextile, trine, or conjunct the Moon. A day when your Sun is receiving favorable aspects is preferred.

## Legal Matters

Good Moon-Jupiter aspects improve the outcome in legal decisions. To gain damages through a lawsuit, begin the process during the increasing Moon. To avoid paying damages, a court date during the decreasing Moon is desirable. Good Moon-Sun aspects strengthen your chance of success. A well-aspected Moon in Cancer or Leo, making good aspects to the Sun, brings the best results in custody cases. In divorce cases, a favorable Moon-Venus aspect is best.

## Loan (Ask for)

A first and second quarter phase favors the lender, the third and fourth quarters favor the borrower. Good aspects of Jupiter and

Venus to the Moon are favorable to both, as is having the Moon in Leo or Taurus.

## Machinery, Appliances, or Tools (Buy)

Tools, machinery, and other implements should be bought on days when your lunar cycle is favorable and when Mars and Uranus are trine, sextile, or conjunct the Moon. Any quarter of the Moon is suitable. When buying gas or electrical appliances, the Moon should be in Aquarius.

## Make a Will

Let the Moon be in a fixed sign (Taurus, Leo, Scorpio, or Aquarius) to ensure permanence. If the Moon is in a cardinal sign (Aries, Cancer, Libra, or Capricorn), the will could be altered. Let the Moon be waxing—increasing in light—and in good aspect to Saturn, Venus, or Mercury. In case the will is made in an emergency during illness and the Moon is slow in motion, void-of-course, combust, or under the Sun's beams, the testator will die and the will remain unaltered. There is some danger that it will be lost or stolen, however.

## Marriage

The best time for marriage to take place is when the Moon is increasing, but not yet full. Good signs for the Moon to be in are Taurus, Cancer, Leo, or Libra.

The Moon in Taurus produces the most steadfast marriages, but if the partners later want to separate, they may have a difficult time. Make sure that the Moon is well aspected, especially to Venus or Jupiter. Avoid aspects to Mars, Uranus, or Pluto and the signs Aries, Gemini, Virgo, Scorpio, or Aquarius.

The values of the signs are as follows:

- Aries is not favored for marriage
- Taurus from 0 to 19 degrees is good, the remaining degrees are less favorable

- Cancer is unfavorable unless you are marrying a widow
- Leo is favored, but it may cause one party to deceive the other as to his or her money or possessions
- Virgo is not favored except when marrying a widow
- Libra is good for engagements but not for marriage
- Scorpio from 0 to 15 degrees is good, but the last 15 degrees are entirely unfortunate. The woman may be fickle, envious, and quarrelsome
- Sagittarius is neutral
- Capricorn, from 0 to 10 degrees, is difficult for marriage; however, the remaining degrees are favorable, especially when marrying a widow
- Aquarius is not favored
- Pisces is favored, although marriage under this sign can incline a woman to chatter a lot

These effects are strongest when the Moon is in the sign. If the Moon and Venus are in a cardinal sign, happiness between the couple may not continue long.

On no account should the Moon apply to Saturn or Mars, even by good aspect.

## Medical Treatment for the Eyes
Let the Moon be increasing in light and motion and making favorable aspects to Venus or Jupiter and be unaspected by Mars. Keep the Moon out of Taurus, Capricorn, or Virgo. If an aspect between the Moon and Mars is unavoidable, let it be separating.

## Medical Treatment for the Head
If possible, have Mars and Saturn free of hard aspects. Let the Moon be in Aries or Taurus, decreasing in light, in conjunction or aspect with Venus or Jupiter and free of hard aspects. The Sun should not be in any aspect to the Moon.

## Medical Treatment for the Nose

Let the Moon be in Cancer, Leo, or Virgo and not aspecting Mars or Saturn and also not in conjunction with a retrograde or weak planet.

## Mining

Saturn rules mining. Begin work when Saturn is marked conjunct, trine, or sextile. Mine for gold when the Sun is marked conjunct, trine, or sextile. Mercury rules quicksilver, Venus rules copper, Jupiter rules tin, Saturn rules lead and coal, Uranus rules radioactive elements, Neptune rules oil, the Moon rules water. Mine for these items when the ruling planet is marked conjunct, trine, or sextile.

## Move to New Home

If you have a choice, and sometimes you don't, make sure that Mars is not aspecting the Moon. Move on a day favorable to your Sun sign or when the Moon is conjunct, sextile, or trine the Sun.

## Mow Lawn

Mow in the first and second quarters (waxing phase) to increase growth and lushness, and in the third and fourth quarters (waning phase) to decrease growth.

## Negotiate

When you are choosing a time to negotiate, consider what the meeting is about and what you want to have happen. If it is agreement or compromise between two parties that you desire, have the Moon be in the sign of Libra. When you are making contracts, it is best to have the Moon in the same element. For example, if your concern is communication, then elect a time when the Moon is in an air sign. If, on the other hand, your concern is about possessions, an earth sign would be more appropriate.

Fixed signs are unfavorable, with the exception of Leo; so are cardinal signs, except for Capricorn. If you are negotiating the end of something, use the rules that apply to ending habits.

## Occupational Training

When you begin training, see that your lunar cycle is favorable that day and that the planet ruling your occupation is marked conjunct or trine.

## Paint

Paint buildings during the waning Libra or Aquarius Moon. If the weather is hot, paint when the Moon is in Taurus. If the weather is cold, paint when the Moon is in Leo. Schedule the painting to start in the fourth quarter as the wood is drier and paint will penetrate wood better. Avoid painting around the New Moon, though, as the wood is likely to be damp, making the paint subject to scalding when hot weather hits it. If the temperature is below 70°F, it is not advisable to paint while the Moon is in Cancer, Scorpio, or Pisces as the paint is apt to creep, check, or run.

## Party (Host or attend)

A party timed so the Moon is in Gemini, Leo, Libra, or Sagittarius, with good aspects to Venus and Jupiter, will be fun and well attended. There should be no aspects between the Moon and Mars or Saturn.

## Pawn

Do not pawn any article when Jupiter is receiving a square or opposition from Saturn or Mars or when Jupiter is within 17 degrees of the Sun, for you will have little chance to redeem the items.

## Pick Mushrooms

Mushrooms, one of the most promising traditional medicines in the world, should be gathered at the Full Moon.

# Plant

Root crops, like carrots and potatoes, are best if planted in the sign Taurus or Capricorn. Beans, peas, tomatoes, peppers, and other fruit-bearing plants are best if planted in a sign that supports seed growth. Leaf plants, like lettuce, broccoli, or cauliflower, are best planted when the Moon is in a water sign.

It is recommended that you transplant during a decreasing Moon, when forces are streaming into the lower part of the plant. This helps root growth.

# Promotion (Ask for)

Choose a day favorable to your Sun sign. Mercury should be marked conjunct, trine, or sextile. Avoid days when Mars or Saturn is aspected.

# Prune

Prune during the third and fourth quarter of a Scorpio Moon to retard growth and to promote better fruit. Prune when the Moon is in cardinal Capricorn to promote healing.

# Reconcile with People

If the reconciliation is with a woman, let Venus be strong and well aspected. If elders or superiors are involved, see that Saturn is receiving good aspects; if the reconciliation is between young people or between an older and younger person, see that Mercury is well aspected.

# Romance

There is less control of when a romance starts, but romances begun under an increasing Moon are more likely to be permanent or satisfying, while those begun during the decreasing Moon tend to transform the participants. The tone of the relationship can be guessed from the sign the Moon is in. Romances begun with the Moon in Aries may be impulsive. Those begun in Capricorn will

2016 © Minerva Studio Image from BigStockPhoto.com

take greater effort to bring to a desirable conclusion, but they may be very rewarding. Good aspects between the Moon and Venus will have a positive influence on the relationship. Avoid unfavorable aspects to Mars, Uranus, and Pluto. A decreasing Moon, particularly the fourth quarter, facilitates ending a relationship and causes the least pain.

## Roof a Building

Begin roofing a building during the third or fourth quarter, when the Moon is in Aries or Aquarius. Shingles laid during the New Moon have a tendency to curl at the edges.

## Sauerkraut

The best-tasting sauerkraut is made just after the Full Moon in the fruitful signs of Cancer, Scorpio, or Pisces.

## Select a Child's Sex

Count from the last day of menstruation to the first day of the next cycle and divide the interval between the two dates in half. Pregnancy in the first half produces females, but copulation should take place with the Moon in a feminine sign. Pregnancy in the latter half, up to three days before the beginning of menstruation, produces males, but copulation should take place with the Moon in a masculine sign. The three-day period before the next period again produces females.

## Sell or Canvass

Begin these activities during a day favorable to your Sun sign. Otherwise, sell on days when Jupiter, Mercury, or Mars is trine, sextile, or conjunct the Moon. Avoid days when Saturn is square or opposing the Moon, for that always hinders business and causes discord. If the Moon is passing from the first quarter to full, it is best to have the Moon swift in motion and in good aspect with Venus and/or Jupiter.

## Sign Papers

Sign contracts or agreements when the Moon is increasing in a fruitful sign and on a day when the Moon is making favorable aspects to Mercury. Avoid days when Mars, Saturn, or Neptune are square or opposite the Moon.

## Spray and Weed

Spray pests and weeds during the fourth quarter when the Moon is in the barren sign Leo or Aquarius and making favorable aspects to Pluto. Weed during a waning Moon in a barren sign.

## Staff (Fire)

Have the Moon in the third or fourth quarter, but not full. The Moon should not be square any planets.

## Staff (Hire)

The Moon should be in the first or second quarter, and preferably in the sign of Gemini or Virgo. The Moon should be conjunct, trine, or sextile Mercury or Jupiter.

## Stocks (Buy)

The Moon should be in Taurus or Capricorn, and there should be a sextile or trine to Jupiter or Saturn.

## Surgical Procedures

Blood flow, like ocean tides, appears to be related to Moon phases. To reduce hemorrhage after a surgery, schedule it within one week before or after a New Moon. Schedule surgery to occur during the increase of the Moon if possible, as wounds heal better and vitality is greater than during the decrease of the Moon. Avoid surgery within one week before or after the Full Moon. Select a date when the Moon is past the sign governing the part of the body involved in the operation. For example, abdominal operations should be done when the Moon is in Sagittarius, Capricorn, or Aquarius. The further removed the Moon sign is from the sign ruling the afflicted part of the body, the better.

For successful operations, avoid times when the Moon is applying to any aspect of Mars. (This tends to promote inflammation and complications.) See the Lunar Aspectarian on odd pages 137–159 to find days with negative Mars aspects and positive Venus and Jupiter aspects. Never operate with the Moon in the same sign as a person's Sun sign or Ascendant. Let the Moon be in a fixed sign and avoid square or opposing aspects. The Moon should not be void-of-course. Cosmetic surgery should be done in the increase of the Moon, when the Moon is not square or in opposition to Mars. Avoid days when the Moon is square or opposing Saturn or the Sun.

## Travel (Air)

Start long trips when the Moon is making favorable aspects to the Sun. For enjoyment, aspects to Jupiter are preferable; for visiting, look for favorable aspects to Mercury. To prevent accidents, avoid squares or oppositions to Mars, Saturn, Uranus, or

Pluto. Choose a day when the Moon is in Sagittarius or Gemini and well aspected to Mercury, Jupiter, or Uranus. Avoid adverse aspects of Mars, Saturn, or Uranus.

## Visit

On setting out to visit a person, let the Moon be in aspect with any retrograde planet, for this ensures that the person you're visiting will be at home. If you desire to stay a long time in a place, let the Moon be in good aspect to Saturn. If you desire to leave the place quickly, let the Moon be in a cardinal sign.

## Wean Children

To wean a child successfully, do so when the Moon is in Sagittarius, Capricorn, Aquarius, or Pisces—signs that do not rule vital human organs. By observing this astrological rule, much trouble for parents and child may be avoided.

## Weight (Reduce)

If you want to lose weight, the best time to get started is when the Moon is in the third or fourth quarter and in the barren sign of Virgo. Review the section on How to Use the Moon Tables and Lunar Aspectarian beginning on page 136 to help you select a date that is favorable to begin your weight-loss program.

## Wine and Drink Other Than Beer

Start brewing when the Moon is in Pisces or Taurus. Sextiles or trines to Venus are favorable, but avoid aspects to Mars or Saturn.

## Write

Write for pleasure or publication when the Moon is in Gemini. Mercury should be making favorable aspects to Uranus and Neptune.

# How to Use the Moon Tables and Lunar Aspectarian

Timing activities is one of the most important things you can do to ensure success. In many Eastern countries, timing by the planets is so important that practically no event takes place without first setting up a chart for it. Weddings have occurred in the middle of the night because the influences were at the best then. You may not want to take it that far, but you can still make use of the influences of the Moon whenever possible. It's easy and it works!

*Llewellyn's Moon Sign Book* has information to help you plan just about any activity: weddings, fishing, making purchases, cutting your hair, traveling, and more. We provide the guidelines you need to pick the best day out of the several from which you have to choose. The Moon Tables are the *Moon Sign Book's* primary method for choosing dates. Following are instructions, examples, and directions on how to read the Moon Tables. More advanced information on using the tables containing the Lunar Aspectarian and favorable and unfavorable days (found on odd-numbered pages opposite the Moon Tables), Moon void-of-course and retrograde information to choose the dates best for you is also included.

## The Five Basic Steps

### Step 1: Directions for Choosing Dates

Look up the directions for choosing dates for the activity that you wish to begin, then go to step 2.

### Step 2: Check the Moon Tables

You'll find two tables for each month of the year beginning on page 136. The Moon Tables (on the left-hand pages) include the day, date, and sign the Moon is in; the element and nature of the sign; the Moon's phase; and when it changes sign or phase. If there is a time listed after a date, that time is the time when the Moon moves into that zodiac sign. Until then, the Moon is considered to be in the sign for the previous day.

The abbreviation Full signifies Full Moon and New signifies New Moon. The times listed with dates indicate when the Moon changes sign. The times listed after the phase indicate when the Moon changes phase.

Turn to the month you would like to begin your activity. You will be using the Moon's sign and phase information most often when you begin choosing your own dates. Use the Time Zone Map on page 164 and the Time Zone Conversions table on page 165 to convert time to your own time zone.

When you find dates that meet the criteria for the correct Moon phase and sign for your activity, you may have completed the process. For certain simple activities, such as getting a haircut, the phase and sign information is all that is needed. If the directions for your activity include information on certain lunar aspects, however, you should consult the Lunar Aspectarian. An example of this would be if the directions told you not to perform a certain activity when the Moon is square (Q) Jupiter.

## Step 3: Check the Lunar Aspectarian

On the pages opposite the Moon Tables you will find tables containing the Lunar Aspectarian and Favorable and Unfavorable Days. The Lunar Aspectarian gives the aspects (or angles) of the Moon to other planets. Some aspects are favorable, while others are not. To use the Lunar Aspectarian, find the planet that the directions list as favorable for your activity, and run down the column to the date desired. For example, you should avoid aspects to Mars if you are planning surgery. So you would look for Mars across the top and then run down that column looking for days where there are no aspects to Mars (as signified by empty boxes). If you want to find a *favorable* aspect (sextile (X) or trine (T)) to Mercury, run your finger down the column under Mercury until you find an X or T. *Adverse* aspects to planets are squares (Q) or oppositions (O). A conjunction (C) is sometimes beneficial, sometimes not, depending on the activity or planets involved.

## Step 4: Favorable and Unfavorable Days

The tables listing favorable and unfavorable days are helpful when you want to choose your personal best dates because your Sun sign is taken into consideration. The twelve Sun signs are listed on the right side of the tables. Once you have determined which days meet your criteria for phase, sign, and aspects, you can determine whether or not those days are positive for you by checking the favorable and unfavorable days for your Sun sign.

To find out if a day is positive for you, find your Sun sign and then look down the column. If it is marked F, it is very favorable. The Moon is in the same sign as your Sun on a favorable day. If it is marked f, it is slightly favorable; U is very unfavorable; and u means slightly unfavorable. A day marked very unfavorable (U) indicates that the Moon is in the sign opposing your Sun.

Once you have selected good dates for the activity you are about to begin, you can go straight to "Using What You've Learned," beginning on the next page. To learn how to fine-tune your selections even further, read on.

## Step 5: Void-of-Course Moon and Retrogrades

This last step is perhaps the most advanced portion of the procedure. It is generally considered poor timing to make decisions, sign important papers, or start special activities during a Moon void-of-course period or during a Mercury retrograde. Once you have chosen the best date for your activity based on steps one through four, you can check the Void-of-Course tables, beginning on page 76, to find out if any of the dates you have chosen have void periods.

The Moon is said to be void-of-course after it has made its last aspect to a planet within a particular sign, but before it has moved into the next sign. Put simply, the Moon is "resting" during the void-of-course period, so activities initiated at this time generally don't come to fruition. You will notice that there are many void periods during the year, and it is nearly impossible to avoid all of them. Some people choose to ignore these altogether and do not take them into consideration when planning activities.

Next, you can check the Retrograde Planets tables on page 160 to see what planets are retrograde during your chosen date(s).

A planet is said to be retrograde when it appears to move backward in the sky as viewed from Earth. Generally, the farther a planet is away from the Sun, the longer it can stay retrograde. Some planets will retrograde for several months at a time. Avoiding retrogrades is not as important in lunar planning as avoiding the Moon void-of-course, with the exception of the planet Mercury.

Mercury rules thought and communication, so it is advisable not to sign important papers, initiate important business or legal work, or make crucial decisions during these times. As with the Moon void-of-course, it is difficult to avoid all planetary retrogrades when beginning events, and you may choose to ignore this step of the process. Following are some examples using some or all of the steps outlined above.

## Using What You've Learned

Let's say it's a new year and you want to have your hair cut. It's thin and you would like it to look fuller, so you find the directions for hair care and you see that for thicker hair you should cut hair while the Moon is Full and in the sign of Taurus, Cancer, or Leo. You should avoid the Moon in Aries, Gemini, or Virgo. Look at the January Moon Table on page 136. You see that the Full Moon is on January 12 at 6:34 am. The Moon is in Leo that day after 7:08 pm and remains in Leo until January 14 at 10:52 pm, so January 12–14 meets both the phase and sign criteria.

Let's move on to a more difficult example using the sign and phase of the Moon. You want to buy a permanent home. After checking the instructions for purchasing a house: "Home (Buy new)" on page 118, you see that you should buy a home when the Moon is in Taurus, Cancer, or Leo. You need to get a loan, so you should also look under "Loan (Ask for)" on page 119. Here it says that the third and fourth quarters favor the borrower (you). You are going to buy the house in October, so go to page 154. The Moon is in the third quarter October 5–12 and fourth quarter October 12–19. The Moon is in Taurus from 7:56 pm on October 6 until October 8 at 9:44 pm; in Cancer from 11:38 pm October 10 until October 13 at 2:41 am; and in Leo from October 13 at 2:41 am until October 15 at 7:19 am. The best days for obtaining a loan would be October 6, 7, 8, 10, 11, 12, 13, 14, or 15.

Just match up the best sign and phase (quarter) to come up with the best date. With all activities, be sure to check the favorable and unfavorable days for your Sun sign in the table adjoining the Lunar Aspectarian. If there is a choice between several dates, pick the one most favorable for you. Because buying a home is an important business decision, you may also wish to see if the Moon is void or if Mercury is retrograde during these dates.

Now let's look at an example that uses signs, phases, and aspects. Our example is starting new home construction. We will use the month of May. Look under "Build (Start foundation)" on page 110 and you'll see that the Moon should be in the first quarter of a fixed sign—Leo, Taurus, Aquarius, or Scorpio. You should select a time when the Moon is not making unfavorable aspects to Saturn. (Conjunctions are usually considered unfavorable if they are to Mars, Saturn, or Neptune.) Look in the May Moon Table. You will see that the Moon is in the first quarter May 25–31 and in Leo from 8:12 am on May 29 until 12:16pm on May 31. Now, look to the May Lunar Aspectarian. We see that there is a favorable trine to Saturn on May 31 and a challenging opposition on May 27. Therefore, May 31 would be the best date to start a foundation.

## A Note About Time and Time Zones

All tables in the Moon Sign Book use Eastern Time. You must calculate the difference between your time zone and the Eastern Time Zone. Please refer to the Time Zone Conversions chart on page 165 for help with time conversions. The sign the Moon is in at midnight is the sign shown in the Aspectarian and Favorable and Unfavorable Days tables.

### *How Does the Time Matter?*

Due to the three-hour time difference between the East and West Coasts of the United States, those of you living on the East Coast may be, for example, under the influence of a Virgo Moon, while those of you living on the West Coast will still have a Leo Moon influence.

We follow a commonly held belief among astrologers: whatever sign the Moon is in at the start of a day—12:00 am Eastern Time—is considered the dominant influence of the day. That sign is indicated in the Moon Tables. If the date you select for an activity shows the Moon changing signs, you can decide how important the sign change may be for your specific election and adjust your election date and time accordingly.

### Use Common Sense

Some activities depend on outside factors. Obviously, you can't go out and plant when there is a foot of snow on the ground. You should adjust to the conditions at hand. If the weather was bad during the first quarter, when it was best to plant crops, do it during the second quarter while the Moon is in a fruitful sign. If the Moon is not in a fruitful sign during the first or second quarter, choose a day when it is in a semi-fruitful sign. The best advice is to choose either the sign or phase that is most favorable, when the two don't coincide.

### To Summarize

First, look up the activity under the proper heading, then look for the information given in the tables. Choose the best date considering the number of positive factors in effect. If most of the dates are favorable, there is no problem choosing the one that will fit your schedule. However, if there aren't any really good dates, pick the ones with the least number of negative influences. Please keep in mind that the information found here applies in the broadest sense to the events you want to plan or are considering. To be the most effective, when you use electional astrology, you should also consider your own birth chart in relation to a chart drawn for the time or times you have under consideration. The best advice we can offer you is: read the entire introduction to each section.

# January Moon Table

| Date | Sign | Element | Nature | Phase |
|------|------|---------|--------|-------|
| 1 Sun | Aquarius | Air | Barren | 1st |
| 2 Mon 4:57 am | Pisces | Water | Fruitful | 1st |
| 3 Tue | Pisces | Water | Fruitful | 1st |
| 4 Wed 11:20 am | Aries | Fire | Barren | 1st |
| 5 Thu | Aries | Fire | Barren | 2nd 2:47 pm |
| 6 Fri 3:18 pm | Taurus | Earth | Semi-fruitful | 2nd |
| 7 Sat | Taurus | Earth | Semi-fruitful | 2nd |
| 8 Sun 5:06 pm | Gemini | Air | Barren | 2nd |
| 9 Mon | Gemini | Air | Barren | 2nd |
| 10 Tue 5:49 pm | Cancer | Water | Fruitful | 2nd |
| 11 Wed | Cancer | Water | Fruitful | 2nd |
| 12 Thu 7:08 pm | Leo | Fire | Barren | Full 6:34 am |
| 13 Fri | Leo | Fire | Barren | 3rd |
| 14 Sat 10:52 pm | Virgo | Earth | Barren | 3rd |
| 15 Sun | Virgo | Earth | Barren | 3rd |
| 16 Mon | Virgo | Earth | Barren | 3rd |
| 17 Tue 6:16 am | Libra | Air | Semi-fruitful | 3rd |
| 18 Wed | Libra | Air | Semi-fruitful | 3rd |
| 19 Thu 5:09 pm | Scorpio | Water | Fruitful | 4th 5:13 pm |
| 20 Fri | Scorpio | Water | Fruitful | 4th |
| 21 Sat | Scorpio | Water | Fruitful | 4th |
| 22 Sun 5:45 am | Sagittarius | Fire | Barren | 4th |
| 23 Mon | Sagittarius | Fire | Barren | 4th |
| 24 Tue 5:43 pm | Capricorn | Earth | Semi-fruitful | 4th |
| 25 Wed | Capricorn | Earth | Semi-fruitful | 4th |
| 26 Thu | Capricorn | Earth | Semi-fruitful | 4th |
| 27 Fri 3:37 am | Aquarius | Air | Barren | New 7:07 pm |
| 28 Sat | Aquarius | Air | Barren | 1st |
| 29 Sun 11:10 am | Pisces | Water | Fruitful | 1st |
| 30 Mon | Pisces | Water | Fruitful | 1st |
| 31 Tue 4:46 pm | Aries | Fire | Barren | 1st |

# January Aspectarian/Favorable & Unfavorable Days

| Date | Sun | Mercury | Venus | Mars | Jupiter | Saturn | Uranus | Neptune | Pluto |
|---|---|---|---|---|---|---|---|---|---|
| 1 | | | | | T | X | X | | |
| 2 | | X | C | | | | | C | |
| 3 | X | | | C | | Q | | | X |
| 4 | | Q | | | | | | | |
| 5 | Q | | | | | C | | | Q |
| 6 | | T | X | | O | T | | | |
| 7 | T | | | X | | | | X | T |
| 8 | | | | | | | | | |
| 9 | | | Q | Q | | | | Q | |
| 10 | | O | | | T | O | X | | |
| 11 | | | T | T | | | | T | O |
| 12 | O | | | | Q | Q | | | |
| 13 | | | | | | | | | |
| 14 | | | | | X | T | T | | |
| 15 | | T | O | | | | | O | |
| 16 | | | | O | | Q | | | T |
| 17 | T | Q | | | | | | | |
| 18 | | | | | | O | | | Q |
| 19 | Q | | | | C | X | | | |
| 20 | | X | | | | | | T | |
| 21 | | | T | T | | | | | X |
| 22 | X | | | | | | | | |
| 23 | | | Q | | | | T | Q | |
| 24 | | | | Q | X | C | | | |
| 25 | | C | | | | | X | | |
| 26 | | | X | | Q | | Q | | C |
| 27 | C | | | X | | | | | |
| 28 | | | | | T | | X | | |
| 29 | | | | | | X | | | |
| 30 | | X | | | | | | C | X |
| 31 | | | C | C | | Q | | | |

| Date | Aries | Taurus | Gemini | Cancer | Leo | Virgo | Libra | Scorpio | Sagittarius | Capricorn | Aquarius | Pisces |
|---|---|---|---|---|---|---|---|---|---|---|---|---|
| 1 | f | u | f | | U | | f | u | f | | F | |
| 2 | f | u | f | | U | | f | u | f | | F | |
| 3 | | f | u | f | | U | | f | u | f | | F |
| 4 | | f | u | f | | U | | f | u | f | | F |
| 5 | F | | f | u | f | | U | | f | u | f | |
| 6 | F | | f | u | f | | U | | f | u | f | |
| 7 | | F | | f | u | f | | U | | f | u | f |
| 8 | | F | | f | u | f | | U | | .f | u | f |
| 9 | f | | F | | f | u | f | | U | | f | u |
| 10 | f | | F | | f | u | f | | U | | f | u |
| 11 | u | f | | F | | f | u | f | | U | | f |
| 12 | u | f | | F | | f | u | f | | U | | f |
| 13 | f | u | f | | F | | f | u | f | | U | |
| 14 | f | u | f | | F | | f | u | f | | U | |
| 15 | | f | u | f | | F | | f | u | f | | U |
| 16 | | f | u | f | | F | | f | u | f | | U |
| 17 | | f | u | f | | F | | f | u | f | | U |
| 18 | U | | f | u | f | | F | | f | u | f | |
| 19 | U | | f | u | f | | F | | f | u | f | |
| 20 | | U | | f | u | f | | F | | f | u | f |
| 21 | | U | | f | u | f | | F | | f | u | f |
| 22 | | U | | f | u | f | | F | | f | u | f |
| 23 | f | | U | | f | u | f | | F | | f | u |
| 24 | f | | U | | f | u | f | | F | | f | u |
| 25 | u | f | | U | | f | u | f | | F | | f |
| 26 | u | f | | U | | f | u | f | | F | | f |
| 27 | u | f | | U | | f | u | f | | F | | f |
| 28 | f | u | f | | U | | f | u | f | | F | |
| 29 | f | u | f | | U | | f | u | f | | F | |
| 30 | | f | u | f | | U | | f | u | f | | F |
| 31 | | f | u | f | | U | | f | u | f | | F |

# February Moon Table

| Date | Sign | Element | Nature | Phase |
|------|------|---------|--------|-------|
| 1 Wed | Aries | Fire | Barren | 1st |
| 2 Thu 8:50 pm | Taurus | Earth | Semi-fruitful | 1st |
| 3 Fri | Taurus | Earth | Semi-fruitful | 2nd 11:19 pm |
| 4 Sat 11:44 pm | Gemini | Air | Barren | 2nd |
| 5 Sun | Gemini | Air | Barren | 2nd |
| 6 Mon | Gemini | Air | Barren | 2nd |
| 7 Tue 2:03 am | Cancer | Water | Fruitful | 2nd |
| 8 Wed | Cancer | Water | Fruitful | 2nd |
| 9 Thu 4:41 am | Leo | Fire | Barren | 2nd |
| 10 Fri | Leo | Fire | Barren | Full 7:33 pm |
| 11 Sat 8:52 am | Virgo | Earth | Barren | 3rd |
| 12 Sun | Virgo | Earth | Barren | 3rd |
| 13 Mon 3:43 pm | Libra | Air | Semi-fruitful | 3rd |
| 14 Tue | Libra | Air | Semi-fruitful | 3rd |
| 15 Wed | Libra | Air | Semi-fruitful | 3rd |
| 16 Thu 1:41 am | Scorpio | Water | Fruitful | 3rd |
| 17 Fri | Scorpio | Water | Fruitful | 3rd |
| 18 Sat 1:52 pm | Sagittarius | Fire | Barren | 4th 2:33 pm |
| 19 Sun | Sagittarius | Fire | Barren | 4th |
| 20 Mon | Sagittarius | Fire | Barren | 4th |
| 21 Tue 2:08 am | Capricorn | Earth | Semi-fruitful | 4th |
| 22 Wed | Capricorn | Earth | Semi-fruitful | 4th |
| 23 Thu 12:17 pm | Aquarius | Air | Barren | 4th |
| 24 Fri | Aquarius | Air | Barren | 4th |
| 25 Sat 7:24 pm | Pisces | Water | Fruitful | 4th |
| 26 Sun | Pisces | Water | Fruitful | New 9:58 am |
| 27 Mon 11:52 pm | Aries | Fire | Barren | 1st |
| 28 Tue | Aries | Fire | Barren | 1st |

# February Aspectarian/Favorable & Unfavorable Days

| Date | Sun | Mercury | Venus | Mars | Jupiter | Saturn | Uranus | Neptune | Pluto |
|------|-----|---------|-------|------|---------|--------|--------|---------|-------|
| 1 | X | | | | | | | | |
| 2 | | Q | | | O | T | C | | Q |
| 3 | Q | | | | | | | X | |
| 4 | | T | | | | | | | T |
| 5 | | | X | X | | | | Q | |
| 6 | T | | | | T | O | X | | |
| 7 | | | Q | Q | | | | T | |
| 8 | | | | | Q | | Q | | O |
| 9 | | O | T | T | | | | | |
| 10 | O | | | | X | | T | | |
| 11 | | | | | | | T | | |
| 12 | | | | | | | | O | T |
| 13 | | | | | | Q | | | |
| 14 | | T | O | O | | | | | |
| 15 | T | | | | C | X | O | | Q |
| 16 | | | | | | | | | |
| 17 | | Q | | | | | | T | X |
| 18 | Q | | | | | | | | |
| 19 | | | T | | | | | Q | |
| 20 | | X | | T | X | C | T | | |
| 21 | X | | | | | | | | |
| 22 | | | Q | Q | Q | | Q | X | C |
| 23 | | | | | | | | | |
| 24 | | | X | | | | | | |
| 25 | | C | | X | T | X | X | | |
| 26 | C | | | | | | C | | |
| 27 | | | | | | Q | | | X |
| 28 | | | C | | | | | | |

| Date | Aries | Taurus | Gemini | Cancer | Leo | Virgo | Libra | Scorpio | Sagittarius | Capricorn | Aquarius | Pisces |
|------|-------|--------|--------|--------|-----|-------|-------|---------|-------------|-----------|----------|--------|
| 1 | F | | f | u | f | | U | | f | u | f | |
| 2 | F | | f | u | f | | U | | f | u | f | |
| 3 | | F | | f | u | f | | U | | f | u | f |
| 4 | | F | | f | u | f | | U | | f | u | f |
| 5 | f | | F | | f | u | f | | U | | f | u |
| 6 | f | | F | | f | u | f | | U | | f | u |
| 7 | u | f | | F | | f | u | f | | U | | f |
| 8 | u | f | | F | | f | u | f | | U | | f |
| 9 | u | f | | F | | f | u | f | | U | | f |
| 10 | f | u | f | | F | | f | u | f | | U | |
| 11 | f | u | f | | F | | f | u | f | | U | |
| 12 | | f | u | f | | F | | f | u | f | | U |
| 13 | | f | u | f | | F | | f | u | f | | U |
| 14 | U | | f | u | f | | F | | f | u | f | |
| 15 | U | | f | u | f | | F | | f | u | f | |
| 16 | | U | | f | u | f | | F | | f | u | f |
| 17 | | U | | f | u | f | | F | | f | u | f |
| 18 | | U | | f | u | f | | F | | f | u | f |
| 19 | f | | U | | f | u | f | | F | | f | u |
| 20 | f | | U | | f | u | f | | F | | f | u |
| 21 | u | f | | U | | f | u | f | | F | | f |
| 22 | u | f | | U | | f | u | f | | F | | f |
| 23 | u | f | | U | | f | u | f | | F | | f |
| 24 | f | u | f | | U | | f | u | f | | F | |
| 25 | f | u | f | | U | | f | u | f | | F | |
| 26 | | f | u | f | | U | | f | u | f | | F |
| 27 | | f | u | f | | U | | f | u | f | | F |
| 28 | F | | f | u | f | | U | | f | u | f | |

# March Moon Table

| Date | Sign | Element | Nature | Phase |
|---|---|---|---|---|
| 1 Wed | Aries | Fire | Barren | 1st |
| 2 Thu 2:43 am | Taurus | Earth | Semi-fruitful | 1st |
| 3 Fri | Taurus | Earth | Semi-fruitful | 1st |
| 4 Sat 5:05 am | Gemini | Air | Barren | 1st |
| 5 Sun | Gemini | Air | Barren | 2nd 6:32 am |
| 6 Mon 7:54 am | Cancer | Water | Fruitful | 2nd |
| 7 Tue | Cancer | Water | Fruitful | 2nd |
| 8 Wed 11:45 am | Leo | Fire | Barren | 2nd |
| 9 Thu | Leo | Fire | Barren | 2nd |
| 10 Fri 5:07 pm | Virgo | Earth | Barren | 2nd |
| 11 Sat | Virgo | Earth | Barren | 2nd |
| 12 Sun | Virgo | Earth | Barren | Full 10:54 am |
| 13 Mon 1:28 am | Libra | Air | Semi-fruitful | 3rd |
| 14 Tue | Libra | Air | Semi-fruitful | 3rd |
| 15 Wed 11:11 am | Scorpio | Water | Fruitful | 3rd |
| 16 Thu | Scorpio | Water | Fruitful | 3rd |
| 17 Fri 11:00 pm | Sagittarius | Fire | Barren | 3rd |
| 18 Sat | Sagittarius | Fire | Barren | 3rd |
| 19 Sun | Sagittarius | Fire | Barren | 3rd |
| 20 Mon 11:31 am | Capricorn | Earth | Semi-fruitful | 4th 11:58 am |
| 21 Tue | Capricorn | Earth | Semi-fruitful | 4th |
| 22 Wed 10:28 pm | Aquarius | Air | Barren | 4th |
| 23 Thu | Aquarius | Air | Barren | 4th |
| 24 Fri | Aquarius | Air | Barren | 4th |
| 25 Sat 6:06 am | Pisces | Water | Fruitful | 4th |
| 26 Sun | Pisces | Water | Fruitful | 4th |
| 27 Mon 10:11 am | Aries | Fire | Barren | New 10:57 pm |
| 28 Tue | Aries | Fire | Barren | 1st |
| 29 Wed 11:48 am | Taurus | Earth | Semi-fruitful | 1st |
| 30 Thu | Taurus | Earth | Semi-fruitful | 1st |
| 31 Fri 12:40 pm | Gemini | Air | Barren | 1st |

# March Aspectarian/Favorable & Unfavorable Days

| Date | Sun | Mercury | Venus | Mars | Jupiter | Saturn | Uranus | Neptune | Pluto |
|------|-----|---------|-------|------|---------|--------|--------|---------|-------|
| 1 | | | | C | O | T | C | | Q |
| 2 | | X | | | | | | X | |
| 3 | X | | | | | | | | T |
| 4 | | | | | | | | | |
| 5 | Q | Q | X | | T | | X | Q | |
| 6 | | | | X | | O | | | |
| 7 | T | T | Q | | Q | | Q | T | O |
| 8 | | | | Q | | | | | |
| 9 | | | T | | | | | | |
| 10 | | | | T | X | T | T | | |
| 11 | | | | | | | | O | |
| 12 | O | O | | | | | Q | | T |
| 13 | | | O | | | | | | |
| 14 | | | | | C | | O | | Q |
| 15 | | | | O | | | X | | |
| 16 | | | | | | | | T | |
| 17 | T | | | | | | | | X |
| 18 | | T | T | | | | | Q | |
| 19 | | | | | X | T | | | |
| 20 | Q | | | | | C | | | |
| 21 | | Q | Q | T | | | | X | |
| 22 | | | | | Q | | Q | | C |
| 23 | X | | X | Q | | | | | |
| 24 | | X | | | T | | X | | |
| 25 | | | | | | | X | | |
| 26 | | | | X | | | | C | X |
| 27 | C | | C | | | Q | | | |
| 28 | | | | O | | | | | Q |
| 29 | | C | | | | T | C | | |
| 30 | | | | C | | | | X | T |
| 31 | | | X | | | | | | |

| Date | Aries | Taurus | Gemini | Cancer | Leo | Virgo | Libra | Scorpio | Sagittarius | Capricorn | Aquarius | Pisces |
|------|-------|--------|--------|--------|-----|-------|-------|---------|-------------|-----------|----------|--------|
| 1 | F | | f | u | f | | U | | f | u | f | |
| 2 | | F | | f | u | f | | U | | f | u | f |
| 3 | | F | | f | u | f | | U | | f | u | f |
| 4 | | F | | f | u | f | | U | | f | u | f |
| 5 | f | | F | | f | u | f | | U | | f | u |
| 6 | f | | F | | f | u | f | | U | | f | u |
| 7 | u | f | | F | | f | u | f | | U | | f |
| 8 | u | f | | F | | f | u | f | | U | | f |
| 9 | f | u | f | | F | | f | u | f | | U | |
| 10 | f | u | f | | F | | f | u | f | | U | |
| 11 | | f | u | f | | F | | f | u | f | | U |
| 12 | | f | u | f | | F | | f | u | f | | U |
| 13 | U | | f | u | f | | F | | f | u | f | |
| 14 | U | | f | u | f | | F | | f | u | f | |
| 15 | U | | f | u | f | | F | | f | u | f | |
| 16 | | U | | f | u | f | | F | | f | u | f |
| 17 | | U | | f | u | f | | F | | f | u | f |
| 18 | f | | U | | f | u | f | | F | | f | u |
| 19 | f | | U | | f | u | f | | F | | f | u |
| 20 | f | | U | | f | u | f | | F | | f | u |
| 21 | u | f | | U | | f | u | f | | F | | f |
| 22 | u | f | | U | | f | u | f | | F | | f |
| 23 | f | u | f | | U | | f | u | f | | F | |
| 24 | f | u | f | | U | | f | u | f | | F | |
| 25 | f | u | f | | U | | f | u | f | | F | |
| 26 | | f | u | f | | U | | f | u | f | | F |
| 27 | | f | u | f | | U | | f | u | f | | F |
| 28 | F | | f | u | f | | U | | f | u | f | |
| 29 | F | | f | u | f | | U | | f | u | f | |
| 30 | | F | | f | u | f | | U | | f | u | f |
| 31 | | F | | f | u | f | | U | | f | u | f |

## April Moon Table

| Date | Sign | Element | Nature | Phase |
|------|------|---------|--------|-------|
| 1 Sat | Gemini | Air | Barren | 1st |
| 2 Sun 2:27 pm | Cancer | Water | Fruitful | 1st |
| 3 Mon | Cancer | Water | Fruitful | 2nd 2:39 pm |
| 4 Tue 6:13 pm | Leo | Fire | Barren | 2nd |
| 5 Wed | Leo | Fire | Barren | 2nd |
| 6 Thu | Leo | Fire | Barren | 2nd |
| 7 Fri 12:20 am | Virgo | Earth | Barren | 2nd |
| 8 Sat | Virgo | Earth | Barren | 2nd |
| 9 Sun 8:34 am | Libra | Air | Semi-fruitful | 2nd |
| 10 Mon | Libra | Air | Semi-fruitful | 2nd |
| 11 Tue 6:42 pm | Scorpio | Water | Fruitful | Full 2:08 am |
| 12 Wed | Scorpio | Water | Fruitful | 3rd |
| 13 Thu | Scorpio | Water | Fruitful | 3rd |
| 14 Fri 6:27 am | Sagittarius | Fire | Barren | 3rd |
| 15 Sat | Sagittarius | Fire | Barren | 3rd |
| 16 Sun 7:05 pm | Capricorn | Earth | Semi-fruitful | 3rd |
| 17 Mon | Capricorn | Earth | Semi-fruitful | 3rd |
| 18 Tue | Capricorn | Earth | Semi-fruitful | 3rd |
| 19 Wed 6:52 am | Aquarius | Air | Barren | 4th 5:57 am |
| 20 Thu | Aquarius | Air | Barren | 4th |
| 21 Fri 3:43 pm | Pisces | Water | Fruitful | 4th |
| 22 Sat | Pisces | Water | Fruitful | 4th |
| 23 Sun 8:32 pm | Aries | Fire | Barren | 4th |
| 24 Mon | Aries | Fire | Barren | 4th |
| 25 Tue 9:56 pm | Taurus | Earth | Semi-fruitful | 4th |
| 26 Wed | Taurus | Earth | Semi-fruitful | New 8:16 am |
| 27 Thu 9:39 pm | Gemini | Air | Barren | 1st |
| 28 Fri | Gemini | Air | Barren | 1st |
| 29 Sat 9:48 pm | Cancer | Water | Fruitful | 1st |
| 30 Sun | Cancer | Water | Fruitful | 1st |

# April Aspectarian/Favorable & Unfavorable Days

| Date | Sun | Mercury | Venus | Mars | Jupiter | Saturn | Uranus | Neptune | Pluto |
|---|---|---|---|---|---|---|---|---|---|
| 1 | X | | | | T | | | Q | |
| 2 | | X | Q | | | O | X | | |
| 3 | Q | | | X | Q | | | T | O |
| 4 | | | T | | | | | Q | |
| 5 | T | Q | | | | | | | |
| 6 | | | | Q | X | T | T | | |
| 7 | | T | | | | | | | |
| 8 | | | | T | | | | O | T |
| 9 | | | O | | | Q | | | |
| 10 | | | | | C | | | | Q |
| 11 | O | | | | | X | O | | |
| 12 | | O | | | | | | T | |
| 13 | | | O | | | | | | X |
| 14 | | | T | | | | | | |
| 15 | | | | | X | | | Q | |
| 16 | T | T | Q | | | C | T | | |
| 17 | | | | | | | | X | |
| 18 | | | | | Q | | Q | | C |
| 19 | Q | Q | X | T | | | | | |
| 20 | | | | | T | | | | |
| 21 | X | X | | Q | | X | X | | |
| 22 | | | | | | | C | | |
| 23 | | | C | X | | Q | | | X |
| 24 | | | | O | | | | | |
| 25 | | C | | | | T | C | | Q |
| 26 | C | | | | | | X | | |
| 27 | | | X | | | | | | T |
| 28 | | | C | T | | | Q | | |
| 29 | | X | Q | | | O | X | | |
| 30 | X | | | | Q | | | T | |

| Date | Aries | Taurus | Gemini | Cancer | Leo | Virgo | Libra | Scorpio | Sagittarius | Capricorn | Aquarius | Pisces |
|---|---|---|---|---|---|---|---|---|---|---|---|---|
| 1 | f | | F | | f | u | f | | U | | f | u |
| 2 | f | | F | | f | u | f | | U | | f | u |
| 3 | u | f | | F | | f | u | f | | U | | f |
| 4 | u | f | | F | | f | u | f | | U | | f |
| 5 | f | u | f | | F | | f | u | f | | U | |
| 6 | f | u | f | | F | | f | u | f | | U | |
| 7 | | f | u | f | | F | | f | u | f | | U |
| 8 | | f | u | f | | F | | f | u | f | | U |
| 9 | | f | u | f | | F | | f | u | f | | U |
| 10 | U | | f | u | f | | F | | f | u | f | |
| 11 | U | | f | u | f | | F | | f | u | f | |
| 12 | | U | | f | u | f | | F | | f | u | f |
| 13 | | U | | f | u | f | | F | | f | u | f |
| 14 | | U | | f | u | f | | F | | f | u | f |
| 15 | f | | U | | f | u | f | | F | | f | u |
| 16 | f | | U | | f | u | f | | F | | f | u |
| 17 | u | f | | U | | f | u | f | | F | | f |
| 18 | u | f | | U | | f | u | f | | F | | f |
| 19 | u | f | | U | | f | u | f | | F | | f |
| 20 | f | u | f | | U | | f | u | f | | F | |
| 21 | f | u | f | | U | | f | u | f | | F | |
| 22 | | f | u | f | | U | | f | u | f | | F |
| 23 | | f | u | f | | U | | f | u | f | | F |
| 24 | F | | f | u | f | | U | | f | u | f | |
| 25 | F | | f | u | f | | U | | f | u | f | |
| 26 | | F | | f | u | f | | U | | f | u | f |
| 27 | | F | | f | u | f | | U | | f | u | f |
| 28 | f | | F | | f | u | f | | U | | f | u |
| 29 | f | | F | | f | u | f | | U | | f | u |
| 30 | u | f | | F | | f | u | f | | U | | f |

# May Moon Table

| Date | Sign | Element | Nature | Phase |
|------|------|---------|--------|-------|
| 1 Mon | Cancer | Water | Fruitful | 1st |
| 2 Tue 12:12 am | Leo | Fire | Barren | 2nd 10:47 pm |
| 3 Wed | Leo | Fire | Barren | 2nd |
| 4 Thu 5:47 am | Virgo | Earth | Barren | 2nd |
| 5 Fri | Virgo | Earth | Barren | 2nd |
| 6 Sat 2:20 pm | Libra | Air | Semi-fruitful | 2nd |
| 7 Sun | Libra | Air | Semi-fruitful | 2nd |
| 8 Mon | Libra | Air | Semi-fruitful | 2nd |
| 9 Tue 1:01 am | Scorpio | Water | Fruitful | 2nd |
| 10 Wed | Scorpio | Water | Fruitful | Full 5:42 pm |
| 11 Thu 12:59 pm | Sagittarius | Fire | Barren | 3rd |
| 12 Fri | Sagittarius | Fire | Barren | 3rd |
| 13 Sat | Sagittarius | Fire | Barren | 3rd |
| 14 Sun 1:37 am | Capricorn | Earth | Semi-fruitful | 3rd |
| 15 Mon | Capricorn | Earth | Semi-fruitful | 3rd |
| 16 Tue 1:50 pm | Aquarius | Air | Barren | 3rd |
| 17 Wed | Aquarius | Air | Barren | 3rd |
| 18 Thu 11:52 pm | Pisces | Water | Fruitful | 4th 8:33 pm |
| 19 Fri | Pisces | Water | Fruitful | 4th |
| 20 Sat | Pisces | Water | Fruitful | 4th |
| 21 Sun 6:10 am | Aries | Fire | Barren | 4th |
| 22 Mon | Aries | Fire | Barren | 4th |
| 23 Tue 8:33 am | Taurus | Earth | Semi-fruitful | 4th |
| 24 Wed | Taurus | Earth | Semi-fruitful | 4th |
| 25 Thu 8:15 am | Gemini | Air | Barren | New 3:44 pm |
| 26 Fri | Gemini | Air | Barren | 1st |
| 27 Sat 7:25 am | Cancer | Water | Fruitful | 1st |
| 28 Sun | Cancer | Water | Fruitful | 1st |
| 29 Mon 8:12 am | Leo | Fire | Barren | 1st |
| 30 Tue | Leo | Fire | Barren | 1st |
| 31 Wed 12:16 pm | Virgo | Earth | Barren | 1st |

# May Aspectarian/Favorable & Unfavorable Days

| Date | Sun | Mercury | Venus | Mars | Jupiter | Saturn | Uranus | Neptune | Pluto |
|---|---|---|---|---|---|---|---|---|---|
| 1 |  | Q |  |  |  |  |  | Q | O |
| 2 | Q |  | T | X |  |  |  |  |  |
| 3 |  | T |  |  | X |  | T |  |  |
| 4 |  |  | Q |  |  | T |  |  |  |
| 5 | T |  |  |  |  |  |  | O | T |
| 6 |  |  | O |  | Q |  |  |  |  |
| 7 |  |  |  | T | C |  |  |  |  |
| 8 |  | O |  |  |  | X | O |  | Q |
| 9 |  |  |  |  |  |  |  |  |  |
| 10 | O |  |  |  |  |  |  | T | X |
| 11 |  |  |  |  |  |  |  |  |  |
| 12 |  |  | T | O | X |  |  | Q |  |
| 13 |  | T |  |  |  | C | T |  |  |
| 14 |  |  | Q |  |  |  |  |  |  |
| 15 |  |  |  |  | Q |  |  | X | C |
| 16 | T | Q |  |  |  |  |  | Q |  |
| 17 |  |  | X |  | T |  |  |  |  |
| 18 | Q |  |  | T |  | X | X |  |  |
| 19 |  | X |  |  |  |  |  |  |  |
| 20 |  |  |  | Q |  | Q |  | C | X |
| 21 | X |  |  |  |  |  |  |  |  |
| 22 |  |  | C | X | O |  |  |  | Q |
| 23 |  | C |  |  |  | T | C |  |  |
| 24 |  |  |  |  |  |  |  | X | T |
| 25 | C |  |  |  |  |  |  |  |  |
| 26 |  |  | X | C | T |  |  | Q |  |
| 27 |  |  |  |  |  | O | X |  |  |
| 28 |  | X | Q |  | Q |  |  | T | O |
| 29 | X |  |  |  |  |  | Q |  |  |
| 30 |  | Q |  |  | X |  |  |  |  |
| 31 |  |  | T | X |  | T | T |  |  |

| Date | Aries | Taurus | Gemini | Cancer | Leo | Virgo | Libra | Scorpio | Sagittarius | Capricorn | Aquarius | Pisces |
|---|---|---|---|---|---|---|---|---|---|---|---|---|
| 1 | u | f |  | F |  | f | u | f |  | U |  | f |
| 2 | f | u | f |  | F |  | f | u | f |  | U |  |
| 3 | f | u | f |  | F |  | f | u | f |  | U |  |
| 4 | f | u | f |  | F |  | f | u | f |  | U |  |
| 5 |  | f | u | f |  | F |  | f | u | f |  | U |
| 6 |  | f | u | f |  | F |  | f | u | f |  | U |
| 7 | U |  | f | u | f |  | F |  | f | u | f |  |
| 8 | U |  | f | u | f |  | F |  | f | u | f |  |
| 9 |  | U |  | f | u | f |  | F |  | f | u | f |
| 10 |  | U |  | f | u | f |  | F |  | f | u | f |
| 11 |  | U |  | f | u | f |  | F |  | f | u | f |
| 12 | f |  | U |  | f | u | f |  | F |  | f | u |
| 13 | f |  | U |  | f | u | f |  | F |  | f | u |
| 14 | u | f |  | U |  | f | u | f |  | F |  | f |
| 15 | u | f |  | U |  | f | u | f |  | F |  | f |
| 16 | u | f |  | U |  | f | u | f |  | F |  | f |
| 17 | f | u | f |  | U |  | f | u | f |  | F |  |
| 18 | f | u | f |  | U |  | f | u | f |  | F |  |
| 19 |  | f | u | f |  | U |  | f | u | f |  | F |
| 20 |  | f | u | f |  | U |  | f | u | f |  | F |
| 21 |  | f | u | f |  | U |  | f | u | f |  | F |
| 22 | F |  | f | u | f |  | U |  | f | u | f |  |
| 23 | F |  | f | u | f |  | U |  | f | u | f |  |
| 24 |  | F |  | f | u | f |  | U |  | f | u | f |
| 25 |  | F |  | f | u | f |  | U |  | f | u | f |
| 26 | f |  | F |  | f | u | f |  | U |  | f | u |
| 27 | f |  | F |  | f | u | f |  | U |  | f | u |
| 28 | u | f |  | F |  | f | u | f |  | U |  | f |
| 29 | u | f |  | F |  | f | u | f |  | U |  | f |
| 30 | f | u | f |  | F |  | f | u | f |  | U |  |
| 31 | f | u | f |  | F |  | f | u | f |  | U |  |

# June Moon Table

| Date | Sign | Element | Nature | Phase |
|------|------|---------|--------|-------|
| 1 Thu | Virgo | Earth | Barren | 2nd 8:42 am |
| 2 Fri 8:04 pm | Libra | Air | Semi-fruitful | 2nd |
| 3 Sat | Libra | Air | Semi-fruitful | 2nd |
| 4 Sun | Libra | Air | Semi-fruitful | 2nd |
| 5 Mon 6:46 am | Scorpio | Water | Fruitful | 2nd |
| 6 Tue | Scorpio | Water | Fruitful | 2nd |
| 7 Wed 6:59 pm | Sagittarius | Fire | Barren | 2nd |
| 8 Thu | Sagittarius | Fire | Barren | 2nd |
| 9 Fri | Sagittarius | Fire | Barren | Full 9:10 am |
| 10 Sat 7:36 am | Capricorn | Earth | Semi-fruitful | 3rd |
| 11 Sun | Capricorn | Earth | Semi-fruitful | 3rd |
| 12 Mon 7:45 pm | Aquarius | Air | Barren | 3rd |
| 13 Tue | Aquarius | Air | Barren | 3rd |
| 14 Wed | Aquarius | Air | Barren | 3rd |
| 15 Thu 6:17 am | Pisces | Water | Fruitful | 3rd |
| 16 Fri | Pisces | Water | Fruitful | 3rd |
| 17 Sat 1:55 pm | Aries | Fire | Barren | 4th 7:33 am |
| 18 Sun | Aries | Fire | Barren | 4th |
| 19 Mon 5:53 pm | Taurus | Earth | Semi-fruitful | 4th |
| 20 Tue | Taurus | Earth | Semi-fruitful | 4th |
| 21 Wed 6:44 pm | Gemini | Air | Barren | 4th |
| 22 Thu | Gemini | Air | Barren | 4th |
| 23 Fri 6:07 pm | Cancer | Water | Fruitful | New 10:31 pm |
| 24 Sat | Cancer | Water | Fruitful | 1st |
| 25 Sun 6:06 pm | Leo | Fire | Barren | 1st |
| 26 Mon | Leo | Fire | Barren | 1st |
| 27 Tue 8:41 pm | Virgo | Earth | Barren | 1st |
| 28 Wed | Virgo | Earth | Barren | 1st |
| 29 Thu | Virgo | Earth | Barren | 1st |
| 30 Fri 3:02 am | Libra | Air | Semi-fruitful | 2nd 8:51 pm |

# June Aspectarian/Favorable & Unfavorable Days

| Date | Sun | Mercury | Venus | Mars | Jupiter | Saturn | Uranus | Neptune | Pluto |
|---|---|---|---|---|---|---|---|---|---|
| 1 | Q | | | | | | | O | T |
| 2 | | T | | Q | | Q | | | |
| 3 | T | | | | C | | | | |
| 4 | | | | | X | | | | Q |
| 5 | | | O | T | | | O | | |
| 6 | | | | | | | | T | X |
| 7 | | O | | | | | | | |
| 8 | | | | | X | | Q | | |
| 9 | O | | | | | C | | | |
| 10 | | | T | O | | | T | | |
| 11 | | | | | Q | | | X | C |
| 12 | | | | | | | Q | | |
| 13 | | T | Q | | T | | | | |
| 14 | T | | | | | X | | | |
| 15 | | | | T | | X | | | |
| 16 | | Q | X | | | | | C | X |
| 17 | Q | | | | | | Q | | |
| 18 | | | | Q | O | | | | Q |
| 19 | X | X | | | | | T | C | |
| 20 | | | C | X | | | | X | |
| 21 | | | | | | | | | T |
| 22 | | | | | T | | Q | | |
| 23 | C | | | | | O | X | | |
| 24 | | C | | C | Q | | | T | O |
| 25 | | | X | | | | Q | | |
| 26 | | | | | X | | | | |
| 27 | | | Q | | | T | T | | |
| 28 | X | | | | | | | O | |
| 29 | | X | T | X | | Q | | | T |
| 30 | Q | | | | | | | | |

| Date | Aries | Taurus | Gemini | Cancer | Leo | Virgo | Libra | Scorpio | Sagittarius | Capricorn | Aquarius | Pisces |
|---|---|---|---|---|---|---|---|---|---|---|---|---|
| 1 | | f | u | f | | F | | f | u | f | | U |
| 2 | | f | u | f | | F | | f | u | f | | U |
| 3 | U | | f | u | f | | F | | f | u | f | |
| 4 | U | | f | u | f | | F | | f | u | f | |
| 5 | U | | f | u | f | | F | | f | u | f | |
| 6 | | U | | f | u | f | | F | | f | u | f |
| 7 | | U | | f | u | f | | F | | f | u | f |
| 8 | f | | U | | f | u | f | | F | | f | u |
| 9 | f | | U | | f | u | f | | F | | f | u |
| 10 | f | | U | | f | u | f | | F | | f | u |
| 11 | u | f | | U | | f | u | f | | F | | f |
| 12 | u | f | | U | | f | u | f | | F | | f |
| 13 | f | u | f | | U | | f | u | f | | F | |
| 14 | f | u | f | | U | | f | u | f | | F | |
| 15 | f | u | f | | U | | f | u | f | | F | |
| 16 | | f | u | f | | U | | f | u | f | | F |
| 17 | | f | u | f | | U | | f | u | f | | F |
| 18 | F | | f | u | f | | U | | f | u | f | |
| 19 | F | | f | u | f | | U | | f | u | f | |
| 20 | | F | | f | u | f | | U | | f | u | f |
| 21 | | F | | f | u | f | | U | | f | u | f |
| 22 | f | | F | | f | u | f | | U | | f | u |
| 23 | f | | F | | f | u | f | | U | | f | u |
| 24 | u | f | | F | | f | u | f | | U | | f |
| 25 | u | f | | F | | f | u | f | | U | | f |
| 26 | f | u | f | | F | | f | u | f | | U | |
| 27 | f | u | f | | F | | f | u | f | | U | |
| 28 | | f | u | f | | F | | f | u | f | | U |
| 29 | | f | u | f | | F | | f | u | f | | U |
| 30 | | f | u | f | | F | | f | u | f | | U |

# July Moon Table

| Date | Sign | Element | Nature | Phase |
|------|------|---------|--------|-------|
| 1 Sat | Libra | Air | Semi-fruitful | 2nd |
| 2 Sun 12:59 pm | Scorpio | Water | Fruitful | 2nd |
| 3 Mon | Scorpio | Water | Fruitful | 2nd |
| 4 Tue | Scorpio | Water | Fruitful | 2nd |
| 5 Wed 1:08 am | Sagittarius | Fire | Barren | 2nd |
| 6 Thu | Sagittarius | Fire | Barren | 2nd |
| 7 Fri 1:45 pm | Capricorn | Earth | Semi-fruitful | 2nd |
| 8 Sat | Capricorn | Earth | Semi-fruitful | 2nd |
| 9 Sun | Capricorn | Earth | Semi-fruitful | Full 12:07 am |
| 10 Mon 1:35 am | Aquarius | Air | Barren | 3rd |
| 11 Tue | Aquarius | Air | Barren | 3rd |
| 12 Wed 11:51 am | Pisces | Water | Fruitful | 3rd |
| 13 Thu | Pisces | Water | Fruitful | 3rd |
| 14 Fri 7:52 pm | Aries | Fire | Barren | 3rd |
| 15 Sat | Aries | Fire | Barren | 3rd |
| 16 Sun | Aries | Fire | Barren | 4th 3:26 pm |
| 17 Mon 1:04 am | Taurus | Earth | Semi-fruitful | 4th |
| 18 Tue | Taurus | Earth | Semi-fruitful | 4th |
| 19 Wed 3:31 am | Gemini | Air | Barren | 4th |
| 20 Thu | Gemini | Air | Barren | 4th |
| 21 Fri 4:09 am | Cancer | Water | Fruitful | 4th |
| 22 Sat | Cancer | Water | Fruitful | 4th |
| 23 Sun 4:34 am | Leo | Fire | Barren | New 5:46 am |
| 24 Mon | Leo | Fire | Barren | 1st |
| 25 Tue 6:32 am | Virgo | Earth | Barren | 1st |
| 26 Wed | Virgo | Earth | Barren | 1st |
| 27 Thu 11:37 am | Libra | Air | Semi-fruitful | 1st |
| 28 Fri | Libra | Air | Semi-fruitful | 1st |
| 29 Sat 8:23 pm | Scorpio | Water | Fruitful | 1st |
| 30 Sun | Scorpio | Water | Fruitful | 2nd 11:23 am |
| 31 Mon | Scorpio | Water | Fruitful | 2nd |

# July Aspectarian/Favorable & Unfavorable Days

| Date | Sun | Mercury | Venus | Mars | Jupiter | Saturn | Uranus | Neptune | Pluto |
|---|---|---|---|---|---|---|---|---|---|
| 1 |  | Q |  | Q | C | X |  |  | Q |
| 2 |  |  |  |  |  |  |  | O |  |
| 3 | T |  |  |  |  |  |  | T |  |
| 4 |  | T |  | T |  |  |  |  | X |
| 5 |  |  | O |  |  |  |  |  |  |
| 6 |  |  |  |  | X | C |  | Q |  |
| 7 |  |  |  |  |  |  |  | T |  |
| 8 |  |  |  |  | Q |  |  | X |  |
| 9 | O |  |  | O |  |  | Q |  | C |
| 10 |  | O | T |  |  |  |  |  |  |
| 11 |  |  |  |  | T | X |  |  |  |
| 12 |  |  |  |  |  |  | X |  |  |
| 13 |  |  | Q |  |  |  |  | C | X |
| 14 | T |  |  | T |  | Q |  |  |  |
| 15 |  |  | X |  | O |  |  |  |  |
| 16 | Q | T |  | Q |  | T | C |  | Q |
| 17 |  |  |  |  |  |  |  |  |  |
| 18 | X | Q |  |  |  |  |  | X | T |
| 19 |  |  |  | X |  |  |  |  |  |
| 20 |  | X | C |  | T | O |  | Q |  |
| 21 |  |  |  |  |  | X |  |  |  |
| 22 |  |  |  |  | Q |  |  | T | O |
| 23 | C |  |  | C |  |  | Q |  |  |
| 24 |  |  | X |  | X | T |  |  |  |
| 25 |  | C |  |  |  | T |  |  |  |
| 26 |  |  |  |  | Q |  |  | O | T |
| 27 | X |  | Q | X |  |  |  |  |  |
| 28 |  |  |  |  | C |  |  |  | Q |
| 29 |  |  | T |  |  | X | O |  |  |
| 30 | Q | X |  | Q |  |  |  | T |  |
| 31 |  |  |  |  |  |  |  |  | X |

| Date | Aries | Taurus | Gemini | Cancer | Leo | Virgo | Libra | Scorpio | Sagittarius | Capricorn | Aquarius | Pisces |
|---|---|---|---|---|---|---|---|---|---|---|---|---|
| 1 | U |  | f | u | f |  | F |  | f | u | f |  |
| 2 | U |  | f | u | f |  | F |  | f | u | f |  |
| 3 |  | U |  | f | u | f |  | F |  | f | u | f |
| 4 |  | U |  | f | u | f |  | F |  | f | u | f |
| 5 | f |  | U |  | f | u | f |  | F |  | f | u |
| 6 | f |  | U |  | f | u | f |  | F |  | f | u |
| 7 | f |  | U |  | f | u | f |  | F |  | f | u |
| 8 | u | f |  | U |  | f | u | f |  | F |  | f |
| 9 | u | f |  | U |  | f | u | f |  | F |  | f |
| 10 | f | u | f |  | U |  | f | u | f |  | F |  |
| 11 | f | u | f |  | U |  | f | u | f |  | F |  |
| 12 | f | u | f |  | U |  | f | u | f |  | F |  |
| 13 |  | f | u | f |  | U |  | f | u | f |  | F |
| 14 |  | f | u | f |  | U |  | f | u | f |  | F |
| 15 | F |  | f | u | f |  | U |  | f | u | f |  |
| 16 | F |  | f | u | f |  | U |  | f | u | f |  |
| 17 |  | F |  | f | u | f |  | U |  | f | u | f |
| 18 |  | F |  | f | u | f |  | U |  | f | u | f |
| 19 |  | F |  | f | u | f |  | U |  | f | u | f |
| 20 | f |  | F |  | f | u | f |  | U |  | f | u |
| 21 | f |  | F |  | f | u | f |  | U |  | f | u |
| 22 | u | f |  | F |  | f | u | f |  | U |  | f |
| 23 | u | f |  | F |  | f | u | f |  | U |  | f |
| 24 | f | u | f |  | F |  | f | u | f |  | U |  |
| 25 | f | u | f |  | F |  | f | u | f |  | U |  |
| 26 |  | f | u | f |  | F |  | f | u | f |  | U |
| 27 |  | f | u | f |  | F |  | f | u | f |  | U |
| 28 | U |  | f | u | f |  | F |  | f | u | f |  |
| 29 | U |  | f | u | f |  | F |  | f | u | f |  |
| 30 |  | U |  | f | u | f |  | F |  | f | u | f |
| 31 |  | U |  | f | u | f |  | F |  | f | u | f |

# August Moon Table

| Date | Sign | Element | Nature | Phase |
|------|------|---------|--------|-------|
| 1 Tue 8:01 am | Sagittarius | Fire | Barren | 2nd |
| 2 Wed | Sagittarius | Fire | Barren | 2nd |
| 3 Thu 8:37 pm | Capricorn | Earth | Semi-fruitful | 2nd |
| 4 Fri | Capricorn | Earth | Semi-fruitful | 2nd |
| 5 Sat | Capricorn | Earth | Semi-fruitful | 2nd |
| 6 Sun 8:15 am | Aquarius | Air | Barren | 2nd |
| 7 Mon | Aquarius | Air | Barren | Full 2:11 pm |
| 8 Tue 5:56 pm | Pisces | Water | Fruitful | 3rd |
| 9 Wed | Pisces | Water | Fruitful | 3rd |
| 10 Thu | Pisces | Water | Fruitful | 3rd |
| 11 Fri 1:22 am | Aries | Fire | Barren | 3rd |
| 12 Sat | Aries | Fire | Barren | 3rd |
| 13 Sun 6:40 am | Taurus | Earth | Semi-fruitful | 3rd |
| 14 Mon | Taurus | Earth | Semi-fruitful | 4th 9:15 pm |
| 15 Tue 10:06 am | Gemini | Air | Barren | 4th |
| 16 Wed | Gemini | Air | Barren | 4th |
| 17 Thu 12:13 pm | Cancer | Water | Fruitful | 4th |
| 18 Fri | Cancer | Water | Fruitful | 4th |
| 19 Sat 1:55 pm | Leo | Fire | Barren | 4th |
| 20 Sun | Leo | Fire | Barren | 4th |
| 21 Mon 4:25 pm | Virgo | Earth | Barren | New 2:30 pm |
| 22 Tue | Virgo | Earth | Barren | 1st |
| 23 Wed 9:05 pm | Libra | Air | Semi-fruitful | 1st |
| 24 Thu | Libra | Air | Semi-fruitful | 1st |
| 25 Fri | Libra | Air | Semi-fruitful | 1st |
| 26 Sat 4:53 am | Scorpio | Water | Fruitful | 1st |
| 27 Sun | Scorpio | Water | Fruitful | 1st |
| 28 Mon 3:48 pm | Sagittarius | Fire | Barren | 1st |
| 29 Tue | Sagittarius | Fire | Barren | 2nd 4:13 am |
| 30 Wed | Sagittarius | Fire | Barren | 2nd |
| 31 Thu 4:18 am | Capricorn | Earth | Semi-fruitful | 2nd |

# August Aspectarian/Favorable & Unfavorable Days

| Date | Sun | Mercury | Venus | Mars | Jupiter | Saturn | Uranus | Neptune | Pluto |
|------|-----|---------|-------|------|---------|--------|--------|---------|-------|
| 1 | | Q | | | | | | | |
| 2 | T | | | T | X | | | Q | |
| 3 | | | | | | C | T | | |
| 4 | | T | O | | | | | X | |
| 5 | | | | | Q | | | | C |
| 6 | | | | | | | Q | | |
| 7 | O | | | O | T | | | | |
| 8 | | | | | | X | X | | |
| 9 | | O | T | | | | | C | |
| 10 | | | | | Q | | | | X |
| 11 | | | | | | | | | |
| 12 | T | | Q | T | O | T | | | Q |
| 13 | | | | | | | C | | |
| 14 | Q | T | X | Q | | | | X | T |
| 15 | | | | | | | | | |
| 16 | | Q | | X | T | O | | Q | |
| 17 | X | | | | | | X | | |
| 18 | | X | | | Q | | | T | O |
| 19 | | | C | | | | Q | | |
| 20 | | | | C | X | | | | |
| 21 | C | | | | | T | T | | |
| 22 | | C | | | | | | O | T |
| 23 | | | X | | | Q | | | |
| 24 | | | | | | | | | |
| 25 | | | | X | C | X | | | Q |
| 26 | X | X | Q | | | | O | | |
| 27 | | | | | | | | T | X |
| 28 | | Q | T | Q | | | | | |
| 29 | Q | | | | | | | Q | |
| 30 | | | | T | X | C | | | |
| 31 | T | T | | | | | | T | |

| Date | Aries | Taurus | Gemini | Cancer | Leo | Virgo | Libra | Scorpio | Sagittarius | Capricorn | Aquarius | Pisces |
|------|-------|--------|--------|--------|-----|-------|-------|---------|-------------|-----------|----------|--------|
| 1 | | U | | f | u | f | | F | | f | u | f |
| 2 | f | | U | | f | u | f | | F | | f | u |
| 3 | f | | U | | f | u | f | | F | | f | u |
| 4 | u | f | | U | | f | u | f | | F | | f |
| 5 | u | f | | U | | f | u | f | | F | | f |
| 6 | u | f | | U | | f | u | f | | F | | f |
| 7 | f | u | f | | U | | f | u | f | | F | |
| 8 | f | u | f | | U | | f | u | f | | F | |
| 9 | | f | u | f | | U | | f | u | f | | F |
| 10 | | f | u | f | | U | | f | u | f | | F |
| 11 | F | | f | u | f | | U | | f | u | f | |
| 12 | F | | f | u | f | | U | | f | u | f | |
| 13 | F | | f | u | f | | U | | f | u | f | |
| 14 | | F | | f | u | f | | U | | f | u | f |
| 15 | | F | | f | u | f | | U | | f | u | f |
| 16 | f | | F | | f | u | f | | U | | f | u |
| 17 | f | | F | | f | u | f | | U | | f | u |
| 18 | u | f | | F | | f | u | f | | U | | f |
| 19 | u | f | | F | | f | u | f | | U | | f |
| 20 | f | u | f | | F | | f | u | f | | U | |
| 21 | f | u | f | | F | | f | u | f | | U | |
| 22 | | f | u | f | | F | | f | u | f | | U |
| 23 | | f | u | f | | F | | f | u | f | | U |
| 24 | U | | f | u | f | | F | | f | u | f | |
| 25 | U | | f | u | f | | F | | f | u | f | |
| 26 | U | | f | u | f | | F | | f | u | f | |
| 27 | | U | | f | u | f | | F | | f | u | f |
| 28 | | U | | f | u | f | | F | | f | u | f |
| 29 | f | | U | | f | u | f | | F | | f | u |
| 30 | f | | U | | f | u | f | | F | | f | u |
| 31 | f | | U | | f | u | f | | F | | f | u |

# September Moon Table

| Date | Sign | Element | Nature | Phase |
|------|------|---------|--------|-------|
| 1 Fri | Capricorn | Earth | Semi-fruitful | 2nd |
| 2 Sat 4:06 pm | Aquarius | Air | Barren | 2nd |
| 3 Sun | Aquarius | Air | Barren | 2nd |
| 4 Mon | Aquarius | Air | Barren | 2nd |
| 5 Tue 1:28 am | Pisces | Water | Fruitful | 2nd |
| 6 Wed | Pisces | Water | Fruitful | Full 3:03 am |
| 7 Thu 8:01 am | Aries | Fire | Barren | 3rd |
| 8 Fri | Aries | Fire | Barren | 3rd |
| 9 Sat 12:23 pm | Taurus | Earth | Semi-fruitful | 3rd |
| 10 Sun | Taurus | Earth | Semi-fruitful | 3rd |
| 11 Mon 3:29 pm | Gemini | Air | Barren | 3rd |
| 12 Tue | Gemini | Air | Barren | 3rd |
| 13 Wed 6:12 pm | Cancer | Water | Fruitful | 4th 2:25 am |
| 14 Thu | Cancer | Water | Fruitful | 4th |
| 15 Fri 9:09 pm | Leo | Fire | Barren | 4th |
| 16 Sat | Leo | Fire | Barren | 4th |
| 17 Sun | Leo | Fire | Barren | 4th |
| 18 Mon 12:52 am | Virgo | Earth | Barren | 4th |
| 19 Tue | Virgo | Earth | Barren | 4th |
| 20 Wed 6:06 am | Libra | Air | Semi-fruitful | New 1:30 am |
| 21 Thu | Libra | Air | Semi-fruitful | 1st |
| 22 Fri 1:40 pm | Scorpio | Water | Fruitful | 1st |
| 23 Sat | Scorpio | Water | Fruitful | 1st |
| 24 Sun | Scorpio | Water | Fruitful | 1st |
| 25 Mon 12:01 am | Sagittarius | Fire | Barren | 1st |
| 26 Tue | Sagittarius | Fire | Barren | 1st |
| 27 Wed 12:24 pm | Capricorn | Earth | Semi-fruitful | 2nd 10:54 pm |
| 28 Thu | Capricorn | Earth | Semi-fruitful | 2nd |
| 29 Fri | Capricorn | Earth | Semi-fruitful | 2nd |
| 30 Sat 12:40 am | Aquarius | Air | Barren | 2nd |

# September Aspectarian/Favorable & Unfavorable Days

| Date | Sun | Mercury | Venus | Mars | Jupiter | Saturn | Uranus | Neptune | Pluto |
|------|-----|---------|-------|------|---------|--------|--------|---------|-------|
| 1 | | | | | | | | X | C |
| 2 | | | | Q | | Q | | | |
| 3 | | | O | | | | | | |
| 4 | | O | | | T | X | X | | |
| 5 | | | | O | | | | | |
| 6 | O | | | | | Q | | C | X |
| 7 | | | | | | | | | |
| 8 | | | T | | | T | | | Q |
| 9 | | T | | T | O | | C | | |
| 10 | T | | Q | | | | | X | T |
| 11 | | Q | Q | | | | | | |
| 12 | | | | | | | | Q | |
| 13 | Q | | X | | T | O | X | | |
| 14 | | X | | X | | | | T | O |
| 15 | X | | | | Q | | Q | | |
| 16 | | | | | | | | | |
| 17 | | | C | | X | T | T | | |
| 18 | | C | C | | | | O | | |
| 19 | | | | | Q | | | | T |
| 20 | C | | | | | | | | |
| 21 | | | | | X | | | | Q |
| 22 | | X | | | C | O | | | |
| 23 | | | X | | | | | T | X |
| 24 | | X | | | | | | | |
| 25 | X | | Q | | | | | | |
| 26 | | | Q | | C | | Q | | |
| 27 | Q | Q | | | X | | T | | |
| 28 | | | T | T | | | | X | C |
| 29 | | | | Q | | Q | | | |
| 30 | T | T | | | | | | | |

| Date | Aries | Taurus | Gemini | Cancer | Leo | Virgo | Libra | Scorpio | Sagittarius | Capricorn | Aquarius | Pisces |
|------|-------|--------|--------|--------|-----|-------|-------|---------|-------------|-----------|----------|--------|
| 1 | u | f | | U | | f | u | f | | F | | f |
| 2 | u | f | | U | | f | u | f | | F | | f |
| 3 | f | u | f | | U | | f | u | f | | F | |
| 4 | f | u | f | | U | | f | u | f | | F | |
| 5 | | f | u | f | | U | | f | u | f | | F |
| 6 | | f | u | f | | U | | f | u | f | | F |
| 7 | | f | u | f | | U | | f | u | f | | F |
| 8 | F | | f | u | f | | U | | f | u | f | |
| 9 | F | | f | u | f | | U | | f | u | f | |
| 10 | | F | | f | u | f | | U | | f | u | f |
| 11 | | F | | f | u | f | | U | | f | u | f |
| 12 | f | | F | | f | u | f | | U | | f | u |
| 13 | f | | F | | f | u | f | | U | | f | u |
| 14 | u | f | | F | | f | u | f | | U | | f |
| 15 | u | f | | F | | f | u | f | | U | | f |
| 16 | f | u | f | | F | | f | u | f | | U | |
| 17 | f | u | f | | F | | f | u | f | | U | |
| 18 | | f | u | f | | F | | f | u | f | | U |
| 19 | | f | u | f | | F | | f | u | f | | U |
| 20 | | f | u | f | | F | | f | u | f | | U |
| 21 | U | | f | u | f | | F | | f | u | f | |
| 22 | U | | f | u | f | | F | | f | u | f | |
| 23 | | U | | f | u | f | | F | | f | u | f |
| 24 | | U | | f | u | f | | F | | f | u | f |
| 25 | f | | U | | f | u | f | | F | | f | u |
| 26 | f | | U | | f | u | f | | F | | f | u |
| 27 | f | | U | | f | u | f | | F | | f | u |
| 28 | u | f | | U | | f | u | f | | F | | f |
| 29 | u | f | | U | | f | u | f | | F | | f |
| 30 | f | u | f | | U | | f | u | f | | F | |

# October Moon Table

| Date | Sign | Element | Nature | Phase |
|------|------|---------|--------|-------|
| 1 Sun | Aquarius | Air | Barren | 2nd |
| 2 Mon 10:26 am | Pisces | Water | Fruitful | 2nd |
| 3 Tue | Pisces | Water | Fruitful | 2nd |
| 4 Wed 4:40 pm | Aries | Fire | Barren | 2nd |
| 5 Thu | Aries | Fire | Barren | Full 2:40 pm |
| 6 Fri 7:56 pm | Taurus | Earth | Semi-fruitful | 3rd |
| 7 Sat | Taurus | Earth | Semi-fruitful | 3rd |
| 8 Sun 9:44 pm | Gemini | Air | Barren | 3rd |
| 9 Mon | Gemini | Air | Barren | 3rd |
| 10 Tue 11:38 pm | Cancer | Water | Fruitful | 3rd |
| 11 Wed | Cancer | Water | Fruitful | 3rd |
| 12 Thu | Cancer | Water | Fruitful | 4th 8:25 am |
| 13 Fri 2:41 am | Leo | Fire | Barren | 4th |
| 14 Sat | Leo | Fire | Barren | 4th |
| 15 Sun 7:19 am | Virgo | Earth | Barren | 4th |
| 16 Mon | Virgo | Earth | Barren | 4th |
| 17 Tue 1:35 pm | Libra | Air | Semi-fruitful | 4th |
| 18 Wed | Libra | Air | Semi-fruitful | 4th |
| 19 Thu 9:41 pm | Scorpio | Water | Fruitful | New 3:12 pm |
| 20 Fri | Scorpio | Water | Fruitful | 1st |
| 21 Sat | Scorpio | Water | Fruitful | 1st |
| 22 Sun 7:57 am | Sagittarius | Fire | Barren | 1st |
| 23 Mon | Sagittarius | Fire | Barren | 1st |
| 24 Tue 8:12 pm | Capricorn | Earth | Semi-fruitful | 1st |
| 25 Wed | Capricorn | Earth | Semi-fruitful | 1st |
| 26 Thu | Capricorn | Earth | Semi-fruitful | 1st |
| 27 Fri 8:59 am | Aquarius | Air | Barren | 2nd 6:22 pm |
| 28 Sat | Aquarius | Air | Barren | 2nd |
| 29 Sun 7:46 pm | Pisces | Water | Fruitful | 2nd |
| 30 Mon | Pisces | Water | Fruitful | 2nd |
| 31 Tue | Pisces | Water | Fruitful | 2nd |

# October Aspectarian/Favorable & Unfavorable Days

| Date | Sun | Mercury | Venus | Mars | Jupiter | Saturn | Uranus | Neptune | Pluto |
|---|---|---|---|---|---|---|---|---|---|
| 1 | | | | | | X | | | |
| 2 | | | | | T | | X | | |
| 3 | | | O | O | | | | C | X |
| 4 | | | | | Q | | | | |
| 5 | O | O | | | | | | | Q |
| 6 | | | | | | O | T | C | |
| 7 | | | | | | | X | | |
| 8 | | | T | T | | | | | T |
| 9 | | | | | | | | Q | |
| 10 | T | T | Q | Q | T | O | X | | |
| 11 | | | | | | | | T | |
| 12 | Q | Q | | X | | | | Q | O |
| 13 | | | X | Q | | | | | |
| 14 | X | | | | T | | | | |
| 15 | | X | | X | | T | | | |
| 16 | | | | | | | | O | T |
| 17 | | | C | C | | Q | | | |
| 18 | | | | | | | | | Q |
| 19 | C | | | | | | X | O | |
| 20 | | C | | C | | | | T | |
| 21 | | | | | | | | | X |
| 22 | | | X | | | | | | |
| 23 | | | X | | | | | Q | |
| 24 | | | | Q | | C | T | | |
| 25 | X | | | | X | | | X | |
| 26 | | X | Q | | | | | | C |
| 27 | Q | | | T | Q | | Q | | |
| 28 | | Q | T | | | | | | |
| 29 | | | | | | X | X | | |
| 30 | T | | | | T | | | C | |
| 31 | | T | | | Q | | | | X |

| Date | Aries | Taurus | Gemini | Cancer | Leo | Virgo | Libra | Scorpio | Sagittarius | Capricorn | Aquarius | Pisces |
|---|---|---|---|---|---|---|---|---|---|---|---|---|
| 1 | f | u | f | | U | | f | u | f | | F | |
| 2 | f | u | f | | U | | f | u | f | | F | |
| 3 | | f | u | f | | U | | f | u | f | | F |
| 4 | | f | u | f | | U | | f | u | f | | F |
| 5 | F | | f | u | f | | U | | f | u | f | |
| 6 | F | | f | u | f | | U | | f | u | f | |
| 7 | | F | | f | u | f | | U | | f | u | f |
| 8 | | F | | f | u | f | | U | | f | u | f |
| 9 | f | | F | | f | u | f | | U | | f | u |
| 10 | f | | F | | f | u | f | | U | | f | u |
| 11 | u | f | | F | | f | u | f | | U | | f |
| 12 | u | f | | F | | f | u | f | | U | | f |
| 13 | f | u | f | | F | | f | u | f | | U | |
| 14 | f | u | f | | F | | f | u | f | | U | |
| 15 | f | u | f | | F | | f | u | f | | U | |
| 16 | | f | u | f | | F | | f | u | f | | U |
| 17 | | f | u | f | | F | | f | u | f | | U |
| 18 | U | | f | u | f | | F | | f | u | f | |
| 19 | U | | f | u | f | | F | | f | u | f | |
| 20 | | U | | f | u | f | | F | | f | u | f |
| 21 | | U | | f | u | f | | F | | f | u | f |
| 22 | | U | | f | u | f | | F | | f | u | f |
| 23 | f | | U | | f | u | f | | F | | f | u |
| 24 | f | | U | | f | u | f | | F | | f | u |
| 25 | u | f | | U | | f | u | f | | F | | f |
| 26 | u | f | | U | | f | u | f | | F | | f |
| 27 | u | f | | U | | f | u | f | | F | | f |
| 28 | f | u | f | | U | | f | u | f | | F | |
| 29 | f | u | f | | U | | f | u | f | | F | |
| 30 | | f | u | f | | U | | f | u | f | | F |
| 31 | | f | u | f | | U | | f | u | f | | F |

# November Moon Table

| Date | Sign | Element | Nature | Phase |
|------|------|---------|--------|-------|
| 1 Wed 2:43 am | Aries | Fire | Barren | 2nd |
| 2 Thu | Aries | Fire | Barren | 2nd |
| 3 Fri 5:46 am | Taurus | Earth | Semi-fruitful | 2nd |
| 4 Sat | Taurus | Earth | Semi-fruitful | Full 1:23 am |
| 5 Sun 5:26 am | Gemini | Air | Barren | 3rd |
| 6 Mon | Gemini | Air | Barren | 3rd |
| 7 Tue 5:45 am | Cancer | Water | Fruitful | 3rd |
| 8 Wed | Cancer | Water | Fruitful | 3rd |
| 9 Thu 7:29 am | Leo | Fire | Barren | 3rd |
| 10 Fri | Leo | Fire | Barren | 4th 3:36 pm |
| 11 Sat 11:41 am | Virgo | Earth | Barren | 4th |
| 12 Sun | Virgo | Earth | Barren | 4th |
| 13 Mon 6:26 pm | Libra | Air | Semi-fruitful | 4th |
| 14 Tue | Libra | Air | Semi-fruitful | 4th |
| 15 Wed | Libra | Air | Semi-fruitful | 4th |
| 16 Thu 3:19 am | Scorpio | Water | Fruitful | 4th |
| 17 Fri | Scorpio | Water | Fruitful | 4th |
| 18 Sat 1:59 pm | Sagittarius | Fire | Barren | New 6:42 am |
| 19 Sun | Sagittarius | Fire | Barren | 1st |
| 20 Mon | Sagittarius | Fire | Barren | 1st |
| 21 Tue 2:14 am | Capricorn | Earth | Semi-fruitful | 1st |
| 22 Wed | Capricorn | Earth | Semi-fruitful | 1st |
| 23 Thu 3:14 pm | Aquarius | Air | Barren | 1st |
| 24 Fri | Aquarius | Air | Barren | 1st |
| 25 Sat | Aquarius | Air | Barren | 1st |
| 26 Sun 3:04 am | Pisces | Water | Fruitful | 2nd 12:03 pm |
| 27 Mon | Pisces | Water | Fruitful | 2nd |
| 28 Tue 11:30 am | Aries | Fire | Barren | 2nd |
| 29 Wed | Aries | Fire | Barren | 2nd |
| 30 Thu 3:38 pm | Taurus | Earth | Semi-fruitful | 2nd |

# November Aspectarian/Favorable & Unfavorable Days

| Date | Sun | Mercury | Venus | Mars | Jupiter | Saturn | Uranus | Neptune | Pluto |
|------|-----|---------|-------|------|---------|--------|--------|---------|-------|
| 1 | | | | O | | | | | |
| 2 | | | O | | | T | C | | Q |
| 3 | | | | | O | | | | |
| 4 | O | | | | | | | X | T |
| 5 | | O | | T | | | | Q | |
| 6 | | | | | O | X | | | |
| 7 | | | T | Q | T | | | | |
| 8 | T | | | | | | | T | O |
| 9 | | T | Q | | Q | | Q | | |
| 10 | Q | | | X | | | | | |
| 11 | | | X | | | T | T | | |
| 12 | | Q | | | X | | | O | T |
| 13 | X | | | | | Q | | | |
| 14 | | X | | C | | | | | |
| 15 | | | | | X | O | | | Q |
| 16 | | | | C | | | | | |
| 17 | | | C | | | | | T | X |
| 18 | C | | | | | | | | |
| 19 | | | | | | | | Q | |
| 20 | | C | | X | | C | T | | |
| 21 | | | | | X | | | | |
| 22 | | | X | Q | | | | X | C |
| 23 | X | | | | | | Q | | |
| 24 | | | | | Q | | | | |
| 25 | | X | Q | T | | X | X | | |
| 26 | Q | | | | T | | | | |
| 27 | | | | | | | | C | X |
| 28 | | Q | T | | | Q | | | |
| 29 | T | | | | | | | | Q |
| 30 | | T | | O | | T | C | | |

| Date | Aries | Taurus | Gemini | Cancer | Leo | Virgo | Libra | Scorpio | Sagittarius | Capricorn | Aquarius | Pisces |
|------|-------|--------|--------|--------|-----|-------|-------|---------|-------------|-----------|----------|--------|
| 1 | F | | f | u | f | | U | | f | u | f | |
| 2 | F | | f | u | f | | U | | f | u | f | |
| 3 | F | | f | u | f | | U | | f | u | f | |
| 4 | | F | | f | u | f | | U | | f | u | f |
| 5 | | F | | f | u | f | | U | | f | u | f |
| 6 | f | | F | | f | u | f | | U | | f | u |
| 7 | f | | F | | f | u | f | | U | | f | u |
| 8 | u | f | | F | | f | u | f | | U | | f |
| 9 | u | f | | F | | f | u | f | | U | | f |
| 10 | f | u | f | | F | | f | u | f | | U | |
| 11 | f | u | f | | F | | f | u | f | | U | |
| 12 | | f | u | f | | F | | f | u | f | | U |
| 13 | | f | u | f | | F | | f | u | f | | U |
| 14 | U | | f | u | f | | F | | f | u | f | |
| 15 | U | | f | u | f | | F | | f | u | f | |
| 16 | U | | f | u | f | | F | | f | u | f | |
| 17 | | U | | f | u | f | | F | | f | u | f |
| 18 | | U | | f | u | f | | F | | f | u | f |
| 19 | f | | U | | f | u | f | | F | | f | u |
| 20 | f | | U | | f | u | f | | F | | f | u |
| 21 | u | f | | U | | f | u | f | | F | | f |
| 22 | u | f | | U | | f | u | f | | F | | f |
| 23 | u | f | | U | | f | u | f | | F | | f |
| 24 | f | u | f | | U | | f | u | f | | F | |
| 25 | f | u | f | | U | | f | u | f | | F | |
| 26 | f | u | f | | U | | f | u | f | | F | |
| 27 | | f | u | f | | U | | f | u | f | | F |
| 28 | | f | u | f | | U | | f | u | f | | F |
| 29 | F | | f | u | f | | U | | f | u | f | |
| 30 | F | | f | u | f | | U | | f | u | f | |

# December Moon Table

| Date | Sign | Element | Nature | Phase |
|------|------|---------|--------|-------|
| 1 Fri | Taurus | Earth | Semi-fruitful | 2nd |
| 2 Sat 4:21 pm | Gemini | Air | Barren | 2nd |
| 3 Sun | Gemini | Air | Barren | Full 10:47 am |
| 4 Mon 3:37 pm | Cancer | Water | Fruitful | 3rd |
| 5 Tue | Cancer | Water | Fruitful | 3rd |
| 6 Wed 3:37 pm | Leo | Fire | Barren | 3rd |
| 7 Thu | Leo | Fire | Barren | 3rd |
| 8 Fri 6:09 pm | Virgo | Earth | Barren | 3rd |
| 9 Sat | Virgo | Earth | Barren | 3rd |
| 10 Sun | Virgo | Earth | Barren | 4th 2:51 am |
| 11 Mon 12:01 am | Libra | Air | Semi-fruitful | 4th |
| 12 Tue | Libra | Air | Semi-fruitful | 4th |
| 13 Wed 8:59 am | Scorpio | Water | Fruitful | 4th |
| 14 Thu | Scorpio | Water | Fruitful | 4th |
| 15 Fri 8:07 pm | Sagittarius | Fire | Barren | 4th |
| 16 Sat | Sagittarius | Fire | Barren | 4th |
| 17 Sun | Sagittarius | Fire | Barren | 4th |
| 18 Mon 8:33 am | Capricorn | Earth | Semi-fruitful | New 1:30 am |
| 19 Tue | Capricorn | Earth | Semi-fruitful | 1st |
| 20 Wed 9:29 pm | Aquarius | Air | Barren | 1st |
| 21 Thu | Aquarius | Air | Barren | 1st |
| 22 Fri | Aquarius | Air | Barren | 1st |
| 23 Sat 9:42 am | Pisces | Water | Fruitful | 1st |
| 24 Sun | Pisces | Water | Fruitful | 1st |
| 25 Mon 7:27 pm | Aries | Fire | Barren | 1st |
| 26 Tue | Aries | Fire | Barren | 2nd 4:20 am |
| 27 Wed | Aries | Fire | Barren | 2nd |
| 28 Thu 1:23 am | Taurus | Earth | Semi-fruitful | 2nd |
| 29 Fri | Taurus | Earth | Semi-fruitful | 2nd |
| 30 Sat 3:31 am | Gemini | Air | Barren | 2nd |
| 31 Sun | Gemini | Air | Barren | 2nd |

# December Aspectarian/Favorable & Unfavorable Days

| Date | Sun | Mercury | Venus | Mars | Jupiter | Saturn | Uranus | Neptune | Pluto |
|---|---|---|---|---|---|---|---|---|---|
| 1 | | | | | O | | | X | T |
| 2 | | | O | | | | | | |
| 3 | O | | | | | | | Q | |
| 4 | | O | | T | | O | X | | |
| 5 | | | | | T | | | T | O |
| 6 | | | | Q | | Q | | | |
| 7 | T | | T | | Q | | | | |
| 8 | | T | | X | | T | T | | |
| 9 | | | Q | | X | | | O | |
| 10 | Q | Q | | | | Q | | | T |
| 11 | | | | | | | | | |
| 12 | X | X | X | | | | | O | Q |
| 13 | | | | C | | X | | | |
| 14 | | | | | C | | | T | X |
| 15 | | | | | | | | | |
| 16 | | | | | | | | Q | |
| 17 | | C | C | | | | T | | |
| 18 | C | | | X | | C | | | |
| 19 | | | | | X | | | X | C |
| 20 | | | | | | Q | | | |
| 21 | | X | | Q | | | | | |
| 22 | | | | | Q | | X | | |
| 23 | X | | X | | | X | | | |
| 24 | | Q | | T | T | | | C | X |
| 25 | | | Q | | Q | | | | |
| 26 | Q | T | | | | | | | |
| 27 | | | | | | | C | | Q |
| 28 | T | | T | O | | T | | X | |
| 29 | | | | | O | | | | T |
| 30 | | | | | | | | Q | |
| 31 | | O | | | | | | X | |

| Date | Aries | Taurus | Gemini | Cancer | Leo | Virgo | Libra | Scorpio | Sagittarius | Capricorn | Aquarius | Pisces |
|---|---|---|---|---|---|---|---|---|---|---|---|---|
| 1 | F | | f | u | f | | U | | | f | u | f |
| 2 | F | | f | u | f | | U | | | f | u | f |
| 3 | f | F | | f | u | f | | U | | | f | u |
| 4 | f | F | | f | u | f | | U | | | f | u |
| 5 | u | f | F | | f | u | f | | U | | | f |
| 6 | u | f | F | | f | u | f | | U | | | f |
| 7 | f | u | f | F | | f | u | f | | U | | |
| 8 | f | u | f | F | | f | u | f | | U | | |
| 9 | | f | u | f | F | | f | u | f | | U | |
| 10 | | f | u | f | F | | f | u | f | | U | |
| 11 | | | f | u | f | F | | f | u | f | | U |
| 12 | | | f | u | f | F | | f | u | f | | U |
| 13 | | | f | u | f | F | | f | u | f | | U |
| 14 | U | | | f | u | f | F | | f | u | f | |
| 15 | U | | | f | u | f | F | | f | u | f | |
| 16 | | U | | | f | u | f | F | | f | u | f |
| 17 | | U | | | f | u | f | F | | f | u | f |
| 18 | | U | | | f | u | f | F | | f | u | f |
| 19 | f | | U | | | f | u | f | F | | f | u |
| 20 | f | | U | | | f | u | f | F | | f | u |
| 21 | u | f | | U | | | f | u | f | F | | f |
| 22 | u | f | | U | | | f | u | f | F | | f |
| 23 | u | f | | U | | | f | u | f | F | | f |
| 24 | f | u | f | | U | | | f | u | f | F | |
| 25 | f | u | f | | U | | | f | u | f | F | |
| 26 | | f | u | f | | U | | | f | u | f | F |
| 27 | | f | u | f | | U | | | f | u | f | F |
| 28 | F | | f | u | f | | U | | | f | u | f |
| 29 | F | | f | u | f | | U | | | f | u | f |
| 30 | F | | f | u | f | | U | | | f | u | f |
| 31 | f | F | | f | u | f | | U | | | f | u |

# 2017 Retrograde Planets

| Planet | Begin | Eastern | Pacific | End | Eastern | Pacific |
|---|---|---|---|---|---|---|
| Mercury | 12/19/16 | 5:55 am | **2:55 am** | 1/8/17 | 4:43 am | **1:43 am** |
| Jupiter | 2/5/17 | | **10:52 pm** | 6/9/17 | 10:03 am | **7:03 am** |
| | 2/6/17 | 1:52 am | | | | |
| Venus | 3/4/17 | 4:09 am | **1:09 am** | 4/15/17 | 6:18 am | **3:18 am** |
| Saturn | 4/5/17 | | **10:06 pm** | 8/25/17 | 8:08 pm | **5:08 am** |
| | 4/6/17 | 1:06 am | | | | |
| Mercury | 4/9/17 | 7:14 pm | **4:14 pm** | 5/3/17 | 12:33 pm | **9:33 am** |
| Pluto | 4/20/17 | 8:49 am | **5:49 am** | 9/28/17 | 3:36 pm | **12:36 pm** |
| Neptune | 6/16/17 | 7:09 am | **4:09 am** | 11/22/17 | 9:21 am | **6:21 pm** |
| Uranus | 8/2/17 | | **10:31 pm** | 1/2/18 | 9:13 am | **6:13 am** |
| | 8/3/17 | 1:31 am | | | | |
| Mercury | 8/12/17 | 9:00 pm | **6:00 pm** | 9/5/17 | 7:29 am | **4:29 pm** |
| Mercury | 12/2/17 | | **11:34 pm** | 12/22/17 | 8:51 pm | **5:51 pm** |
| | 12/3/17 | 2:34 am | | | | |

Eastern Time in plain type, **Pacific Time in bold type**

| | Dec 16 | Jan 17 | Feb | Mar | Apr | May | Jun | Jul | Aug | Sep | Oct | Nov | Dec | Jan 18 |
|---|---|---|---|---|---|---|---|---|---|---|---|---|---|---|
| ☿ | ▓ | | | | ▓ | | | | ▓ | | | | ▓ | |
| ♃ | | | ▓ | ▓ | ▓ | ▓ | ▓ | | | | | | | |
| ♀ | | | | ▓ | ▓ | | | | | | | | | |
| ♄ | | | | | ▓ | ▓ | ▓ | ▓ | ▓ | | | | | |
| ♇ | | | | | ▓ | ▓ | ▓ | ▓ | ▓ | ▓ | | | | |
| ♆ | | | | | | | ▓ | ▓ | ▓ | ▓ | ▓ | ▓ | | |
| ♅ | | | | | | | | | ▓ | ▓ | ▓ | ▓ | ▓ | ▓ |

# Egg-Setting Dates

| To Have Eggs by this Date | Sign | Qtr. | Date to Set Eggs |
|---|---|---|---|
| Jan 6, 3:18 pm–Jan 8, 5:06 pm | Taurus | 2nd | Dec 16, 2016 |
| Jan 10, 5:49 pm–Jan 12, 6:34 am | Cancer | 2nd | Dec 20, 2016 |
| Jan 29, 11:10 am–Jan 31, 4:46 pm | Pisces | 1st | Jan 08, 2017 |
| Feb 2, 8:50 pm–Feb 4, 11:44 pm | Taurus | 1st | Jan 12 |
| Feb 7, 2:03 am–Feb 9, 4:41 am | Cancer | 2nd | Jan 17 |
| Feb 26, 9:58 am–Feb 27, 11:52 pm | Pisces | 1st | Feb 05 |
| Mar 2, 2:43 am–Mar 4, 5:05 am | Taurus | 1st | Feb 09 |
| Mar 6, 7:54 am–Mar 8, 11:45 am | Cancer | 2nd | Feb 13 |
| Mar 29, 11:48 am–Mar 31, 12:40 pm | Taurus | 1st | Mar 08 |
| Apr 2, 2:27 pm–Apr 4, 6:13 pm | Cancer | 1st | Mar 12 |
| Apr 9, 8:34 am–Apr 11, 2:08 am | Libra | 2nd | Mar 19 |
| Apr 26, 8:16 am–Apr 27, 9:39 pm | Taurus | 1st | Apr 05 |
| Apr 29, 9:48 pm–May 2, 12:12 am | Cancer | 1st | Apr 08 |
| May 6, 2:20 pm–May 9, 1:01 am | Libra | 2nd | Apr 15 |
| May 27, 7:25 am–May 29, 8:12 am | Cancer | 1st | May 06 |
| Jun 2, 8:04 pm–Jun 5, 6:46 am | Libra | 2nd | May 12 |
| Jun 23, 10:31 pm–Jun 25, 6:06 pm | Cancer | 1st | Jun 02 |
| Jun 30, 3:02 am–Jul 2, 12:59 pm | Libra | 1st | Jun 09 |
| Jul 27, 11:37 am–Jul 29, 8:23 pm | Libra | 1st | Jul 06 |
| Aug 23, 9:05 pm–Aug 26, 4:53 am | Libra | 1st | Aug 02 |
| Sep 5, 1:28 am–Sep 6, 3:03 am | Pisces | 2nd | Aug 15 |
| Sep 20, 6:06 am–Sep 22, 1:40 pm | Libra | 1st | Aug 30 |
| Oct 2, 10:26 am–Oct 4, 4:40 pm | Pisces | 2nd | Sep 11 |
| Oct 19, 3:12 pm–Oct 19, 9:41 pm | Libra | 1st | Sep 28 |
| Oct 29, 7:46 pm–Nov 1, 2:43 am | Pisces | 2nd | Oct 08 |
| Nov 3, 5:46 am–Nov 4, 1:23 am | Taurus | 2nd | Oct 13 |
| Nov 26, 3:04 am–Nov 28, 11:30 am | Pisces | 1st | Nov 05 |
| Nov 30, 3:38 am–Dec 2, 4:21 pm | Taurus | 2nd | Nov 09 |
| Dec 23, 9:42 am–Dec 25, 7:27 pm | Pisces | 1st | Dec 02 |
| Dec 28, 1:23 am–Dec 30, 3:31 am | Taurus | 2nd | Dec 07 |

# Dates to Hunt and Fish

| Date | Quarter | Sign |
|------|---------|------|
| Jan 2, 4:57 am–Jan 4, 11:20 am | 1st | Pisces |
| Jan 10, 5:49 pm–Jan 12, 7:08 pm | 2nd | Cancer |
| Jan 19, 5:09 pm–Jan 22, 5:45 am | 3rd | Scorpio |
| Jan 29, 11:10 am–Jan 31, 4:46 pm | 1st | Pisces |
| Feb 7, 2:03 am–Feb 9, 4:41 am | 2nd | Cancer |
| Feb 16, 1:41 am–Feb 18, 1:52 pm | 3rd | Scorpio |
| Feb 18, 1:52 pm–Feb 21, 2:08 am | 3rd | Sagittarius |
| Feb 25, 7:24 pm–Feb 27, 11:52 pm | 4th | Pisces |
| Mar 6, 7:54 am–Mar 8, 11:45 am | 2nd | Cancer |
| Mar 15, 11:11 am–Mar 17, 11:00 pm | 3rd | Scorpio |
| Mar 17, 11:00 pm–Mar 20, 11:31 am | 3rd | Sagittarius |
| Mar 25, 6:06 am–Mar 27, 10:11 am | 4th | Pisces |
| Apr 2, 2:27 pm–Apr 4, 6:13 pm | 1st | Cancer |
| Apr 11, 6:42 pm–Apr 14, 6:27 am | 3rd | Scorpio |
| Apr 14, 6:27 am–Apr 16, 7:05 am | 3rd | Sagittarius |
| Apr 21, 3:43 pm–Apr 23, 8:32 pm | 4th | Pisces |
| Apr 29, 9:48 pm–May 2, 12:12 am | 1st | Cancer |
| May 9, 1:01 am–May 11, 12:59 pm | 2nd | Scorpio |
| May 11, 12:59 pm–May 14, 1:37 am | 3rd | Sagittarius |
| May 18, 11:52 pm–May 21, 6:10 am | 4th | Pisces |
| May 27, 7:25 am–May 29, 8:12 am | 1st | Cancer |
| Jun 5, 6:46 am–Jun 7, 6:59 pm | 2nd | Scorpio |
| Jun 7, 6:59 pm–Jun 10, 7:36 am | 2nd | Sagittarius |
| Jun 15, 6:17 am–Jun 17, 1:55 pm | 3rd | Pisces |
| Jun 23, 6:07 pm–Jun 25, 6:06 pm | 4th | Cancer |
| Jul 2, 12:59 pm–Jul 5, 1:08 am | 2nd | Scorpio |
| Jul 5, 1:08 am–Jul 7, 1:45 pm | 2nd | Sagittarius |
| Jul 12, 11:51 am–Jul 14, 7:52 pm | 3rd | Pisces |
| Jul 14, 7:52 pm–Jul 17, 1:04 am | 3rd | Aries |
| Jul 21, 4:09 am–Jul 23, 4:34 am | 4th | Cancer |
| Jul 29, 8:23 pm–Aug 1, 8:01 am | 1st | Scorpio |
| Aug 1, 8:01 am–Aug 3, 8:37 pm | 2nd | Sagittarius |
| Aug 8, 5:56 pm–Aug 11, 1:22 am | 3rd | Pisces |
| Aug 11, 1:22 am–Aug 13, 6:40 am | 3rd | Aries |
| Aug 17, 12:13 pm–Aug 19, 1:55 pm | 4th | Cancer |
| Aug 26, 4:53 am–Aug 28, 3:48 pm | 1st | Scorpio |
| Sep 5, 1:28 am–Sep 7, 8:01 am | 2nd | Pisces |
| Sep 7, 8:01 am–Sep 9, 12:23 pm | 3rd | Aries |
| Sep 13, 6:12 pm–Sep 15, 9:09 pm | 4th | Cancer |
| Sep 22, 1:40 pm–Sep 25, 12:01 am | 1st | Scorpio |
| Oct 2, 10:26 am–Oct 4, 4:40 pm | 2nd | Pisces |
| Oct 4, 4:40 pm–Oct 6, 7:56 pm | 2nd | Aries |
| Oct 10, 11:38 pm–Oct 13, 2:41 am | 3rd | Cancer |
| Oct 19, 9:41 pm–Oct 22, 7:57 am | 1st | Scorpio |
| Oct 29, 7:46 pm–Nov 1, 2:43 am | 2nd | Pisces |
| Nov 1, 2:43 am–Nov 3, 5:46 am | 2nd | Aries |
| Nov 7, 5:45 am–Nov 9, 7:29 am | 3rd | Cancer |
| Nov 16, 3:19 am–Nov 18, 1:59 pm | 4th | Scorpio |
| Nov 26, 3:04 am–Nov 28, 11:30 am | 1st | Pisces |
| Nov 28, 11:30 am–Nov 30, 3:38 pm | 2nd | Aries |
| Dec 4, 3:37 pm–Dec 6, 3:37 pm | 3rd | Cancer |
| Dec 13, 8:59 am–Dec 15, 8:07 pm | 4th | Scorpio |
| Dec 23, 9:42 am–Dec 25, 7:27 pm | 1st | Pisces |

# Dates to Destroy Weeds and Pests

| Date | Sign | Qtr. |
|---|---|---|
| Jan 12, 7:08 pm–Jan 14, 10:52 pm | Leo | 3rd |
| Jan 14, 10:52 pm–Jan 17, 6:16 am | Virgo | 3rd |
| Jan 22, 5:45 am–Jan 24, 5:43 pm | Sagittarius | 4th |
| Jan 27, 3:37 am–Jan 27, 7:07 pm | Aquarius | 4th |
| Feb 10, 7:33 pm–Feb 11, 8:52 am | Leo | 3rd |
| Feb 11, 8:52 am–Feb 13, 3:43 pm | Virgo | 3rd |
| Feb 18, 1:52 pm–Feb 18, 2:33 pm | Sagittarius | 3rd |
| Feb 18, 2:33 pm–Feb 21, 2:08 am | Sagittarius | 4th |
| Feb 23, 12:17 pm–Feb 25, 7:24 pm | Aquarius | 4th |
| Mar 12, 10:54 am–Mar 13, 1:28 am | Virgo | 3rd |
| Mar 17, 11:00 pm–Mar 20, 11:31 am | Sagittarius | 3rd |
| Mar 22, 10:28 pm–Mar 25, 6:06 am | Aquarius | 4th |
| Mar 27, 10:11 am–Mar 27, 10:57 pm | Aries | 4th |
| Apr 14, 6:27 am–Apr 16, 7:05 pm | Sagittarius | 3rd |
| Apr 19, 6:52 am–Apr 21, 3:43 pm | Aquarius | 4th |
| Apr 23, 8:32 pm–Apr 25, 9:56 pm | Aries | 4th |
| May 11, 12:59 pm–May, 14 1:37 am | Sagittarius | 3rd |
| May 16, 1:50 pm–May, 18 8:33 pm | Aquarius | 3rd |
| May 18, 8:33 pm–May, 18 11:52 pm | Aquarius | 4th |
| May 21, 6:10 am–May, 23 8:33 am | Aries | 4th |
| May 25, 8:15 am–May, 25 3:44 pm | Gemini | 4th |
| Jun 9, 9:10 am–Jun 10, 7:36 am | Sagittarius | 3rd |
| Jun 12, 7:45 pm–Jun 15, 6:17 am | Aquarius | 3rd |
| Jun 17, 1:55 pm–Jun 19, 5:53 pm | Aries | 4th |
| Jun 21, 6:44 pm–Jun 23, 6:07 pm | Gemini | 4th |
| Jul 10, 1:35 am–Jul 12, 11:51 am | Aquarius | 3rd |
| Jul 14, 7:52 pm–Jul 16, 3:26 pm | Aries | 3rd |
| Jul 16, 3:26 pm–Jul 17, 1:04 am | Aries | 4th |
| Jul 19, 3:31 am–Jul 21, 4:09 am | Gemini | 4th |
| Jul 23, 4:34 am–Jul 23, 5:46 am | Leo | 4th |
| Aug 7, 2:11 pm–Aug 8, 5:56 pm | Aquarius | 3rd |
| Aug 11, 1:22 am–Aug 13, 6:40 am | Aries | 3rd |
| Aug 15, 10:06 am–Aug 17, 12:13 pm | Gemini | 4th |
| Aug 19, 1:55 pm–Aug 21, 2:30 pm | Leo | 4th |
| Sep 7, 8:01 am–Sep 9, 12:23 pm | Aries | 3rd |
| Sep 11, 3:29 pm–Sep 13, 2:25 am | Gemini | 3rd |
| Sep 13, 2:25 am–Sep 13, 6:12 pm | Gemini | 4th |
| Sep 15, 9:09 pm–Sep 18, 12:52 am | Leo | 4th |
| Sep 18, 12:52 am–Sep 20, 1:30 am | Virgo | 4th |
| Oct 5, 2:40 pm–Oct 6, 7:56 pm | Aries | 3rd |
| Oct 8, 9:44 pm–Oct 10, 11:38 pm | Gemini | 3rd |
| Oct 13, 2:41 am–Oct 15, 7:19 am | Leo | 4th |
| Oct 15, 7:19 am–Oct 17, 1:35 pm | Virgo | 4th |
| Nov 5, 5:26 am–Nov 7, 5:45 am | Gemini | 3rd |
| Nov 9, 7:29 am–Nov 10, 3:36 pm | Leo | 3rd |
| Nov 10, 3:36 pm–Nov 11, 11:41 am | Leo | 4th |
| Nov 11, 11:41 am–Nov 13, 6:26 pm | Virgo | 4th |
| Dec 3, 10:47 am–Dec 4, 3:37 pm | Gemini | 3rd |
| Dec 6, 3:37 pm–Dec 8, 6:09 pm | Leo | 3rd |
| Dec 8, 6:09 pm–Dec 10, 2:51 am | Virgo | 3rd |
| Dec 10, 2:51 am–Dec 11, 12:01 am | Virgo | 4th |
| Dec 15, 8:07 pm–Dec 18, 1:30 am | Sagittarius | 4th |

# Time Zone Map

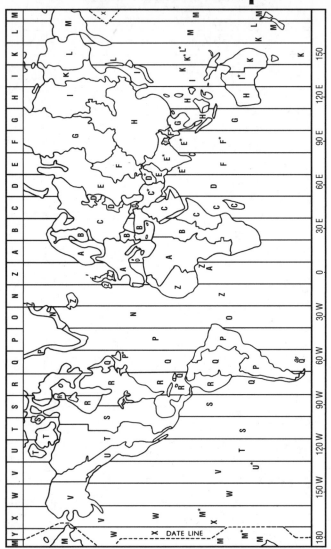

# Time Zone Conversions

(R)  EST—Used in book
(S)  CST—Subtract 1 hour
(T)  MST—Subtract 2 hours
(U)  PST—Subtract 3 hours
(V)  Subtract 4 hours
(V*) Subtract 4½ hours
(U*) Subtract 3½ hours
(W)  Subtract 5 hours
(X)  Subtract 6 hours
(Y)  Subtract 7 hours
(Q)  Add 1 hour
(P)  Add 2 hours
(P*) Add 2½ hours
(O)  Add 3 hours
(N)  Add 4 hours
(Z)  Add 5 hours
(A)  Add 6 hours
(B)  Add 7 hours
(C)  Add 8 hours
(C*) Add 8½ hours

(D)  Add 9 hours
(D*) Add 9½ hours
(E)  Add 10 hours
(E*) Add 10½ hours
(F)  Add 11 hours
(F*) Add 11½ hours
(G)  Add 12 hours
(H)  Add 13 hours
(I)  Add 14 hours
(I*)  Add 14½ hours
(K)  Add 15 hours
(K*) Add 15½ hours
(L)  Add 16 hours
(L*) Add 16½ hours
(M)  Add 17 hours
(M*) Add 18 hours
(P*) Add 2½ hours

---

**Important!**

All times given in the *Moon Sign Book* are set in Eastern Time. The conversions shown here are for standard times only. Use the time zone conversions map and table to calculate the difference in your time zone. You must make the adjustment for your time zone and adjust for Daylight Saving Time where applicable.

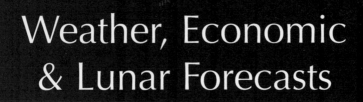

# Weather, Economic & Lunar Forecasts

# Forecasting the Weather

*by Kris Brandt Riske*

Astrometeorology—astrological weather forecasting—reveals seasonal and weekly weather trends based on the cardinal ingresses (Summer and Winter Solstices, and Spring and Autumn Equinoxes) and the four monthly lunar phases. The planetary alignments and the longitudes and latitudes they influence have the strongest effect, but the zodiacal signs are also involved in creating weather conditions.

The components of a thunderstorm, for example, are heat, wind, and electricity. A Mars-Jupiter configuration generates the necessary heat and Mercury adds wind and electricity. A severe thunderstorm, and those that produce tornados, usually involve Mercury, Mars, Uranus, or Neptune. The zodiacal signs add their energy to the planetary mix to increase or decrease the chance for weather phenomena and their severity.

In general, the fire signs (Aries, Leo, Sagittarius) indicate heat and dryness, both of which peak when Mars, the planet with a similar nature, is in these signs. Water signs (Cancer, Scorpio, Pisces) are conducive to precipitation, and air signs (Gemini, Libra, Aquarius) are conducive to cool temperatures and wind. Earth signs (Taurus, Virgo, Capricorn) vary from wet to dry, heat to cold. The signs and their prevailing weather conditions are listed here:

Aries: Heat, dry, wind
Taurus: Moderate temperatures, precipitation
Gemini: Cool temperatures, wind, dry
Cancer: Cold, steady precipitation
Leo: Heat, dry, lightning
Virgo: Cold, dry, windy
Libra: Cool, windy, fair
Scorpio: Extreme temperatures, abundant precipitation
Sagittarius: Warm, fair, moderate wind
Capricorn: Cold, wet, damp
Aquarius: Cold, dry, high pressure, lightning
Pisces: Wet, cool, low pressure

Take note of the Moon's sign at each lunar phase. It reveals the prevailing weather conditions for the next six to seven days. The same is true of Mercury and Venus. These two influential weather planets transit the entire zodiac each year, unless retrograde patterns add their influence.

## Planetary Influences

People relied on astrology to forecast weather for thousands of years. They were able to predict drought, floods, and temperature variations through interpreting planetary alignments. In recent years there has been a renewed interest in astrometeorology.

A weather forecast can be composed for any date—tomorrow, next week, or a thousand years in the future. According to astrometeorology, each planet governs certain weather phenomena. When certain planets are aligned with other planets, weather—precipitation, cloudy or clear skies, tornados, hurricanes, and other conditions—are generated.

## Sun and Moon

The Sun governs the constitution of the weather and, like the Moon, it serves as a trigger for other planetary configurations that result in weather events. When the Sun is prominent in a cardinal ingress or lunar phase chart, the area is often warm and sunny. The Moon can bring or withhold moisture, depending upon its sign placement.

## Mercury

Mercury is also a triggering planet, but its main influence is wind direction and velocity. In its stationary periods, Mercury reflects high winds, and its influence is always prominent in major weather events, such as hurricanes and tornadoes, when it tends to lower the temperature.

## Venus

Venus governs moisture, clouds, and humidity. It brings warming trends that produce sunny, pleasant weather if in positive aspect to other planets. In some signs—Libra, Virgo, Gemini, Sagittarius—Venus is drier. It is at its wettest when placed in Cancer, Scorpio, Pisces, or Taurus.

## Mars

Mars is associated with heat, drought, and wind, and can raise the temperature to record-setting levels when in a fire sign (Aries, Leo, Sagittarius). Mars is also the planet that provides the spark that generates thunderstorms and is prominent in tornado and hurricane configurations.

## Jupiter

Jupiter, a fair-weather planet, tends toward higher temperatures when in Aries, Leo, or Sagittarius. It is associated with high-pressure systems and is a contributing factor at times to dryness. Storms are often amplified by Jupiter.

## Saturn

Saturn is associated with low-pressure systems, cloudy to overcast skies, and excessive precipitation. Temperatures drop when Saturn is involved. Major winter storms always have a strong Saturn influence, as do storms that produce a slow, steady downpour for hours or days.

## Uranus

Like Jupiter, Uranus indicates high-pressure systems. It reflects descending cold air and, when prominent, is responsible for a jet stream that extends far south. Uranus can bring drought in winter, and it is involved in thunderstorms, tornados, and hurricanes.

## Neptune

Neptune is the wettest planet. It signals low-pressure systems and is dominant when hurricanes are in the forecast. When Neptune is strongly placed, flood danger is high. It's often associated with winter thaws. Temperatures, humidity, and cloudiness increase where Neptune influences weather.

## Pluto

Pluto is associated with weather extremes, as well as unseasonably warm temperatures and drought. It reflects the high winds involved in major hurricanes, storms, and tornados.

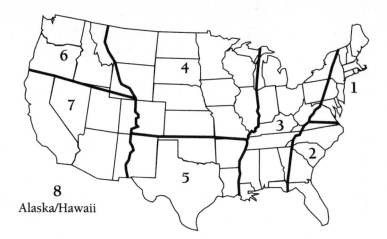

# Weather Forecast for 2017

*by Kris Brandt Riske*

## Winter

Precipitation and temperatures will range from average to above in Zone 1. Coastal areas of Zone 2 and northern Florida will see abundant precipitation at times with seasonal temperatures. Cloudy skies, wind, and unseasonably cool temperatures will be the norm in Zone 3 along with periods of severe thunderstorms with tornado potential.

Precipitation will also be abundant at times in eastern areas of Zones 4 and 5 along with a high potential for flooding. Western areas of Zones 4 and 5 will be warmer than average, while the remainder of these zones will range from seasonal to below. Storms will bring heavy precipitation at times to the eastern Rocky Mountains/foothills in Zones 4 and 5, and these storms will also impact the rest of the states in these zones; strong thunderstorms are possible during warmer weeks. Temperatures in Zone 6 will be average to above, with moisture average to below.

Eastern areas of Zone 7 will see above average precipitation, while moisture in western and central areas will range from seasonal to below. Temperatures in Alaska (Zone 8) will be seasonal to below with abundant precipitation and periodic strong storms. Much of Hawaii (Zone 8) will see low precipitation and high temperatures.

## New Moon, January 1–4

**Zone 1:** Temperatures are seasonal to below, skies are cloudy, and the zone sees precipitation, heaviest in northern areas.

**Zone 2:** Skies are partly cloudy to cloudy and windy with precipitation in much of the zone, which is heaviest in central and southern areas with tornado potential, and temperatures range from seasonal to below.

**Zone 3:** Western and central parts of the zone are stormy with high winds and precipitation, central areas could see strong thunderstorms with tornado potential; eastern areas are partly cloudy.

**Zone 4:** Precipitation in western and central areas moves into eastern parts of the zone, some abundant, temperatures are seasonal to below, and skies are variably cloudy.

**Zone 5:** The zone is fair to partly cloudy and windy with scattered precipitation and seasonal temperatures.

**Zone 6:** Eastern skies are fair, western and central skies are partly cloudy to cloudy with precipitation, and temperatures are seasonal to below.

**Zone 7:** Western areas see scattered precipitation under partly cloudy to cloudy skies, central areas are mostly fair, eastern areas are windy and colder with precipitation later in the week, and temperatures are generally seasonal.

**Zone 8:** Central and eastern Alaska are windy with precipitation, skies are partly cloudy to cloudy, and temperatures are seasonal. Hawaii is fair to partly cloudy and seasonal, and windy central and east with scattered showers.

## 1st Quarter Moon, January 5–11

**Zone 1:** The zone is partly cloudy and windy with precipitation north, and temperatures are seasonal to below.

**Zone 2:** Skies are variably cloudy and windy and temperatures are seasonal to below; southern and central areas see precipitation.

**Zone 3:** Central areas see precipitation, skies are generally partly cloudy, and temperatures are seasonal to below; eastern areas are coldest.

**Zone 4:** Most skies are fair to partly cloudy and windy, but western parts of the zone are cold and stormy, central areas see scattered precipitation; temperatures range from seasonal to below.

**Zone 5:** Western and central parts of the zone see scattered precipitation, and the zone is windy and variably cloudy with temperatures ranging from seasonal to below.

**Zone 6:** Central areas are windy, skies are generally fair to partly cloudy, eastern areas are stormy with precipitation, and temperatures range from seasonal to below.

**Zone 7:** Western and central skies are variably cloudy with scattered precipitation with temperatures ranging from seasonal to below; eastern areas have storm potential.

**Zone 8:** Central and eastern Alaska are windy as a front moves through the area, western and central parts of the state see precipitation, some abundant, and temperatures are seasonal. Much of Hawaii sees precipitation, some locally heavy. Skies are partly cloudy to cloudy, and temperatures are seasonal.

## Full Moon, January 12–18

**Zone 1:** Temperatures are seasonal and skies are partly cloudy and windy with scattered precipitation.

**Zone 2:** Temperatures range from seasonal to below and much of the zone sees precipitation, with the heaviest in central and southern areas, under partly cloudy to cloudy skies; strong thunderstorms are possible.

**Zone 3:** Skies are variably cloudy, temperatures range from seasonal to below, central areas are windy with precipitation, eastern areas are windy, and strong thunderstorms with heavy precipitation are possible west.

**Zone 4:** Western and central parts of the zone are windy, skies are mostly fair to partly cloudy, temperatures range from seasonal to below, and eastern areas could see heavy precipitation.

**Zone 5:** Temperatures are seasonal, skies are fair to partly cloudy, and western areas are windy.

**Zone 6:** Skies are partly cloudy to cloudy and windy, temperatures are seasonal, and western and central areas see precipitation.

**Zone 7:** The zone is seasonal with much cloudiness and heavy precipitation in northern coastal areas that moves into central and eastern areas.

**Zone 8:** Temperatures in Alaska are seasonal to below, western areas see precipitation, eastern and central areas are windy, and skies are partly cloudy to cloudy. Much of Hawaii is windy, skies are partly cloudy to cloudy, and western areas see precipitation.

### 3rd Quarter Moon, January 19–26

**Zone 1:** Temperatures are seasonal and skies are partly cloudy to cloudy and windy with precipitation.

**Zone 2:** Temperatures range from seasonal to below, northern areas see precipitation, and central and southern parts of the zone could be stormy with locally heavy precipitation and strong thunderstorms.

**Zone 3:** Windy conditions prevail as a front moves across much of the zone, bringing precipitation under variably cloudy skies with seasonal temperatures.

**Zone 4:** Precipitation in western areas moves into central parts of the zone, stormy conditions with abundant precipitation are possible in the mountains, temperatures are seasonal to below, and central and eastern areas are fair to partly cloudy.

**Zone 5:** The zone is windy with precipitation in the west, possibly stormy conditions in central areas with high winds and abundant precipitation, and temperatures are seasonal.

**Zone 6:** Partly cloudy skies are windy, temperatures are seasonal, and eastern areas see scattered precipitation.

**Zone 7:** Scattered precipitation accompanies seasonal temperatures and windy skies that are partly cloudy to cloudy.

**Zone 8:** Eastern areas of Alaska are cloudy with precipitation, temperatures are seasonal, and western and central areas are fair to partly cloudy. Hawaii is fair to partly cloudy with temperatures ranging from seasonal to above.

### New Moon, January 27–February 2

**Zone 1:** The zone is seasonal with precipitation, some locally heavy, in northern areas later in the week.

**Zone 2:** Skies are fair to partly cloudy with a chance for precipitation and temperatures are seasonal.

**Zone 3:** Locally heavy precipitation in western areas moves into central parts of the zone, skies are variably cloudy, and temperatures are seasonal; eastern areas see scattered precipitation.

**Zone 4:** Skies are variably cloudy, temperatures are seasonal, western areas are stormy, and eastern parts of the zone could see locally heavy precipitation.

**Zone 5:** Temperatures are seasonal and skies fair to partly cloudy, more cloudy in the east, and potential for abundant precipitation.

**Zone 6:** Stormy conditions are possible in eastern areas, temperatures range from seasonal to below, and western and central skies are partly cloudy.

**Zone 7:** Skies are variably cloudy and much of the zone sees precipitation with stormy conditions possible in eastern areas; temperatures are seasonal to below.

**Zone 8:** Alaska is mostly fair and seasonal with scattered precipitation. Hawaii is windy, seasonal, and fair to partly cloudy.

## 1st Quarter Moon, February 3–9

**Zone 1:** Seasonal temperatures accompany partly cloudy to cloudy skies with scattered precipitation.

**Zone 2:** Northern areas are partly cloudy, temperatures are seasonal to below, and southern and central areas see more cloudiness with precipitation, some locally heavy.

**Zone 3:** Much of the zone sees precipitation under partly cloudy to cloudy skies with temperatures ranging from seasonal to below, and eastern areas are mostly fair.

**Zone 4:** Western and central areas are windy with precipitation and seasonal temperatures, eastern areas are cold, and skies are variably cloudy.

**Zone 5:** Temperatures are seasonal, skies are variably cloudy, central and western area are windy, and western parts of the zone see precipitation.

**Zone 6:** Western skies are mostly fair, central and eastern areas are cloudy with precipitation, and temperatures range from seasonal to below.

**Zone 7:** Much of the zone is cloudy with precipitation, which is heaviest in eastern areas; north coastal areas are mostly fair; and temperatures are seasonal to below.

**Zone 8:** Windy conditions in Alaska accompany seasonal temperatures, skies are partly cloudy to cloudy, and central areas see precipitation. Hawaii is windy, seasonal, and variably cloudy with precipitation in much of the state.

## Full Moon, February 10–17

**Zone 1:** The zone is windy with fair to partly cloudy skies and temperatures range from seasonal to below.

**Zone 2:** Much of the zone is windy with precipitation, some locally heavy in central and southern areas with flood potential, temperatures are seasonal to below, and strong thunderstorms with tornado potential are possible.

**Zone 3:** Temperatures are seasonal to below and cold in western areas, central and eastern areas see precipitation, some locally heavy, and skies are variably cloudy and windy.

**Zone 4:** Skies are partly cloudy to cloudy and windy, temperatures range from seasonal to below, western areas see precipitation, and central and eastern areas see scattered precipitation.

**Zone 5:** The zone is windy and partly cloudy to cloudy, temperatures are seasonal to below, and central areas see precipitation.

**Zone 6:** Temperatures are seasonal, skies are partly cloudy to cloudy, and eastern areas see precipitation.

**Zone 7:** Central and eastern areas are windy as a front moves through under partly cloudy to cloudy skies, bringing scattered precipitation to much of the zone; temperatures are seasonal.

**Zone 8:** Alaskan skies are partly cloudy to cloudy, temperatures are seasonal, eastern areas see precipitation, and central and eastern areas are windy. Hawaii is cloudy and seasonal with showers.

### 3rd Quarter Moon, February 18–25

**Zone 1:** Much of the zone sees precipitation and high winds, especially north; skies are partly cloudy to cloudy; and temperatures are seasonal.

**Zone 2:** Skies are windy and fair to partly cloudy, southern areas see precipitation, and temperatures are seasonal.

**Zone 3:** Seasonal temperatures accompany partly cloudy to cloudy skies with scattered precipitation later in the week and a chance for strong thunderstorms with tornado potential.

**Zone 4:** The zone is fair to partly cloudy and seasonal with scattered precipitation east.

**Zone 5:** Temperatures are seasonal and skies are partly cloudy to cloudy with scattered precipitation and a chance for thunderstorms central.

**Zone 6:** Skies are mostly cloudy and temperatures range from seasonal to below as a front moves through the area bringing scattered precipitation in central and eastern areas.

**Zone 7:** Variable cloudiness accompanies precipitation west and central, some locally heavy, and seasonal temperatures.

**Zone 8:** Western and central Alaska are windy, central Alaska is stormy, and temperatures are seasonal to below. Temperatures in Hawaii are seasonal to below and much of the state is windy with precipitation.

### New Moon, February 26–March 4

**Zone 1:** The zone is fair to partly cloudy and seasonal with a chance for precipitation.

**Zone 2:** Variable cloudiness with precipitation in both central and southern areas, some locally heavy, and seasonal temperatures.

**Zone 3:** Strong thunderstorms with tornado potential are possible in western and central areas along with stormy conditions and high winds; temperatures are seasonal to below, and skies are partly cloudy to cloudy.

**Zone 4:** Much of the zone sees precipitation, some locally heavy in central and east, with potential for strong tornado-producing thunderstorms east; temperatures are seasonal to below.

**Zone 5:** Seasonal temperatures accompany variably cloudy skies with precipitation central and east, some locally heavy, and possible strong thunderstorms with tornado potential.

**Zone 6:** Skies are fair to partly cloudy with more cloudiness east and scattered precipitation, and temperatures range from seasonal to above.

**Zone 7:** Northern coastal areas see precipitation and the zone is windy, seasonal, and partly cloudy to cloudy.

**Zone 8:** Central and eastern Alaska see precipitation with partly cloudy to cloudy skies, western areas are mostly fair, and temperatures are seasonal. Hawaii is mostly fair and seasonal.

### 1st Quarter Moon, March 5–11

**Zone 1:** Seasonal temperatures accompany partly cloudy to cloudy skies.

**Zone 2:** The zone is windy with seasonal temperatures and scattered precipitation.

**Zone 3:** Skies are partly cloudy to cloudy and windy, eastern areas see precipitation later in the week, and western and central areas could see strong thunderstorms with locally heavy precipitation.

**Zone 4:** Strong thunderstorms are possible in eastern areas, temperatures are seasonal, and skies are partly cloudy.

**Zone 5:** Central areas see precipitation, skies are partly cloudy, and temperatures are seasonal but cooler east.

**Zone 6:** Temperatures are seasonal and skies are fair to partly cloudy with precipitation central.

**Zone 7:** Temperatures range from seasonal to above and skies are mostly fair.

**Zone 8:** Later in the week, western Alaska is windy with precipitation, some locally heavy; eastern areas see precipitation; central and eastern areas are mostly fair to partly cloudy; and temperatures are seasonal. Hawaii is seasonal with partly cloudy to cloudy skies.

### Full Moon, March 12–19

**Zone 1:** The zone is fair to partly cloudy with temperatures ranging from seasonal to below.

**Zone 2:** Seasonal temperatures accompany partly cloudy skies with a chance for precipitation.

**Zone 3:** Temperatures range from seasonal to above, skies are fair to partly cloudy and windy, and eastern areas have a chance for precipitation.

**Zone 4:** Northern areas have a chance for precipitation, skies are fair to partly cloudy, and temperatures are seasonal to above.

**Zone 5:** The zone is mostly fair with temperatures ranging from seasonal to above, and eastern areas have a chance for precipitation.

**Zone 6:** Much of the zone sees precipitation, which is abundant in eastern areas; skies are partly cloudy to cloudy, and temperatures are seasonal.

**Zone 7:** Temperatures are seasonal to above, much of the zone sees precipitation, and skies are variably cloudy; southern coastal areas are mostly fair.

**Zone 8:** Alaska is mostly fair to partly cloudy with precipitation west, and temperatures are seasonal. Hawaii is variably cloudy and seasonal with showers west.

## Spring

Temperatures will range from seasonal to below in Zone 1, and northern areas will see an above average number of storms and cloudy days. In Zone 2, temperatures will trend lower than average and there will be stormy periods with above average precipitation. Although eastern areas of Zone 3 will be cooler with more precipitation, western and central parts of this zone will be windy and seasonal with average potential for strong thunderstorms in southern areas. Wind and cloudy skies will prevail across Zones 4 and 5, with central areas seeing major storms that move through these states from the northwestern area of Zone 4. Temperatures in Zones 4 and 5 will range from seasonal to below, with precipitation ranging from seasonal to above. Western parts of Zone 6 will be warmer and drier than central and eastern areas, and precipitation across the zone will range from seasonal to below. Zone 7 will experience temperatures ranging from seasonal to below with major storms in mountain areas; precipitation will be mostly average, but below average in western areas. In Zone 8, temperatures in central Alaska will be below average as this area sees more cloudy days and storms. Eastern Alaska will also see abundant precipitation at times and windy conditions, while western Alaska will be generally seasonal with below average precipitation. Much of Hawaii (Zone 8) will experience an above-average number of cooler days with precipitation.

### 3rd Quarter Moon, March 20–26

**Zone 1:** Skies are fair to partly cloudy with scattered precipitation and seasonal temperatures.

**Zone 2:** Strong thunderstorms with tornado potential are possible in central and southern areas, skies are variably cloudy, and temperatures are seasonal.

**Zone 3:** Temperatures range from seasonal to above, skies are fair to partly cloudy, and the zone sees scattered showers.

**Zone 4:** This zone has a chance for precipitation, skies are fair to partly cloudy, and temperatures are seasonal to above.

**Zone 5:** Fair to partly cloudy skies accompany temperatures ranging from seasonal to above, and eastern areas have a chance for strong thunderstorms.

**Zone 6:** Western areas see precipitation, central areas have a chance for precipitation, eastern areas are mostly fair, skies are variably cloudy, and temperatures are seasonal to above.

**Zone 7:** Western areas see precipitation later in the week, skies are mostly fair to partly cloudy, and temperatures are seasonal to above.

**Zone 8:** Temperatures in Alaska are seasonal, skies are partly cloudy to cloudy, and eastern areas see precipitation. Eastern Hawaii is cloudy, western and central areas are fair to partly cloudy. The state is windy and some areas see scattered thunderstorms.

### New Moon, March 27–April 2

**Zone 1:** Skies are fair to partly cloudy, temperatures are seasonal, and northern areas see scattered precipitation.

**Zone 2:** Seasonal temperatures accompany partly cloudy skies and scattered precipitation.

**Zone 3:** Much of the zone sees scattered showers and thunderstorms with seasonal temperatures, and skies are windy and variably cloudy.

**Zone 4:** Western areas are fair to partly cloudy, central and eastern areas see scattered thunderstorms and precipitation, and temperatures range from seasonal to below.

**Zone 5:** Skies are mostly fair, eastern areas see more cloudiness and scattered thunderstorms, and temperatures are seasonal.

**Zone 6:** Variably cloudy skies and temperatures ranging from seasonal to above accompany a chance for precipitation in central and eastern areas.

**Zone 7:** Temperatures are seasonal to above, skies are mostly fair, and eastern areas are windy with a chance for precipitation.

**Zone 8:** Central and eastern Alaska see precipitation, some locally heavy; skies are variably cloudy, and temperatures are seasonal. Temperatures in Hawaii are seasonal to above and skies are partly cloudy with scattered showers.

### 1st Quarter Moon, April 3–10

**Zone 1:** Much of the zone sees precipitation, some locally heavy, under partly cloudy to cloudy skies; temperatures range from seasonal to below.

**Zone 2:** The zone is fair to partly cloudy and seasonal, and southern areas are windy with a chance for precipitation.

**Zone 3:** Skies are partly cloudy and windy with seasonal temperatures, and central and eastern areas have a chance for precipitation.

**Zone 4:** Temperatures range from seasonal to above and skies are mostly fair; eastern areas have a chance for scattered thunderstorms.

**Zone 5:** Skies are fair and temperatures range from seasonal to above.

**Zone 6:** Seasonal temperatures accompany partly cloudy to cloudy skies, and eastern areas see precipitation, some locally heavy.

**Zone 7:** Western skies are mostly fair, central and eastern areas see precipitation under partly cloudy to cloudy skies, and temperatures are seasonal.

**Zone 8:** Central Alaska sees precipitation, skies are variably cloudy, and temperatures are seasonal. Temperatures in Hawaii are seasonal, skies are windy and partly cloudy to cloudy, and much of the state sees scattered showers.

## Full Moon, April 11–18

**Zone 1:** Precipitation, likely abundant in some areas, accompanies windy conditions and temperatures ranging from seasonal to below.

**Zone 2:** The zone is partly cloudy and windy, central and southern areas are cooler with scattered precipitation, and northern areas are seasonal with precipitation.

**Zone 3:** Temperatures range from seasonal to below under variably cloudy skies and precipitation, some locally heavy, and thunderstorms.

**Zone 4:** Much of the zone sees precipitation and scattered thunderstorms, skies are partly cloudy, and temperatures are seasonal to above.

**Zone 5:** Thunderstorms are possible, especially in western and central areas, with locally heavy precipitation; temperatures are seasonal to above, and skies are fair to partly cloudy.

**Zone 6:** The zone is windy with precipitation, some abundant, under partly cloudy to cloudy skies, and temperatures are seasonal to below.

**Zone 7:** Western and central areas are windy with scattered precipitation, eastern areas are windy with locally heavy precipitation, and skies are partly cloudy to cloudy.

**Zone 8:** Central Alaska is cloudy with precipitation, some abundant, western areas are windy and partly cloudy, eastern areas are fair, and temperatures range from seasonal to below. Hawaii is partly cloudy to cloudy and seasonal with locally heavy precipitation in central parts of the state.

### 3rd Quarter Moon, April 19–25

**Zone 1:** The zone is windy with temperatures ranging from seasonal to above, and northern areas see precipitation, possibly abundant.

**Zone 2:** Fair skies accompany seasonal temperatures.

**Zone 3:** Western and central areas see significant precipitation, skies are variably cloudy, and temperatures are seasonal to below.

**Zone 4:** Western parts of the zone see precipitation, some abundant, central and eastern areas are mostly fair, and temperatures are mostly seasonal.

**Zone 5:** Skies are mostly fair in central and eastern areas with a chance for thunderstorms, western areas see precipitation, and temperatures are seasonal to above.

**Zone 6:** Temperatures are seasonal to above and skies are partly cloudy with a chance for scattered thunderstorms.

**Zone 7:** Western areas have a chance for precipitation, skies are fair to partly cloudy, and temperatures are seasonal to above.

**Zone 8:** Alaska is fair to partly cloudy with temperatures ranging from seasonal to below. Hawaii is windy with scattered thunderstorms and temperatures ranging from seasonal to above.

### New Moon, April 26–May 1

**Zone 1:** Southern areas are fair to partly cloudy, northern areas are cloudy with precipitation, and temperatures are seasonal.

**Zone 2:** Northern skies are fair, central and southern areas see showers and thunderstorms, and temperatures are seasonal.

**Zone 3:** Temperatures range from seasonal to above, skies are mostly fair to partly cloudy, and central parts of the zone see scattered thunderstorms.

**Zone 4:** Much of the zone sees scattered thunderstorms, possibly with tornado potential, skies are fair to partly cloudy, and temperatures are seasonal to above.

**Zone 5:** Fair to partly cloudy skies accompany thunderstorms with tornado potential, and temperatures range from seasonal to above

**Zone 6:** The zone is mostly fair with scattered thunderstorms and temperatures ranging from seasonal to above.

**Zone 7:** Fair skies accompany temperatures ranging from seasonal to above.

**Zone 8:** Alaska is windy and fair with temperatures seasonal to above. Temperatures in Hawaii are seasonal to above, skies are mostly fair and windy, and central areas see scattered precipitation.

### 1st Quarter Moon, May 2–9

**Zone 1:** Skies are fair and temperatures are seasonal to above.

**Zone 2:** Northern areas are fair, central and southern areas see precipitation, and temperatures are seasonal.

**Zone 3:** Temperatures are seasonal to above, western and eastern skies are mostly fair, and central areas are partly cloudy to cloudy with locally heavy precipitation and strong thunderstorms with tornado potential.

**Zone 4:** Much of the zone sees scattered thunderstorms and temperatures ranging from seasonal to above, and central and eastern areas could see strong thunderstorms with tornado potential.

**Zone 5:** Much of the zone sees scattered thunderstorms, central and eastern areas are humid with potential for locally heavy precipitation and tornados, and temperatures are seasonal to above.

**Zone 6:** The zone is mostly fair to partly cloudy and seasonal with precipitation in the west and scattered precipitation in the east.

**Zone 7:** Temperatures are seasonal to above and skies are fair to partly cloudy.

**Zone 8:** Alaska is fair to partly cloudy with temperatures ranging from seasonal to above with precipitation in western areas. Hawaii is windy and fair with temperatures seasonal to above.

## Full Moon, May 10–17

**Zone 1:** The zone is seasonal and windy with a chance for thunderstorms and locally heavy precipitation.

**Zone 2:** Northern areas could see strong thunderstorms, central and southern parts of the zone are mostly fair, and temperatures are seasonal to above.

**Zone 3:** Much of the zone sees scattered thunderstorms, some with tornado potential, and conditions are humid with temperatures ranging from seasonal to above.

**Zone 4:** Western areas are cloudy and cool with precipitation that advances into central areas of the zone, scattered thunderstorms are possible east, and temperatures are seasonal to above.

**Zone 5:** Much of the zone sees precipitation under partly cloudy to cloudy skies and seasonal temperatures.

**Zone 6:** Temperatures are seasonal and much of the zone sees showers and scattered thunderstorms, some with locally heavy precipitation, with skies partly cloudy to cloudy.

**Zone 7:** Skies are partly cloudy to cloudy, temperatures are seasonal to above, and much of the zone sees scattered thunderstorms and showers.

**Zone 8:** Alaska is partly cloudy to cloudy and seasonal with precipitation central and east. Hawaii is variably cloudy and seasonal with showers.

## 3rd Quarter Moon, May 18–24

**Zone 1:** Skies are partly cloudy to cloudy, temperatures are seasonal to above, and northern areas could see locally heavy precipitation.

**Zone 2:** Much of the zone sees precipitation, some locally heavy, strong thunderstorms with tornado potential are possible, and humidity accompanies seasonal temperatures.

**Zone 3:** Western areas are windy, temperatures are seasonal, and central and eastern areas are humid with thunderstorms and possible tornados.

**Zone 4:** Skies are fair to partly cloudy, central and eastern areas have a chance for showers, and temperatures are seasonal to above.

**Zone 5:** Temperatures are seasonal to above, skies are fair to partly cloudy with more cloudiness in eastern areas, and there is a chance for showers and thunderstorms.

**Zone 6:** Much of the zone is windy and partly cloudy with scattered showers and seasonal temperatures.

**Zone 7:** Northern coastal areas see showers, the zone is windy and generally partly cloudy, and temperatures are seasonal to above.

**Zone 8:** Western Alaska is windy, central and eastern parts of the state are cloudy with precipitation, and temperatures are seasonal. Hawaii is seasonal, partly cloudy in central and eastern areas, and cloudy with showers in western areas.

### New Moon, May 25–31

**Zone 1:** The zone is humid and variably cloudy with temperatures ranging from seasonal to above and showers in the north.

**Zone 2:** Northern areas are humid and partly cloudy, central and southern areas are mostly fair, and temperature are seasonal to above.

**Zone 3:** Western parts of the zone are cloudy with showers, central and eastern areas are mostly fair, eastern areas have a chance for precipitation, and temperatures are seasonal.

**Zone 4:** Much of the zone has a chance for scattered showers and thunderstorms under variably cloudy and windy skies, temperatures range from seasonal to above, and central areas could be stormy.

**Zone 5:** Eastern areas could be stormy and much of the zone has a chance for showers and thunderstorms under variably cloudy skies with seasonal temperatures.

**Zone 6:** The zone is seasonal and partly cloudy with a chance for showers in central and eastern areas.

**Zone 7:** Temperatures are seasonal to above and skies are mostly fair.

**Zone 8:** Alaska is seasonal with precipitation and variable cloudiness in western and central areas, and eastern areas are windy and fair. Hawaii is humid and partly cloudy with temperatures ranging from seasonal to above.

### 1st Quarter Moon, June 1–8

**Zone 1:** Skies are fair to partly cloudy, temperatures are seasonal to above, and northern areas see precipitation, some locally heavy.

**Zone 2:** Northern areas are fair, central and southern areas are partly cloudy to cloudy with precipitation and strong thunderstorms with tornado potential, and temperatures range from seasonal to below.

**Zone 3:** Western areas are fair; eastern areas are partly cloudy, central areas are partly cloudy to cloudy with showers and thunderstorms, and temperatures are seasonal to below.

**Zone 4:** Western parts of the zone are fair, central and eastern areas are partly cloudy to cloudy with precipitation, some locally heavy; temperatures are seasonal.

**Zone 5:** The zone is variably cloudy with precipitation, some locally heavy, in central and eastern areas.

**Zone 6:** Much of the zone sees showers and thunderstorms under variably cloudy skies with temperatures ranging from seasonal to above.

**Zone 7:** Western and central parts of the zone are windy with a chance for precipitation, skies are fair to partly cloudy, and temperatures are seasonal to above.

**Zone 8:** Eastern Alaska is cloudy with precipitation, western and central parts of the state are fair to partly cloudy, and temperatures are seasonal to above. Hawaii is fair to partly cloudy with temperatures ranging from seasonal to above.

**Full Moon, June 9–16**
**Zone 1:** The zone is variably cloudy and seasonal with scattered showers.
**Zone 2:** Fair to partly cloudy skies and humidity accompany a chance for precipitation and temperatures ranging from seasonal to above.
**Zone 3:** Temperatures are seasonal to above with a chance for thunderstorms, which could be strong with tornado potential in central areas.
**Zone 4:** Skies are fair to partly cloudy, temperatures range from seasonal to above, and increasing cloudiness later in the week brings precipitation.
**Zone 5:** The zone is mostly fair with temperatures ranging from seasonal to above.
**Zone 6:** Temperatures are seasonal to above, skies are fair to partly cloudy, and central areas have a chance for thunderstorms.
**Zone 7:** The zone is windy and humid with temperatures ranging from seasonal to above, and eastern areas are humid with a chance for thunderstorms.
**Zone 8:** Alaska is fair to partly cloudy and seasonal with more cloudiness in central areas. Hawaii is mostly fair and seasonal.

**3rd Quarter Moon, June 17–22**
**Zone 1:** Temperatures range from seasonal to above under fair to partly cloudy skies with scattered showers and thunderstorms.
**Zone 2:** Central and southern areas are cloudy with precipitation, northern areas are fair, and temperatures are seasonal.
**Zone 3:** Western areas are windy, eastern areas are fair, and central areas see precipitation, some locally heavy. Temperatures are seasonal to below.
**Zone 4:** Fair to partly cloudy skies and humidity accompany a

chance for thunderstorms and temperatures ranging from seasonal to above.

**Zone 5:** Central and eastern areas have a chance for showers and thunderstorms, temperatures are seasonal to above, and skies are fair to partly cloudy.

**Zone 6:** Much of the zone sees showers with strong thunderstorms in eastern areas, variably cloudy skies, and temperatures seasonal to above.

**Zone 7:** Skies are mostly fair and temperatures seasonal to above, northern coastal areas see showers, and eastern parts are humid with scattered thunderstorms and locally heavy precipitation.

**Zone 8:** Western Alaska sees precipitation, central and eastern parts of the state are mostly fair, and temperatures are seasonal to above. Temperatures in Hawaii are seasonal to above with a chance for showers and thunderstorm. Skies are partly cloudy.

## Summer

Zone 1 can expect temperatures and precipitation ranging from seasonal to above with more cloudiness in northern areas and above average potential for tropical storms and hurricanes. Northern and central parts of Zone 2 also have above average potential for tropical storms and hurricanes and will see abundant precipitation at times. Southern areas of Zone 2 will see average precipitation, and temperatures across the zone will range from seasonal to above. Precipitation and temperatures levels will range from seasonal to above across Zone 3, and the Gulf states will also see abundant precipitation at times along with an above average potential for tropical storms and hurricanes. In Zones 4 and 5, temperatures and precipitation will be mostly seasonal with strong thunderstorms in the eastern Plains States. Precipitation in Zone 6 will be average, but eastern areas will see significant downfall at times, while temperatures will range from seasonal to above.

Temperatures in much of Zone 7 will range from seasonal to above under significant high-pressure systems, along with precipitation ranging from seasonal to below except in eastern areas. In Zone 8, Alaska will be generally seasonal with average temperatures and precipitation, although eastern parts of the state will be warmer and drier. Hawaii will experience seasonal temperatures and precipitation.

### New Moon, June 23–29

**Zone 1:** The zone is partly cloudy with temperatures seasonal to above with a chance for precipitation in northern areas and thunderstorms in southern areas.

**Zone 2:** Northern areas see thunderstorms, central and southern areas see showers, skies are partly cloudy, and the zone is humid and seasonal.

**Zone 3:** Conditions are humid, skies are partly cloudy, temperatures range from seasonal to above, and showers and strong thunderstorms are possible across the zone.

**Zone 4:** Skies are partly cloudy, temperatures range from seasonal to above, conditions are humid, and central and eastern areas see scattered thunderstorms, some strong.

**Zone 5:** Central parts of the zone see scattered thunderstorms, some strong with tornado potential. Humidity accompanies temperatures ranging from seasonal to above, and skies are partly cloudy.

**Zone 6:** Much of the zone sees showers and scattered thunderstorms, temperatures range from seasonal to above, and skies are windy and partly cloudy.

**Zone 7:** Temperatures ranging from seasonal to above accompany scattered thunderstorms across much of the zone, eastern areas have a chance for showers, and skies are fair to partly cloudy.

**Zone 8:** Western and central Alaska see precipitation under variably cloudy skies with seasonal temperatures. Temperatures in Hawaii are seasonal to above, skies are partly cloudy and windy, and much of the state sees showers and thunderstorms.

## 1st Quarter Moon, June 30–July 8

**Zone 1:** The zone is humid and windy with scattered showers and thunderstorms, and temperatures range from seasonal to above.

**Zone 2:** Scattered showers and thunderstorms, some strong with tornado potential and locally heavy precipitation, accompany humidity and temperatures that are seasonal to above.

**Zone 3:** Skies are partly cloudy to cloudy and windy, conditions are humid, temperatures are seasonal to above, and central and eastern areas could see showers and strong thunderstorms with tornado potential.

**Zone 4:** Variably cloudy skies and windy conditions accompany showers and scattered thunderstorms, some strong with tornado potential, and temperatures range from seasonal to above.

**Zone 5:** Temperatures range from seasonal to above and the zone sees showers and thunderstorms, and some are strong in eastern areas with tornado potential.

**Zone 6:** Skies are variably cloudy and windy, temperatures are seasonal, and western areas see showers, some with locally heavy precipitation.

**Zone 7:** Western and central areas are partly cloudy to cloudy with scattered showers, temperatures range from seasonal to above, and eastern areas are fair to partly cloudy and humid with a chance for thunderstorms.

**Zone 8:** Temperatures in Alaska are seasonal, skies are mostly fair to partly cloudy, and eastern areas see precipitation. Hawaii is partly cloudy and humid with temperatures ranging from seasonal to above.

## Full Moon, July 9–15

**Zone 1:** The zone is windy, seasonal, and partly cloudy with a chance for precipitation.

**Zone 2:** Central and southern areas see showers and the zone is partly cloudy to cloudy and seasonal.

**Zone 3:** Western and central areas are cloudy with precipitation—some locally heavy, possibly from a tropical storm—eastern areas are partly cloudy and temperatures are seasonal.

**Zone 4:** Skies are cloudy and windy and temperatures are seasonal, and much of the zone sees thunderstorms and precipitation, some locally heavy.

**Zone 5:** Humidity and temperatures ranging from seasonal to above accompany scattered thunderstorms, some strong with tornado potential; locally heavy precipitation in eastern and central parts of the zone, and western areas see showers.

**Zone 6:** Temperatures range from seasonal to above, skies are partly cloudy and windy, and the zone has a chance for showers and thunderstorms.

**Zone 7:** Skies are fair to partly cloudy and temperatures are seasonal to above.

**Zone 8:** Alaskan temperatures are seasonal to above, skies are fair to partly cloudy and windy, and central and eastern areas see scattered precipitation. Hawaii is partly cloudy with temperatures ranging from seasonal to above with a chance for precipitation.

### 3rd Quarter Moon, July 16–22

**Zone 1:** Skies are partly cloudy and windy and temperatures are seasonal.

**Zone 2:** The zone is windy and partly cloudy with a chance for thunderstorms.

**Zone 3:** Scattered precipitation accompanies seasonal temperatures and windy and partly cloudy skies.

**Zone 4:** Western and central parts of the zone see thunderstorms with tornado potential and locally heavy precipitation that could cause flooding, while eastern areas are mostly fair; temperatures are seasonal.

**Zone 5:** Temperatures range from seasonal to below with heavy precipitation and possible flooding and strong thunderstorms with tornado potential in western and central areas. Eastern areas see showers and variably cloudy skies.

**Zone 6:** The zone is seasonal and partly cloudy with a chance for precipitation.

**Zone 7:** Skies are partly cloudy and temperatures are seasonal to above.

**Zone 8:** Skies in Alaska are variably cloudy, temperatures are seasonal, and central areas see locally heavy precipitation. Seasonal temperatures in Hawaii accompany showers, some locally heavy; a tropical storm is possible.

### New Moon, July 23–29

**Zone 1:** The zone is windy and seasonal with showers and thunderstorms, some with locally heavy precipitation.

**Zone 2:** Northern areas are windy with thunderstorms and locally heavy precipitation, central and southern areas are partly cloudy with a chance for showers and thunderstorms, and temperatures are seasonal.

**Zone 3:** Skies are fair to partly cloudy and windy, temperatures range from seasonal to above, and eastern areas have a chance of thunderstorms with locally heavy precipitation.

**Zone 4:** Western areas are fair, central parts of the zone see strong thunderstorms with tornado potential and locally heavy precipitation, eastern areas see showers, temperatures are seasonal, and skies variably cloudy; a tropical storm is possible.

**Zone 5:** Seasonal temperatures accompany abundant precipitation across much of the zone, including strong thunderstorms with tornado potential; a tropical storm is possible.

**Zone 6:** The zone is mostly fair to partly cloudy with temperatures ranging from seasonal to above, and central and eastern areas see scattered thunderstorms.

**Zone 7:** Skies are fair to partly cloudy and windy, northern coastal areas see scattered showers, temperatures are seasonal to above, and central and eastern areas see scattered thunderstorms.

**Zone 8:** Alaska is fair to partly cloudy with temperatures ranging from seasonal to above and precipitation in central areas. Hawaii is fair to partly cloudy, temperatures are seasonal to above, and central parts of the state see scattered thunderstorms.

**1st Quarter Moon, July 30–August 6**

**Zone 1:** The zone is partly cloudy and seasonal.

**Zone 2:** Temperatures ranging from seasonal to above accompany partly cloudy and windy skies.

**Zone 3:** Much of the zone has a chance for showers, and temperatures are seasonal to below.

**Zone 4:** Temperatures are seasonal to below, central and western areas see precipitation, some locally heavy, and strong thunderstorms with hail and tornado potential are possible; eastern areas are cooler and mostly fair.

**Zone 5:** Western and central parts of the zone could see abundant precipitation, possibly from strong thunderstorms with potential for tornados and hail, and temperatures are seasonal to below; eastern areas see showers.

**Zone 6:** The zone is generally fair to partly cloudy and windy with temperatures ranging from seasonal to above and thunderstorms in central areas.

**Zone 7:** Western and central parts of the zone are windy with scattered thunderstorms, eastern areas are humid, temperatures are seasonal to above, and skies are partly cloudy to cloudy.

**Zone 8:** Alaska is fair to partly cloudy and seasonal. Hawaii is partly cloudy, humid, and seasonal.

**Full Moon, August 7–13**

**Zone 1:** Northern areas are windy, skies are variably cloudy, temperatures range from seasonal to below, and the zone sees scattered precipitation.

**Zone 2:** Temperatures range from seasonal to below, skies are partly cloudy to cloudy, and much of the zone sees showers and scattered thunderstorms.

**Zone 3:** Skies are partly cloudy and the zone is seasonal and humid.

**Zone 4:** Temperatures range from seasonal to above, conditions are humid, skies are partly cloudy to cloudy, and western areas see precipitation, some locally heavy with flooding potential.

**Zone 5:** Western and central parts of the zone see precipitation, some locally heavy with flooding potential, and eastern areas see scattered precipitation; temperatures are seasonal to above.

**Zone 6:** Temperatures in zone 6 are seasonal to above, western areas see scattered thunderstorms and showers, and eastern areas see locally heavy precipitation and possibly strong thunderstorms.

**Zone 7:** Partly cloudy to cloudy skies accompany temperatures ranging from seasonal to above, and conditions in eastern areas are humid with scattered thunderstorms.

**Zone 8:** Central Alaska could see abundant precipitation, skies are partly cloudy to cloudy, and temperatures range from seasonal to below. In Hawaii, locally heavy precipitation and thunderstorms accompany seasonal temperatures and variably cloudy and windy skies.

### 3rd Quarter Moon, August 14–20

**Zone 1:** Temperatures range from seasonal to above and the zone is windy and mostly fair.

**Zone 2:** Northern areas are fair, central and southern areas are cloudy with precipitation, conditions are humid, and temperatures are seasonal.

**Zone 3:** Much of the zone is cloudy and humid with precipitation and a possible tropical storm in the Gulf.

**Zone 4:** Western and central areas see showers and central and eastern areas see scattered thunderstorms, temperatures range from seasonal to above, and skies are variably cloudy.

**Zone 5:** Western and central areas see precipitation, eastern areas are windy, temperatures are seasonal, and skies are variably cloudy.

**Zone 6:** The zone is partly cloudy to cloudy with scattered thunderstorms and showers central and east, conditions are windy, and temperatures range from seasonal to above.

**Zone 7:** Partly cloudy and windy skies accompany seasonal temperatures and scattered thunderstorms in central areas.

**Zone 8:** Alaska is fair to partly cloudy and seasonal with precipitation in eastern areas. Hawaii is fair with temperatures ranging from seasonal to above.

### New Moon, August 21–28

**Zone 1:** Temperatures are seasonal under partly cloudy to cloudy skies with precipitation.

**Zone 2:** Much of the zone sees precipitation, which is locally heavy central and south; conditions are humid, and temperatures range from seasonal to below.

**Zone 3:** Western areas are windy and much of the zone sees precipitation, some locally heavy east, and temperatures are seasonal to below.

**Zone 4:** Scattered thunderstorms accompany windy conditions west and central, eastern areas see precipitation and possibly strong thunderstorms, skies are variably cloudy, and temperatures are seasonal.

**Zone 5:** Much of the zone has a chance for showers and scattered thunderstorms, temperatures are seasonal to above, and skies are partly cloudy to cloudy.

**Zone 6:** Central and western areas see precipitation, some locally heavy; skies are partly cloudy to cloudy, and temperatures are seasonal.

**Zone 7:** Temperatures are seasonal, western and central parts of the zone are partly cloudy to cloudy with showers, and eastern areas are humid and partly cloudy with a chance for thunderstorms.

**Zone 8:** Western Alaska is cloudy with precipitation, central and eastern areas are fair and windy, and temperatures are seasonal.

Hawaii is fair to partly cloudy and seasonal with scattered showers.

## 1st Quarter Moon, August 29–September 5

**Zone 1:** Precipitation accompanies partly cloudy to cloudy skies, and temperatures are seasonal to below.

**Zone 2:** Skies are variably cloudy and windy, temperatures are seasonal, and the zone sees showers and strong thunderstorms with tornado potential.

**Zone 3:** Strong tornado-producing thunderstorms are possible in western and central areas with locally heavy precipitation and wind across much of the zone; temperatures are seasonal to below.

**Zone 4:** Northwest areas are cloudy with precipitation, the remainder of the zone is generally partly cloudy with seasonal temperatures, and scattered thunderstorms in the east with potential for locally heavy precipitation.

**Zone 5:** Temperatures range from seasonal to above, skies are fair to partly cloudy, and central areas see scattered thunderstorms.

**Zone 6:** Skies are variably cloudy, central and eastern areas see precipitation, some locally heavy, and temperatures are seasonal to below.

**Zone 7:** Western skies are fair to partly cloudy, central and eastern areas see precipitation, some locally heavy, and temperatures are seasonal to below.

**Zone 8:** Seasonal temperatures in Alaska accompany variably cloudy skies and precipitation central and east. Much of Hawaii sees showers with seasonal temperatures and partly cloudy to cloudy skies.

## Full Moon, September 6–12

**Zone 1:** Northern areas are partly cloudy, southern parts of the zone are windy with precipitation, and temperatures are seasonal.

**Zone 2:** Seasonal temperatures accompany showers and thunderstorms in northern areas, some strong. Central and southern areas are partly cloudy with a chance for thunderstorms.

**Zone 3:** Much of the zone sees precipitation, eastern areas see thunderstorms, some strong, and conditions are windy; temperatures are seasonal.

**Zone 4:** The zone is partly cloudy to cloudy with precipitation, some locally heavy, and temperatures range from seasonal to below.

**Zone 5:** Western areas are partly cloudy, central and eastern areas see more cloudiness with precipitation, and temperatures are seasonal.

**Zone 6:** Variably cloudy skies accompany windy conditions in western and central areas and scattered thunderstorms in central areas.

**Zone 7:** Western areas are windy with scattered thunderstorms in western and central areas, skies are mostly fair to partly cloudy, and temperatures are seasonal to above.

**Zone 8:** Much of Alaska is fair to partly cloudy and seasonal; western areas are windy with precipitation.

### 3rd Quarter Moon, September 13–19

**Zone 1:** Temperatures range from seasonal to below with variably cloudy and windy skies and thunderstorms, some strong.

**Zone 2:** Much of the zone sees scattered showers with a chance for thunderstorms, skies are variably cloudy, and temperatures are seasonal.

**Zone 3:** Seasonal temperatures accompany partly cloudy skies and eastern areas see precipitation, some locally heavy.

**Zone 4:** Western areas see locally heavy precipitation, central parts of the zone see precipitation, eastern areas have a chance for thunderstorms, and temperatures are seasonal to below.

**Zone 5:** Much of the zone sees precipitation along with partly cloudy to cloudy skies and temperatures ranging from seasonal to below.

**Zone 6:** The zone is windy with temperatures ranging from seasonal to above, western areas see showers, and eastern areas see scattered thunderstorms.

**Zone 7:** Precipitation in northern coastal areas moves into central areas, skies are generally fair to partly cloudy, eastern areas are windy with a chance for thunderstorms, and temperatures are seasonal to above.

**Zone 8:** Much of Alaska sees precipitation under partly cloudy to cloudy and windy skies; temperatures are seasonal to below. Hawaii is partly cloudy and seasonal with showers and thunderstorms.

## Autumn

Temperatures in Zone 1 will be seasonal to below with an above average number of storms, including hail and sleet. Coastal areas of Zone 2 will see some significant storms and temperatures and precipitation will range from seasonal to below throughout the zone. Temperatures in Zone 3 will also range from seasonal to below, while precipitation will be average to above, especially in eastern areas. Zones 4 and 5 will see some significant storms in central and eastern areas, bringing abundant precipitation. Storms will also bring precipitation to western areas of Zone 4 that move into central and eastern areas of both zones. Temperatures in Zones 4 and 5 will be seasonal. Precipitation in central and eastern areas of Zone 6 will be seasonal to above, while it will be warmer with below average precipitation in western areas. Temperatures will range from seasonal to above in Zone 7 with precipitation centering north and in the mountains. Precipitation will be below average in much of Zone 7. Precipitation in Zone 8 will be average to below in western and central parts of Alaska, and average to above in eastern areas; temperatures will be seasonal. Temperatures in Hawaii will range from seasonal to below, as will precipitation.

### New Moon, September 20–26

**Zone 1:** Temperatures are seasonal to below and skies are partly cloudy to cloudy with scattered precipitation in southern parts of the zone and locally heavy precipitation in northern parts.

**Zone 2:** Skies are fair to partly cloudy, temperatures are seasonal, and central and southern areas have a chance for precipitation.

**Zone 3:** Western and central parts are cloudy with locally heavy precipitation, possibly from a tropical storm, and temperatures are seasonal to below. Eastern areas are partly cloudy with scattered precipitation later in the week; a tropical storm is possible.

**Zone 4:** Western areas are fair to partly cloudy, and central and eastern areas are variably cloudy with potential for locally heavy precipitation and strong thunderstorms with tornado potential. Temperatures are seasonal to below; a tropical storm is possible.

**Zone 5:** Central and eastern parts of the zone see locally heavy precipitation and strong thunderstorms with tornado potential, temperatures are seasonal to below, and western skies are variably cloudy with showers; a tropical storm is possible.

**Zone 6:** Temperatures range from seasonal to below, skies are partly cloudy to cloudy, and much of the zone sees precipitation, some locally heavy.

**Zone 7:** Eastern areas have a chance for thunderstorms, temperatures are seasonal to above, skies are partly cloudy to cloudy, and much of the zone sees precipitation.

**Zone 8:** Alaska is variably cloudy with temperatures ranging from seasonal to below and precipitation in central and eastern areas. Temperatures in Hawaii range from seasonal to above, skies are partly cloudy to cloudy, and much of the state sees scattered thunderstorms and showers.

### 1st Quarter Moon, September 27–October 4

**Zone 1:** Northern areas see abundant precipitation and the zone is partly cloudy to cloudy with temperatures ranging from seasonal to below; a major storm is possible.

**Zone 2:** Much of the zone sees precipitation, some abundant, and partly cloudy to cloudy skies. Strong thunderstorms with tornado potential are possible in central and southern parts, and temperatures are seasonal to below; a major storm is possible.

**Zone 3:** Skies are variably cloudy, temperatures are seasonal, and western areas could see strong thunderstorms with tornado potential.

**Zone 4:** Western and central parts of the zone see scattered precipitation, and eastern areas and the eastern Plains see precipitation, some locally heavy, along with a chance for strong thunderstorms with tornado potential. Temperatures are seasonal and skies are partly cloudy to cloudy.

**Zone 5:** Temperatures range from seasonal to above with partly cloudy skies and scattered precipitation.

**Zone 6:** Western areas are windy and stormy, central and eastern areas see precipitation, temperatures are seasonal to below, and skies are partly cloudy to cloudy.

**Zone 7:** Skies are fair to partly cloudy, northern coastal and central areas see precipitation, strong thunderstorms are possible in eastern areas, and temperatures are seasonal.

**Zone 8:** Abundant precipitation in central Alaska moves into eastern areas under variably cloudy and windy skies, and temperatures are seasonal. Hawaii is windy and partly cloudy to cloudy with locally heavy precipitation in western areas, and temperatures range from seasonal to below.

### Full Moon, October 5–11

**Zone 1:** The zone is windy and variably cloudy with precipitation and potential for stormy conditions; temperatures range from seasonal to below.

**Zone 2:** Much of the zone sees precipitation with potential for stormy conditions, skies are variably cloudy and windy, and temperatures range from seasonal to below.

**Zone 3:** Much of the zone sees precipitation with stormy conditions possible in eastern areas, skies are variably cloudy, and temperatures range from seasonal to below.

**Zone 4:** The zone is windy and variably cloudy with temperatures ranging from seasonal to below and western areas could be stormy with abundant precipitation.

**Zone 5:** Western areas see precipitation, skies are variably cloudy, temperatures are seasonal to below, and eastern areas see scattered precipitation.

**Zone 6:** Western parts of the zone are cloudy with abundant precipitation, central and eastern areas are partly cloudy with a chance for precipitation, and temperatures are seasonal to below.

**Zone 7:** Western skies are cloudy with abundant precipitation that moves into central parts of the zone. Eastern areas see scattered precipitation and temperatures are seasonal to below.

**Zone 8:** Alaska is partly cloudy to cloudy and seasonal with precipitation in western and central areas. Hawaii is partly cloudy and seasonal with showers in western areas.

### 3rd Quarter Moon, October 12–18

**Zone 1:** Skies are partly cloudy and windy, temperatures are seasonal, and the zone sees scattered precipitation.

**Zone 2:** Northern and central areas are partly cloudy to cloudy with scattered precipitation, southern areas are fair to partly cloudy, and temperatures are seasonal; central areas could see strong thunderstorms with tornado potential.

**Zone 3:** Strong thunderstorms with tornado potential are possible in western and central areas, and eastern areas have a chance for precipitation; skies are variably cloudy.

**Zone 4:** Western parts of the zone are fair to partly cloudy, temperatures are seasonal, and central and eastern areas are partly cloudy to cloudy with precipitation, including potential for strong tornado-producing thunderstorms in eastern areas.

**Zone 5:** Temperatures are seasonal, eastern areas are windy with precipitation under cloudy skies, and western and central areas are partly cloudy.

**Zone 6:** Western areas of the zone are windy with precipitation that moves into central areas, eastern parts of the zone are fair, and temperatures are seasonal to below.

**Zone 7:** Precipitation in western parts of the zone moves into central and eastern areas, temperatures are seasonal, and skies are variably cloudy and windy.

**Zone 8:** Western and central Alaska see precipitation, eastern areas are windy, and temperatures are seasonal. Hawaii is seasonal and partly cloudy with scattered precipitation.

### New Moon, October 19–26

**Zone 1:** Northern areas see scattered precipitation early in the week, much of the zone sees precipitation later in the week, and temperatures are seasonal under variably cloudy and windy skies.

**Zone 2:** Temperatures range from seasonal to above, skies are partly cloudy, and the zone sees scattered precipitation and thunderstorms.

**Zone 3:** Partly cloudy skies accompany seasonal temperatures, scattered precipitation, and windy conditions in eastern areas.

**Zone 4:** Temperatures are seasonal to above, western skies are partly cloudy, and eastern areas have a chance for showers and thunderstorms.

**Zone 5:** Skies are partly cloudy, temperatures are seasonal to above, and the zone has a chance for showers and thunderstorms.

**Zone 6:** Later in the week, western and central areas see locally heavy precipitation. Earlier in the week, locally heavy precipitation in eastern areas accompanies seasonal temperatures and partly cloudy to cloudy skies; western areas are windy.

**Zone 7:** Eastern areas have a chance for thunderstorms and locally heavy precipitation, western and central parts of the zone are windy with precipitation later in the week, and temperatures are seasonal to above.

**Zone 8:** Skies in Alaska are variably cloudy, temperatures are seasonal, and central and western areas could see abundant precipitation. Hawaii is partly cloudy to cloudy with precipitation and temperatures ranging from seasonal to above.

### 1st Quarter Moon, October 27–November 3

**Zone 1:** Skies are partly cloudy and windy, temperatures range from seasonal to below, and the zone sees scattered precipitation.

**Zone 2:** Much of the zone sees precipitation under variably cloudy skies and temperatures ranging from seasonal to below; strong thunderstorms are possible in central and southern areas.

**Zone 3:** Temperatures are seasonal to below, skies are partly cloudy to cloudy, and central and eastern areas see precipitation.

**Zone 4:** Much of the zone sees precipitation as the week unfolds, temperatures are seasonal to below, and skies are partly cloudy to cloudy and windy.

**Zone 5:** Skies are partly cloudy to cloudy and windy with a chance for thunderstorms in central and eastern areas. Showers in western areas accompany temperatures from seasonal to above.

**Zone 6:** The zone is variably cloudy with precipitation and temperatures are seasonal to above.

**Zone 7:** Northern coastal and central areas see precipitation, skies are variably cloudy, temperatures are seasonal to above, and eastern areas have a chance for precipitation.

**Zone 8:** Alaska is partly cloudy with temperatures ranging from seasonal to above. Hawaii sees scattered precipitation under partly cloudy skies and temperatures are seasonal to above.

### Full Moon, November 4–9

**Zone 1:** The zone is partly cloudy to cloudy and windy with precipitation and temperatures ranging from seasonal to below.

**Zone 2:** Northern areas are windy, the zone is fair to partly cloudy, and temperatures are seasonal to above.

**Zone 3:** Partly cloudy to cloudy skies accompany seasonal temperatures.

**Zone 4:** Temperatures range from seasonal to below, skies are partly cloudy to cloudy, and central and eastern areas see precipitation, some locally heavy.

**Zone 5:** Western areas are partly cloudy, central and eastern parts of the zone see more cloudiness and precipitation, and temperatures are seasonal to below.

**Zone 6:** Partly cloudy and windy skies accompany scattered precipitation across the zone, and temperatures range from seasonal to below.

**Zone 7:** Much of the zone is windy and partly cloudy with temperatures ranging from seasonal to above.

**Zone 8:** Alaska is seasonal and partly cloudy, central parts of the state are windy, and eastern areas are cloudy with precipitation. Hawaii is partly cloudy to cloudy, seasonal, and windy with scattered precipitation.

### 3rd Quarter Moon, November 10–17

**Zone 1:** The zone is fair to partly cloudy and windy with scattered precipitation and temperatures are seasonal to below.

**Zone 2:** Seasonal temperatures accompany fair to partly cloudy and windy skies.

**Zone 3:** The zone has a chance for precipitation, skies are partly cloudy to cloudy, and temperatures range from seasonal to below.

**Zone 4:** Much of the zone sees precipitation, some locally heavy in western areas. Skies are partly cloudy to cloudy, and temperatures are seasonal to below.

**Zone 5:** Skies are mostly cloudy, temperatures range from seasonal to below, and much of the zone sees precipitation, some locally heavy.

**Zone 6:** Western and central areas see scattered precipitation, and eastern areas see precipitation later in the week, some locally heavy. Skies are variably cloudy and temperatures are seasonal.

**Zone 7:** Western and central areas are partly cloudy, eastern areas see more cloudiness and precipitation, some locally heavy; temperatures are seasonal but cooler in eastern areas.

**Zone 8:** Temperatures in Alaska range from seasonal to below, skies are mostly fair in western areas, and central and eastern areas see precipitation. Hawaii is partly cloudy and windy with seasonal temperatures and scattered showers.

**New Moon, November 18–25**

**Zone 1:** Temperatures range from seasonal to below, skies are partly cloudy, and the zone sees precipitation later in the week.

**Zone 2:** Temperatures are seasonal, skies are variably cloudy, and central and southern areas have potential for stormy conditions and strong tornado-producing thunderstorms.

**Zone 3:** The zone is windy and variably cloudy with precipitation in western and central areas, and temperatures range from seasonal to below.

**Zone 4:** Central and eastern areas see precipitation, temperatures are seasonal, and skies are partly cloudy to cloudy.

**Zone 5:** Seasonal temperatures accompany windy skies that are partly cloudy to cloudy with precipitation central and east.

**Zone 6:** Much of the zone sees precipitation, conditions are stormy in western parts of the zone, and skies are mostly cloudy. Temperatures are seasonal to below.

**Zone 7:** Much of the zone sees precipitation and stormy conditions, some locally heavy in eastern areas, and temperatures are seasonal to below.

**Zone 8:** Alaska is windy with temperatures ranging from seasonal to below. Hawaii is windy with precipitation, and temperatures range from seasonal to below.

### 1st Quarter Moon, November 26–December 2

**Zone 1:** The zone is stormy with abundant precipitation, and temperatures range from seasonal to below.

**Zone 2:** Northern areas are stormy, southern and central areas see precipitation, and skies are variably cloudy. Temperatures are seasonal but colder in northern areas.

**Zone 3:** Temperatures are seasonal, skies are partly cloudy to cloudy and windy, and western and central areas see precipitation.

**Zone 4:** Temperatures range from seasonal to below, skies are partly cloudy to cloudy and windy, central and western areas see scattered precipitation, and eastern areas see precipitation and possibly sleet.

**Zone 5:** Skies are partly cloudy to cloudy, temperatures range from seasonal to below, and central and eastern parts of the zone see precipitation.

**Zone 6:** Western and central areas are windy with precipitation, some locally heavy, and skies are partly cloudy to cloudy, while eastern areas are mostly fair and temperatures range from seasonal to below.

**Zone 7:** Skies are fair to partly cloudy, temperatures range from seasonal to below, and western and central areas are windy.

**Zone 8:** Alaska is partly cloudy to cloudy with temperatures ranging from seasonal to above, and conditions are windy. Hawaii is fair to partly cloudy and seasonal.

## Full Moon, December 3–9

**Zone 1:** Southern areas are partly cloudy, northern areas see more cloudiness with precipitation, and temperatures are seasonal.

**Zone 2:** The zone is seasonal and fair to partly cloudy.

**Zone 3:** Western and central parts of the zone are windy with precipitation, possibly sleet. Eastern areas are partly cloudy, temperatures are seasonal to below, and southern areas of the zone could see strong thunderstorms with tornado potential.

**Zone 4:** Western areas are stormy with locally heavy precipitation, central and eastern parts of the zone are partly cloudy with a chance for precipitation, and temperatures are seasonal but cooler in eastern areas.

**Zone 5:** Western and central parts of the zone could see strong thunderstorms with tornado potential and stormy conditions, eastern areas are mostly fair with a chance for precipitation, and temperatures range from seasonal to below.

**Zone 6:** Eastern areas have a chance for precipitation, western areas see locally heavy precipitation later in the week, skies are variably cloudy, and temperatures are seasonal.

**Zone 7:** The zone is partly cloudy and seasonal with a chance for precipitation in eastern parts of the zone.

**Zone 8:** Central and eastern Alaska are windy with precipitation, some abundant. Western areas are mostly fair and temperatures are seasonal. Hawaii is partly cloudy to cloudy and seasonal with showers in eastern areas.

## 3rd Quarter Moon, December 10–17

**Zone 1:** Cloudy, windy, and seasonal with abundant precipitation.

**Zone 2:** Sleet and freezing rain are possible, along with strong thunderstorms with tornado potential. Skies are mostly cloudy and temperatures are seasonal.

**Zone 3:** The zone is windy and fair to partly cloudy, temperatures range from seasonal to below, and eastern areas see scattered precipitation.

**Zone 4:** Western skies are partly cloudy to cloudy with scattered precipitation, central and eastern areas are fair to partly cloudy, and temperatures are seasonal to above.

**Zone 5:** Temperatures are seasonal, western skies are partly cloudy to cloudy and windy, and central and eastern areas are fair to partly cloudy.

**Zone 6:** Much of the zone is windy and cloudy with precipitation, some abundant, and temperatures range from seasonal to below.

**Zone 7:** The zone is windy with precipitation in western and central areas, temperatures are seasonal, and skies are mostly cloudy.

**Zone 8:** Alaska is seasonal and partly cloudy to cloudy with precipitation in western areas. Hawaii is partly cloudy to cloudy and seasonal temperatures accompany showers, some locally heavy.

### New Moon, December 18–25

**Zone 1:** Skies are partly cloudy with scattered precipitation and temperatures range from seasonal to below.

**Zone 2:** The zone is partly cloudy and seasonal.

**Zone 3:** Western and central areas are windy, temperatures are seasonal to above, skies are fair to partly cloudy, and western areas have a chance for precipitation later in the week.

**Zone 4:** Much of the zone sees precipitation, which could be abundant in central areas, skies are partly cloudy to cloudy, and temperatures are seasonal.

**Zone 5:** Mostly cloudy skies and temperatures ranging from seasonal to below accompany precipitation across much of the zone, with the heaviest in eastern areas.

**Zone 6:** Temperatures range from seasonal to below, skies are partly cloudy to cloudy, and eastern and central areas are windy with precipitation, some abundant.

**Zone 7:** Skies are partly cloudy to cloudy, temperatures are seasonal to below, and central and eastern areas see precipitation and windy conditions.

**Zone 8:** Alaska is seasonal and windy, western areas are fair, and central and eastern skies are partly cloudy to cloudy with precipitation. Eastern Hawaii is windy with showers and cloudy skies, western and central areas are fair to partly cloudy and windy, and temperatures are seasonal.

### 1st Quarter Moon, December 26–31

**Zone 1:** Temperatures are seasonal to below, conditions are windy, and much of the zone sees precipitation, some locally heavy in northern areas.

**Zone 2:** The zone is partly cloudy with temperatures seasonal to below with a chance for precipitation in central areas.

**Zone 3:** Skies are fair to partly cloudy and temperatures range from seasonal to below.

**Zone 4:** Seasonal temperatures accompany partly cloudy to cloudy and windy skies with precipitation in central areas.

**Zone 5:** Western and central areas are windy, temperatures are seasonal, and central and eastern areas see precipitation and possibly thunderstorms.

**Zone 6:** Western areas are fair to partly cloudy and windy, central and eastern parts of the zone see more cloudiness with precipitation, and temperatures are seasonal.

**Zone 7:** Skies are partly cloudy to cloudy with scattered precipitation, and temperatures are seasonal.

**Zone 8:** Eastern and western Alaska are cloudy with precipitation, central areas are fair to partly cloudy, and temperatures are seasonal. Hawaii is fair to partly cloudy with temperatures ranging from seasonal to above.

### About the Author

*Kris Brandt Riske is the executive director and a professional member of the American Federation of Astrologers (AFA), the oldest US astrological organization, founded in 1938; and a member of the National Council for Geocosmic Research (NCGR). She has a master's degree in journalism and a certificate of achievement in weather forecast-*

212 Weather Forecast for 2017

ing from Penn State. Kris is the author of several books, including Llewellyn's Complete Book of Astrology: The Easy Way to Learn Astrology, Mapping Your Money, and Mapping Your Future. She is also the coauthor of Mapping Your Travels and Relocation and Astrometeorology: Planetary Powers in Weather Forecasting. Her newest book is Llewellyn's Complete Book of Predictive Astrology. She writes for astrology publications and contributes to the annual weather forecast for Llewellyn's Moon Sign Book. In addition to astrometeorology, she specializes in predictive astrology. Kris is an avid NASCAR fan, although she'd rather be a driver than a spectator. In 2011, she fulfilled her dream when she drove a stock car for twelve fast laps. She posts a weather forecast for each of the thirty-six race weekends (qualifying and race day) for NASCAR drivers and fans. Visit her at www.pitstopforecasting.com. Kris also enjoys gardening, reading, jazz, and her three cats.

# Economic Forecast for 2017

*by Christeen Skinner*

Just before the September Equinox in 2015, Saturn made its move into the sign of Sagittarius. By 2017, Saturn moves out of that sign and into Capricorn later that year. Before it does, Saturn will pass through 26–27 degrees Sagittarius and align with the Galactic Center: the first such conjunction of the 21st century.

It made this alignment three times in the 20th century: in 1929, almost thirty years later in 1957, and then again in 1987. Economists will note that each of these years had significant negative activity in stock markets in general, but in particular for the United States. It seems reasonable to suggest that this situation will recur.

As it happens, and owing to retrogradation (where, as viewed from Earth, a planet seems to go backward and forward over a particular zodiac area), Saturn makes this crossing three times between February and May of 2017.

Strengthening the possibility of a downturn during these months, the lunar North Node will be moving by that time from Virgo and on into the sign of Leo. In the 1930s, the financial astrologer Louise McWhirter offered the observation that one particular business cycle correlated with the movement of the lunar nodes through the zodiac signs. The lunar nodes move backward through the twelve signs. This cycle supports the idea that as the nodes move backward from Aquarius to Leo, the general business cycle is up, but once the node moves into Leo, then the trend turns down.

We now have two clear indicators that the first half of 2017 could witness a downward movement in equities. Analysis of the position of the outer planets and their links with the lunations (New and Full Moons) of the period from February to May 2017 underscores this probability. Indeed, at the Full Moon on April 11, the Sun and Uranus conjoin in opposition to the Moon and Jupiter while Pluto stands midway between the two conjunctions. This is a formidable planetary picture that might produce marked market reaction—especially given Pluto's position.

## 19 Capricorn

Analysis of the top ten declines in market values during the 20th century show them to have one thing in common: there is always a planet or planetoid (Chiron) on 19 degrees Capricorn or its opposite. Perhaps it is the case that as slow-moving planets move across this degree, traders hear echoes or reverberations of past dramas and cannot help but repeat those earlier reactions. It seems unlikely that this particular lunation will go unnoticed, and it is probable that this will be recorded in history as being a singularly eventful day on global markets.

Pluto's arrival in Capricorn back in 2008 coincided with bank scandals and the global financial dramas of that period. Efforts to resolve this included quantitative easing—first in the United

States and then in Europe. Despite this action, government debt has increased on both sides of the Atlantic. It may be that the burden of this debt at least leads to a threatened collapse in bond markets in 2017. Critical dates will surely include those days when planetary configurations highlight this sensitive Capricorn degree. Pluto (geocentrically) crosses this sensitive area of the zodiac between February 2017 and the last quarter of 2018. Key dates include mid-February and late May, periods already identified as being potentially "fragile" for stock markets around the world with regard to Saturn's transit of the Galactic Center.

## Venus

As with other planets, there are periods when Venus appears to move backward relative to Earth's passage around the Sun. Venus is retrograde from early March and returns to the degree of its retrograde station mid-May: yet another signal that financial progress could be impeded between February and May.

Whereas Mercury takes on retrograde appearance three times each year, Venus does not have an annual retrograde phase. Analysis of such periods, which occur roughly every eight years, shows that the actual zodiacal area that Venus retrogrades is of great importance. There is greater correlation with stock market negativity when Venus is retrograde in certain signs.

In 2017, Venus's retrograde period begins when it is midway through Aries. Venus then retrogrades back into Pisces, and appears to stand still at 26 degrees Pisces, where it is at right angles to the Galactic Center, before moving back in Aries.

Aries, like Capricorn, is another of the Cardinal signs. The other two signs of this group are Cancer and Libra. When aspects form between these signs, it is as though a loud chord is played through the solar system, one that is hard to ignore. Venus will be at apparent to Pluto (at 19 degrees Capricorn) on May 25—another potentially problematic day across global markets.

Though not impossible, companies launching under a Venus retrograde position do seem to find it difficult to achieve success. This is particularly true when the business involves partnerships. As might be expected, a Venus retrograde does not augur well for development of the relationship, nor should lone traders and entrepreneurs dismiss the potential negative effect on inaugurating new commercial activities under this condition: they may find it hard to build steady cash flow and maintain these activities. They may also find that their initial capitalization was underestimated.

To avoid the full effect of Venus retrograde, it is best to wait until Venus has returned to at least the degree at which that planet was stationed prior to turning retrograde. In this instance, that would mean foregoing the launch of enterprises between Venus's first station on March 4 and perhaps waiting until June 6 when that planet will have not only crossed back over all the retrograde degrees and formed its square aspect to Pluto, but Venus will have arrived in Taurus—a sign that is said to rule.

Venus deviates for 0 degrees latitude by up to 8 degrees in some years. On March 19, 2017, Venus will be at 8 degrees 34' latitude: a maximum. That this event coincides so closely with the March Equinox may be indicative of Venusian-related businesses coming to the front. Those working in the field of mergers and acquisitions should find this a profitable period.

Venus last reached a similar position close to the Equinox in March of 2009. Note that the stock markets across the world were in recovery following major losses at the start of that month.

### Eclipses

Every year is marked by eclipses of the Sun and Moon. In some years there can be as many as five solar eclipses. It is not essential for a solar eclipse to be accompanied by a lunar eclipse, though this is usually the case. In 2017, there are just two: on February

26 and August 21. Each is preceded by a lunar eclipse—on February 11 and August 7.

Though solar eclipses give signals of trends over long periods, lunar eclipses have a different impact. There are many recorded events in history books that coincided with a lunar eclipse. Emotions tend to run high at these sophisticated Full Moons, resulting in strong market reaction. In the six years between the stock market low of March 2009 and the Spring Equinox in 2015, there were 14 lunar eclipses. At first glance there does not seem to be anything "predictable" in the effect these had on the Dow Jones Index. Yet if we look a little deeper, we find that the effect tends to be dramatic in the week *following* the lunar eclipse.

Marked reaction does not happen after every lunar eclipse, underlining the need to consider these eclipses alongside other cycles. Lunar eclipses can be like minute hands on a clock—the final indicators needed to determine probable strong reaction. However, that may well be the case in 2017.

The two lunar eclipses of 2017 could coincide with high drama in equity markets. The first one in February takes place while the Sun is in Aquarius and the Moon is in Leo, while the August lunar eclipse has the positions reversed (Sun in Leo, Moon in Aquarius).

To assess probable impact, we turn to similar eclipses that have taken place across this sign axis. In early March 2009, and following the lunar eclipse of February 9 that year, markets reached a major low. It may once again be that markets will decline following the 2017 lunar eclipse on February 11. This fits neatly with what has already been observed with regard to Saturn's crossing of the Galactic Center degree and Pluto's positioning.

Yet conditions in 2017 are quite different to those of 2009 since the February 11 lunar eclipse precedes a solar eclipse in Pisces, whereas in 2009, the lunar eclipse followed a Capricorn solar eclipse. A solar eclipse in Capricorn brings to mind the image of a goat at the top of mountain that in some sense slips (markets declining from a "top"). In 2009, the Dow then lost almost 2000 points in just a few weeks (partly attributable to other cycles in operation but presumably with the lunar eclipse offering initial momentum).

However, we can look back at the cycle before that: in 1999, a lunar eclipse across the Leo-Aquarius axis came ahead of a solar eclipse in Aquarius. The Dow declined for approximately ten days before recovering its position by the solar eclipse. It may be that a similar rebound following decline is seen in 2017.

Historical analysis of the August eclipse pairing is no less interesting. Again, we first look back to 2009 when the Dow lost approximately 200 points in the fortnight following the lunar eclipse. A cycle earlier, in 1999, we see a similar pattern: a drop of approximately 200 points over a ten-day period following the eclipse before recovery at the solar eclipse.

Again, a similar pattern could emerge in August 2017.

It is, of course, not just the zodiacal axis on which eclipses take place that is important. If there is to be correlating eventfulness, then there is a high probability that this will be due to the presence of planets at right angles to the eclipse axis. It is recognized that the effect of an eclipse can be triggered by a fast-moving planet moving to the accented eclipse degree or the right angle to it (or even semi-right angle).

The February eclipse occurs at 8 degrees Pisces. Mercury arrives at this degree on March 2. As the "planet of commerce," it is not unusual for Mercury to be at the degree of a recent eclipse when important news is announced to shareholders. In this instance, we would be thinking of those business interests that have association with the sign of Pisces. The sectors most likely to hit the headlines include media, pharmaceuticals, and oil. Is it possible that this degree is highlighted in the charts of relevant companies and that there will be talk of take-overs and subsequent volatility in share price? In the case of oil, given prices have already fallen substantially since its high of $140, there might even be talk of price collapse.

There is yet another point of interest in the February solar eclipse chart. Mars and Uranus are conjunct that same day. As with the Sun and Moon, they are at the start of a new cycle. Mars and Uranus—both moving through Mars-ruled Aries—bring to mind an image of a fire-cracker: something startling and revelatory. In any or all of the listed sectors, explosive news could hit the headlines a few days after the solar eclipse, when Mercury reaches the eclipse degree.

The August solar eclipse is quite different: this takes place in the Fire sign of Leo—at 28 degrees of that sign. In this chart, Mercury is retrograde at 8 degrees Virgo—exactly opposing the February eclipse. Again, oil price movement could be headline news. Interestingly, Mercury returns to the degree of the August eclipse just as Mars, in direct motion, does the same. It may be that some related industries are "eclipsed," not on the date of the eclipse itself but almost a month later, on September 2 or 3.

One very strong possibility is that astrology itself will hit the headlines both around the February eclipse and, in a more exaggerated way, in September. It has been recognized that the degree areas of both solar eclipses tend to appear in the charts of astrologers more often than not!

If the February solar eclipse accents media, pharmaceuticals, and oil, then the August Leo eclipse accents precious metals, the leisure industry, and solar power. Again, we might expect companies working in these areas to experience share price volatility in early September as Mercury and Mars trigger the August eclipse degree.

One other interesting connection between the two solar eclipse charts is worth noting: Jupiter's position at 22 degrees and then 20 degrees Libra, respectively. Jupiter is retrograde in the first chart and direct in the second. The accent on this small area of the

2016 © Kzenon image from BigStockPhoto.com

zodiac suggests that companies with this area featured in their chart will find 2017 to be a year of drama. Their CEO will not be "eclipsed," necessarily, but it is likely that expansion (Jupiter) plans will be of much discussion and result in change of leadership when one faction within the company disagrees with the plans of another.

### *Lunar Rhythms*

The Moon's position can be measured by both latitude and declination and position relative to Earth. In fact, if the Moon reaches apogee (farthest from Earth), perigee (nearest Earth), or sits at 0 degrees declination within forty-eight hours of a lunar eclipse, then market reaction tends to be exaggerated.

We know there will be two lunar eclipses in 2017. As with their related solar eclipses, these take place in February and August. The February 10 penumbral lunar eclipse occurs close to the zodiacal position of the fixed star, Regulus. This is one of the Persian royal stars and Regulus is generally deemed a star of good fortune. Around this date, markets may reach a top from which they then decline. This would fit earlier lunar eclipse trading patterns when markets decline in the days following the eclipse.

The lunar eclipse on Monday, August 7, may not bring with it such strong reaction. This eclipse does not conjoin one of the prominent fixed stars, nor is it at either apogee or perigee, so any reaction is likely to be minor, though certainly there could be minor downward movement for a few days.

### 20-Year Business Cycle and Jupiter-Saturn Cycles

Jupiter and Saturn form a conjunction approximately every twenty years. There is a definite pattern to these events with a whole series taking place in fire, earth, air, or water quadriplicity. The conjunction forming in 2020 will be the first in the sign of Aquarius for some centuries. In 2017, we will be approaching the end of the cycle that began in May 2000.

There is an acknowledged 20-year business cycle that some feel correlates with this Jupiter-Saturn cycle. The halfway point (the opposition) goes some way toward explaining a 10-year business cycle also recognized by economists.

Within the 20-year Jupiter-Saturn cycle, there are "punctuation" marks that include those weeks when Jupiter and Saturn appear to be in conjunction by either latitude or declination. These may be viewed as important "seeding" moments and are useful when looking for times to launch new businesses.

As we know, the planets are rarely *on* the ecliptic or indeed *on* the celestial equator. In their path around the Sun, the planets do not move in "straight lines." Planets, together with the Moon, move around the ecliptic line, and some deviate more than others. Pluto deviates greatly, as may be seen on a 120-year graph. Latitude measurement is given as either north or south of the ecliptic. The significant points include maximum latitude (north or south) and the date when the planet or Moon moves from north to south latitude at the zero degree position.

Note that Pluto arrives at this zero crossing next year (2018) and that the last time it was at this point was December 1930.

In January 2017, Jupiter and Saturn form a latitude parallel (conjunction). They make another such aspect on June 22 (at the Summer Solstice) and on October 19. These dates may be viewed as optimum times for forming new businesses, since the combination of Jupiter and Saturn suggests commercial strength.

Though Jupiter spends much of the year in the sign of Libra, it moves to Scorpio on October 10 so that the first two latitude parallels take place with Jupiter in Libra and Saturn in Sagittarius. By the October date, Jupiter will have crossed over into Scorpio. We may deduce from this that the January and June connections will be good for businesses that are related to Libra plus Sagittarius—perhaps anything to do with partying! Or, on a more serious note, global mergers and acquisitions. The October connection, a Scorpio-Sagittarius mix, suggests medical research, genetic engineering, and general manufacturing with an emphasis on heavy moving equipment.

For much of 2017, the two planets are in rough sextile (angle of 60-degree separation). This is generally seen as a positive aspect where optimism (Jupiter) is balanced with realistic (Saturn) thinking. This aspect is exact on August 27. This might have been considered a good date for a commercial launch but it comes within twenty-four hours of a Sun-Mercury conjunction where Mercury is retrograde: a feature to be avoided if possible—especially as Mercury will be in its own sign of Virgo, where the potential for miscommunication tends to increase.

When Jupiter and Saturn reach semi-square aspect (45-degree separation) later in 2017, they form what could be argued to be their last major, hard aspect, marking the conclusion of a cycle that began in May 2000. Given that this aspect occurs close to the December Solstice and is therefore one of the four most powerful days of the year, it may be that another chill economic wind blows in and markets react negatively for a few days around this solstice.

As Pluto moves nearer to the critical 0 degree of latitude by the end of 2017, there is certainly potential for markets to react negatively and for cracks in some business structures to appear.

## Mars

Mars, the red planet, is thought of as energy-giving. As it passes through each of the twelve signs, it seems to give extra life and lift to the business sectors associated with each sign. As its journey around the Sun takes a little over two years, it does not move through every sign every year. On January 1, 2017, Mars is at 10 degrees Pisces and no longer conjunct Neptune. By the end of the year, it is at 14 degrees Scorpio and closing in on a conjunction with Jupiter that forms at the start of 2018. Mars and Neptune together suggest a thrust in media, pharmaceutical, and oil stocks (not necessarily positive), while Mars and Jupiter should bring energy to military and engineering sectors at the end of the year.

Mars does not have a retrograde period in 2017. After completing its transit of Pisces, Mars moves on through Aries, Taurus, Gemini, Cancer, Leo, Virgo, Libra, and almost half the sign of Scorpio. It thus covers 245 degrees of the zodiac: approximately two-thirds of the entire cycle.

We have already noted that 2017 is likely to be a year of market drama. Considering Mars's transits through so many signs, we can see just how many sectors are likely to be caught off guard, energized, but need to fight to maintain established business positions.

A key date in any year is when the Sun is either conjunct or in opposition to Mars. There is no opposition in 2017, but there is a conjunction in Leo on July 27. Since 2008 (when Pluto moved into Capricorn), research shows that as the Sun is moving toward conjunction with Mars, markets tend to rise. If this pattern repeats, then we should expect to see an upward push across all markets through July 2017 until the conjunction on the 27th, after which we should anticipate some loss—perhaps into and through the lunar eclipse on August 7.

It is worth noting that though the Sun conjoins with Mars every two years, the last Sun-Mars conjunction in Leo was in 2002. It is interesting then to look back to August 2002. What we find is that the conjunction coincided with a top from which the Dow declined a little—supporting the concept of seeing markets rise into the actual conjunction.

What we cannot see from looking at the index alone is the extent to which leisure stocks (associated with the sign of Leo) contributed to this. To observe any effect, we would need to look closely at the charts of leisure-industry companies. It is easier to assess possible impact on the price of precious metals through analysis of the gold price (Leo being linked to precious metals). Here we find evidence of something interesting. The gold index shows definite rise into the 2002 Sun-Mars conjunction. What is important is that the level reached that day became a key resistance level in April of the following year. If we use the same formula, then we would expect the gold price as shown by the gold index to rise into July 27 (the Sun-Mars conjunction) and for the level reached that day to be important in 2018.

### Vesta

Vesta is one of the four major asteroids and is usually found to hold prominent position in the charts of traders. Mars and Vesta begin a new cycle (conjunction) under every four years (not too dissimilar to the recognized Juglar or Kuznet business cycles).

The very fine financial astrologer Bill Meridian made particular study of the Mars-Vesta cycle. His initial studies offered a buy-and-sell strategy based on when the two planets were at set degrees. What is interesting is that over a period of time, the degrees of separation he determined have altered—presently about 15–20 degrees from his initial findings. The original study suggested that an optimum time to buy would be when the two planets were at a separation of approximately 240 degrees, while suggesting to sell when the two were approximately 90 degrees apart. It may be that stocks are at a low when Mars and Vesta are 240–260 degrees apart: late January through February 2017. Used with technical indicators, this could be a profitable buying period. Some investors may choose to take profit as the Sun moves into Pisces on February 19.

In 2017, Vesta comes to a direct station when it retrogrades to 20 degrees Cancer (within orb of opposition to 19 degrees Capricorn). This event takes place on Tuesday, March 7—coinciding with Saturn's crossing of the Galactic Center. The chart for that date attracts attention in that this is also the day of a Sun-Mercury conjunction (17 degrees Pisces). It is not unusual for there to be a reversal in this trend at such times, and this may be no exception.

This degree is interesting in that it is directly opposite the position of Mars in the chart for the New York Stock Exchange (NYSE). When this axis is highlighted, market reaction is often observed.

At this point in Vesta's declination cycle, it is considered "out of orb" (i.e., at an angle of more than 23 degrees declination). In response to this, it may be that traders are particularly active and that volatility rules as a result. It is also noteworthy that on March 7, the Moon moves through the sign of Cancer, moving to an opposition with Pluto. This may prove a significant date for the US dollar, whose fortunes could be challenged by the Euro, which could then gain momentum under positive aspects.

## 2017 Quarterly Forecast

### First Quarter

As we've seen, this quarter should be full of significant market activity with volatility in currency markets apparent in early March as Venus approaches retrograde. We have also noted that the Mars-Vesta cycle with Saturn's transit of the Galactic Center degree could coincide with a stock market low around the same time.

We can now use the charts of the New and Full Moons of this quarter to help identify periods of over-reaction. At the Full Moon on January 12, Venus, Mars, Chiron, Neptune, and the South Node are all moving through the sign of Pisces with Mars opposing the degree it held at the inauguration of the NYSE. If we look at the chart when trading has closed on Wall Street that Thursday, we find the opposition between Jupiter and Uranus is prominent—underscoring the probability of this being a day of high volume (sell-off?) trading. This may well present a buying opportunity with gains to be made in the succeeding period through to the Sun's Pisces entry on February 19.

The Full Moon on Sunday, March 12, also puts focus on the sign of Pisces. This Full Moon coincides with Vesta and Pluto reaching their opposition phase. Markets no longer trade Monday through Friday only: we live in a global village where there is 24/7 trading—particularly in the forex markets. It is probable then that Sunday, March 12, and Monday the 13th will prove to be days of high volatility with southeast Asian currencies likely in the spotlight. (These markets work ahead of those in the West, with traders there at work as the aspects are exact.)

This quarter of the year promises a few tricky months but should bring buying opportunities if equities near expected lows.

One final note here: it would be wise to avoid this period for the launch of new businesses. Venus is retrograde from March 4. Venus retrogrades from 13 Aries to 26 Pisces returning to 13 Aries on May 18—almost exactly on the birthday of the NYSE. It would be wise for businesses to wait until that date before committing to new ventures.

### *Second Quarter*

Venus continues retrograde motion until the direct station on April 14. A few days earlier, on April 10, Mercury begins one of its retrograde phases, slightly ahead of the Full Moon on April 11. In this chart, both Mercury (in Taurus) and Venus (in Pisces) are retrograde while Pluto lies at a near-exact right angle to both the Sun and Moon. The implications here are that there will be a decided change of trend. Further, and in taking note of Pluto's position, it may be that bond markets are greatly affected.

There is an old rule that money can be made by buying at the New Moon and selling at the Full Moon. There have been times in the past when this strategy has worked. However, on its own, this is a risky strategy. The overall trend of any market and the aspects made by slow-moving planets in particular must be taken into account.

The clustering of cosmic events at this April Full Moon suggests a treacherous period. Experienced traders may be able to use this knowledge to their advantage: others should perhaps stay clear.

Mercury does not return to the retrograde station position until May 20, just as the Sun arrives in Gemini a few days ahead of a New Moon (May 25) that finds Mars and Saturn at opposition—a complex planetary picture. If technical indicators agree, then this window (between May 20 and 25) could be the time to sell and realize any profits.

### Third Quarter

Harvests could be of major concern during third-quarter months. Throughout July and early August, concern as to whether or not these will reach hoped-for targets is likely to grow. This will surely have a knock-on effect on food prices, which are then likely to increase. Indeed, a very real worry during this quarter will be a rise in the cost of living.

As has been pointed out earlier, retrograde Mercury opposes its position in the February solar eclipse chart during August. This suggests an echo of that earlier time. The Sun-Mars conjunction on July 27 may cause traders to fall into negative mode following the conjunction, and equities may fall as a result.

The Virgo New Moon on September 20 makes for an interesting chart in this quarter. In this chart, Mercury, Venus, and Mars join the Sun and Moon in Virgo. This extraordinary emphasis on one area of the zodiac suggests a focus on businesses providing precision engineering, genetic decoding, servicing, hygiene systems, maintenance, health, laundry, and all day-to-day essential services. It may be that the share price of companies working in these areas experience a small but valuable lift during this New Moon until the next quarter.

### Fourth Quarter

Saturn made Scorpio ingress on October 5, 2013, from which date gold prices plummeted. On October 10, 2017, and within hours of a positive aspect between Saturn and the lunar node, Jupiter arrives in Scorpio. This may mark the start of an escalation in the price of precious metals and in gold particularly. Oil could also gain.

The period between November 8 and November 13 may be an important one, particularly for foreign exchange traders. An announcement made on the 8th (devaluation of a currency?) as Vesta opposes Uranus has the potential to send shock waves through these markets. With Saturn trining Uranus on November 11, winds of political change may be evident.

Arguably the most important feature of this period is Saturn's ingress into its "own" sign of Capricorn on December 20 (coinciding with the solstice). Saturn has been known to "apply the brakes." For a few days, markets are certainly likely to experience a bumpy and negative ride, though a rise into year-end is probable.

**About the Author**

*Christeen Skinner is the author of* Financial Universe (2004) *in which she forecast the banking crisis. She works in London and has a broad clientele—from city traders to entrepreneurs to private investors. She taught for the Faculty of Astrological Studies for a half-nodal cycle, was chair of the Astrological Association of Great Britain, and is a trustee of Urania Trust.*

# New and Full Moon Forecasts for 2017

*by Sally Cragin*

In the 1990s, "seasonal affective disorder" became a more wide-spread term. "SAD" reasoned that moods were directly related to the amount of sunlight in the sky. During the winter, people got more depressed when days were shorter and the Sun hung at a lower angle. Yet a planetary object even closer to Earth affects our tides, our body rhythms, fertility cycles, and even mood changes, but it is seldom considered.

The Moon has captivated poets, philosophers, songwriters, and lovers for millennia and is by far the most notable object in the night sky. This hardy, rocky satellite does a lazy do-si-do around Mother Earth every twenty-nine and a half days, but the

Moon always keeps the same face turned to our planet. Whether gibbous (around three-fourths), a thin crescent, or gloriously full, the Moon commands our attention and our awe.

Symbolized by a black circle, the New Moon is the first (and last) phase of the Moon. When you see a pale crescent with horns pointing to the west, or to the left (in the shape of a "D"), the Moon is waxing. There are about two weeks before the Moon is full. You will then notice that the darkness—or the bites the dragon is eating off the Moon, depending on which mythology you prefer—will be on the right side of the Moon. The waning crescent has horns pointing to the east, or to the right. The New and Full Moons are about fifteen days apart, and beginning projects at or just after the New Moon is considered auspicious. The Full Moon is a time when projects climax or reach a critical point.

The Moon rules Cancer, the fourth sign of the zodiac, whose symbol is the crab. This sign is associated with the home and domestic life in general. If you know any Cancers, think about their attitude toward the home. Do they prefer not to travel? Are they exceedingly domestic—perhaps excellent bakers or cooks? Are they fiercely loyal and extremely sensitive? When you think about the Moon, bear in mind these essential Cancerian qualities come with it at all times. When you feel the pull of the Moon on your own emotions, you're in tune with the Moon. That can be a consolation. "Oh, so that's why I'm feeling unhinged!"

The English language has plenty of words deriving from our satellite neighbor. We associate the Moon with craziness, "Full Moon madness," along with sub rosa activity—someone who moonlights making moonshine would prefer no one knew about it! Yet in astrology, the Moon is considered to have many attributes, most of them positive. In your personal chart, the Moon can represent your mother (and your attitude toward her), your emotional equilibrium, and tendencies for self-protection as well as moodiness.

The ancients were fascinated by the Moon, so luminous and changeable. Early Romans gave the Moon her own sacred feast day, which we call "Monday." Even our nursery rhyme about Jack and Jill can be traced back to a Scandinavian legend about a boy and girl named Hjuki and Bila who were fetching water from a well when the Moon demanded they serve her. She carried off the pair in a pail—thus their adventure relates to the waxing and waning of the Moon. "Hjuki" means increasing and "Bila" means decreasing. The Australian Dieyeries tribe believes that people were created by the Moon, and in many Native American languages, the Moon is regarded as having male gender.

But perhaps most significant is the Moon's twenty-nine-and-a-half-day cycle, which relates very closely to the standard (but not always correct) twenty-eight-day fertility cycle in females. Why not always correct? Well, check your own menstrual records over a one-year period, and see whether your "personal average" isn't closer to twenty-nine days than twenty-eight. For female readers, consider getting a calendar that notes when New, Full, and first and last quarters of the Moon occur, and if there's a correlation to your menstrual cycle. "*Mens*trual" from *mens*, meaning month, and *month* from, of course, *moon*!

### *How to Use the Moon in Your Life and Work*

We all have patterns—some people are up with the birds, while others are night owls. Some folks get seasonal affective disorder when the clocks change in the fall, while others don't seem to care. But whether you are conscious of it or not, the phases of the Moon also strike a responsive chord in your life. As 2017 unfolds, think about planning your weeks and months by using the lunar rhythms of new, first quarter, full, and last quarter Moons, and then back to the New Moon again. Each of those phases is about seven days.

You might start by just paying attention to the waxing and waning patterns. For example, the first three months of the year the Moon is waxing (getting larger) from January 1 through the 12, and then the 27 through February 10, and then the 26 through March 12. Those weeks should find you craving to spend time with creative or energetic compadres, coming up with ideas, embarking on projects, launching partnerships, and so on.

When the Moon wanes during the first three months of the year—January 13 to 26, February 11 to 25, and March 13 to 27—cull extraneous elements from your life. This is a fine time for house-cleaning, decluttering, filing, recycling, or working on projects that require critical distance. You may find your psychological insights become more fine-tuned during this transit.

When the Moon (New or Full) is in your Sun Sign—for example, the Full Moon is in Cancer on January 12—you may feel that all eyes are on you or that you are more emotional and easily overwhelmed. You may also feel like "Superwoman" or "Superman," and a blend of feelings or impulses is common when the Moon conjuncts your Sun Sign. Happy Moon watching!

### Full Moon in Cancer, January 12

Happy New Year! And enjoy this "Cooking Moon" (according to the Choctaw). This Moon directs your attention to health and home, so taking care of your body and the shelter you park it in will be a preoccupying interest. This Full Moon could bring creativity in the kitchen or prompt you to get a massage to ease the winter blahs. In tune with the Moon, and feeling affectionate and emotional, are Pisces, Cancer, and Scorpio. These water babies will have penetrating insights. Seek out their counsel if you are perplexed by a person or situation. Gemini, Taurus, Virgo, and Leo could enjoy feeling covetous, while Capricorn, Libra, Aries, Aquarius, and Sagittarius could be impatient and impulsive. Mind your p's and q's around folks who "wind you up."

### New Moon in Aquarius, January 27

A day of fresh starts, particularly for Aquarius, Gemini, and Libra, who revel in their imaginations. For all—do something trendy: seeing the hot new movie or ordering the cold new drink. Aquarius Moons bring out the "what if..." impulse in others. If you find you're getting off track, enjoy the excursion, and see where the path takes you. Leo, Virgo, Libra, Taurus, and Scorpio may find themselves drawn to people who are contrary and enjoy a loud "airing of views." Capricorn, Sagittarius, Pisces, and Aries: find an opportunity to gamble, and don't look back.

### Full Moon in Leo, February 10

Though this is a short month, it could be a hot one, particularly as the "Trapper's Moon" falls on the weekend, harmonizing with Venus and Mars (in fiery Aries). Romance is not neutral—particularly for Aquarius, Leo, Aries, and Sagittarius—and if you're in a new partnership (passionate or platonic), you'll want to go from zero to sixty immediately. Leo makes even the shy folks roar, and Taurus, Scorpio, Pisces, and Capricorn will not be shy about stating their opinions. Gemini, Cancer, Virgo, and Libra will crave a good party. Maybe you should throw one!

### New Moon in Pisces, February 26

Water sign New Moons prompt sensitivity, irrationality, extra-sensory perception (ESP), and an affinity for those incarcerated (either emotionally or otherwise). Pisces can also inspire us all to create art or enjoy photography. This New Moon is in harmony with dreamy Neptune, so don't keep a rigid schedule, particularly Pisces, Scorpio, Cancer, and Aries. For you folks, everything is more complex than it seems. Virgo, Sagittarius, Gemini, Leo, and Libra should be patient with themselves. Don't sweat the small stuff. However, Capricorn, Taurus, and Aquarius could move faster—and make more decisions—than anticipated. No worries if that happens!

### Full Moon in Virgo, March 12

The Virgin rules the "Fish Moon" (according to our Colonial ancestors), and this Full Moon is all about getting in touch with that perfectionist side that lurks beneath even the most carefree personalities. With the Spring Equinox looming, this month marks the real new year, as the last sign of Pisces gives way to Aries on March 20. However, between this Full Moon and the March 27th New Moon, Sagittarius, Gemini, Aquarius, and Aries could be critical of others, while Venus retrograde in Aries could prompt Libra, Virgo, Taurus, and Capricorn to have a blind spot about how others treat you.

### New Moon in Aries, March 27

The New Moon says "start," and Aries energy is about doing what's in front of you at top speed! It's also a superb day for starting a diet. This may suit Aries, Leo, Sagittarius, and even Taurus just fine, and if you can still be in control, make haste. Libra, Capricorn, Virgo, Cancer, and Scorpio could be awkward socially or just sell themselves short (self-deprecating comments accidentally launched). Taurus, Aquarius, Gemini, and Pisces could find themselves torn between the "get it done now" and "get it done right" impulses.

### Full Moon in Libra, April 11

Also called the "Planter's Moon," it's a superb time to get enraptured by someone who knows how to talk. Couples activities are favored, but communication could be problematic, thanks to Mercury retrograde (which goes direct on May 3). Jupiter, planet of generosity, conjuncts the Moon, so feasting could be in order. Capricorn, Cancer, Taurus, Pisces, and Aries could be confused by conflicting signals. Sagittarius, Leo, Virgo, and Pisces—this is your time to see both sides of a situation. Libra, Aquarius, Gemini, and Scorpio: friend-making brings benefits of all kinds.

### New Moon in Taurus, April 26

Get a grip on your finances during this New Moon. Think about checking out some new bands or musicians. Taurus Moons prompt us to look for love—though we'll settle for a pleasing aesthetic experience. Taurus, Virgo, Capricorn, Pisces, and Cancer have incredible follow-through, so if you want something done, knock on their door. Scorpio, Leo, and Aquarius should hold off on taking action. You don't have all you need. Pisces, Sagittarius, and Libra may be tempted to buy high-end merchandise, but keep those receipts (Mercury's still retrograde).

### Full Moon in Scorpio, May 10

Spring fever is the theme with this sexy Full Moon. Scorpio brings out everyone's desire for sensual experiences. This "Milk Moon" doesn't come with cookies, however, as Scorpio is also the sign for death (transitions) and money. So the plot may thicken for Taurus, Leo, Gemini, and Aquarius—be skeptical if something's "too good to be true." For Libra, Aries, Capricorn, and Virgo, this could be a transitional time for friendships. For Scorpio, Cancer, Pisces, and Sagittarius, your analytical side prevails—listen to your head, not your heart.

### New Moon in Gemini, May 25

The Moon and Mars are in harmony, but the active air sign placement brings restlessness. Can you settle down with a new writing project, or take the initiative in communication? (This is a fine time to ask for more responsibilities or more compensation, particularly for Gemini, Libra, and Aquarius.) For Sagittarius, Virgo, Pisces, and Cancer, don't settle for the first thing—wait for the best thing. Capricorn, Aries, Taurus, Leo, and Scorpio must do something new—the old will not suit.

### Full Moon in Sagittarius, June 9

Take action, but look out for speed bumps. Sagittarius Moons are excellent for pop-up gatherings of folks passionate about education, justice, or health. This "Honey Moon" is also a fine time to get in touch with your need to travel and whom to travel with. Fire sign Moons at the end of the week give you a second (or perhaps third) wind—and they can increase the windiness tendencies of even the most stolid citizens. Keepin' it light: Sagittarius, Leo, Aries, and Capricorn. Keepin' it real: Pisces, Virgo, Gemini, and Cancer. Keepin' the change: Taurus, Aquarius, Scorpio, and Libra.

### New Moon in Cancer, June 23

A sweet and vulnerable time, Cancer Moons prompt us to turn toward home for solace. Anything you can do to make your abode cozier will bring great joy. For Capricorn, Libra, Aquarius, Sagittarius, and Aries, it's an excellent time to get a massage, work with clay (or buy ceramics), or bake bread. Are you ambivalent about a loved one? Taurus, Gemini, Cancer, Leo, Virgo, Scorpio, and Pisces are perceptive and sensitive with a romantic streak that could make for grand declarations.

### Full Moon in Capricorn, July 9

This "Thunder Moon" puts focus on your home just as the previous New Moon did, but with an added emphasis on structure. Squeaky hinges, broken windows—the urge to repair is strong. Fortunately, this Moon also enhances our ability to think logically, do repetitive tasks, and work on structure and construction. They are also helpful for enduring tedium, so you may get into one of those circular conversations over the fence with a neighbor. Willing to do the work: Capricorn, Aquarius, Pisces, Sagittarius, Scorpio, Taurus, and Virgo. Uncharacteristically subdued: Libra, Cancer, Aries, Leo, and Gemini.

### New Moon in Leo, July 23

This weekend is super for parties and get-togethers. During the week, sales calls could be profitable. Time spent with children will be satisfying, particularly if there's humor involved. And you may find some dear friends or family members succumb to Leo's influence as far as preening goes (or full-on tantrums if a haircut doesn't go as planned). Taurus, Scorpio, Pisces, Capricorn, and Aquarius could "overdo" some aspects of their busy lives. Gemini, Cancer, Leo, Virgo, Libra, Sagittarius, and Aries: go the extra mile and be aware that socializing will pay dividends.

### Full Moon in Aquarius, August 7

The "Dog Day Moon" could prompt howling from some folks, but this Full Moon is excellent for meeting old friends, new friends from exotic locales, or finding a completely fanciful solution to a problem. Mars (taking action) is opposing this Moon, so Taurus and Scorpio should lie low. Trend-spotting comes easily to Sagittarius, Leo, Virgo, and Aries, while Capricorn, Aquarius, Libra, Gemini, and Cancer need to stay close to imaginative or inspirational friends.

### New Moon in Leo, August 21

Haircuts could bring joy, and hair-splitting could be irresistible for others. How to respond? With a roar, of course, and then laughter. Mercury retrograde (August 13 to September 5) complicates those communications further. Gemini, Cancer, Leo, Virgo, Libra, Sagittarius, and Aries should look for the easy way out, while Scorpio, Aquarius, Taurus, and Pisces could over-complicate a situation and then want to walk away.

### Full Moon in Pisces, September 6

The "Chrysanthemum Moon," as it's called by the Chinese, is an exciting day for photographers, radiologists, and those who work with the incarcerated or otherwise incapacitated. You might feel nostalgic and seek out a family member to reminisce with. A day for creating art, particularly if you're a Capricorn, Aquarius, Pisces, Aries, Taurus, Cancer, or Scorpio. A day for feeling everything deeply, especially for Gemini, Virgo, Sagittarius, Libra, and Leo.

### New Moon in Virgo, September 20

Fine-tuning fascinates all—even those "big picture" folks who have no time for details. However, be wary of impulses that find you picking at trifles or getting overly involved in minutia. For some, this is a useful time for seeing the fine print or the details that would otherwise be invisible. People may think they're being "helpful," but getting the "wrong end of the stick" in a verbal interaction is likely, particularly for Gemini, Aquarius, Aries, Sagittarius, and Pisces, who may over-share or show their hand too soon. Cancer, Leo, Virgo, Libra, Scorpio, Taurus, and Capricorn can bow out gracefully today—or have a very frank talk with a loved one.

### Full Moon in Aries, October 5

This Moon could make folks excited about stuff that quickly loses its luster, and that Aries energy could inspire you to cook hot and spicy food or barbecue. This "Harvest Moon" brings opportunities for assessing how far you've come since mid-summer. Aries, Leo, Sagittarius, and Taurus may want to draw attention to themselves, while Libra, Capricorn, Scorpio, and Cancer should stick with being observers—not participants. Virgo, Gemini, Aquarius, and Pisces could be distractible—wait a couple of days if you have a project needing endurance.

### New Moon in Libra, October 19

A time for new relationships to begin and partnerships to go to the next level of involvement. The Moon is in harmony with Mars and Venus in Libra, so family gatherings or "good luck" could be the story for Libra, Aquarius, Gemini, and Scorpio. Aries, Cancer, Capricorn, and Taurus might strike others as more committed than you are. Leo, Sagittarius, Pisces, and Virgo may want to retract a commitment.

### Full Moon in Taurus, November 4

The Hunter's Moon could translate to "Shopper's Moon," as the urge to acquire could be overwhelming. For those who enjoy life's rich banquet, you'll want to go back for seconds before your plate is clear. That would include Taurus, Gemini, Capricorn, and Virgo. Scorpio, Leo, Sagittarius, and Aquarius: speaking your mind feels good, so let it rip. Libra, Aries, Gemini, and Pisces: indulge your materialistic side. Shopping and buying stuff feels so good!

### New Moon in Scorpio, November 18

This Moon is excellent for out-of-the-box thinking. However, some folks could respond to this Moon sign with paranoia and misplaced flirtatiousness. It's also superb for intimacy and closer connections. Scorpio, Pisces, Cancer, Libra, Virgo, Capricorn, and Sagittarius should look to cut their losses, while Taurus, Leo, Aquarius, Gemini, and Aries could overreact to a trifle.

### Full Moon in Gemini, December 3

Get more information—about everything—and cultivate peers or siblings. And remember that Mercury is retrograde today through December 22, so try not to utter words you may have to eat later! Aries, Taurus, Gemini, Cancer, Virgo, Leo, Libra, Scorpio, and Capricorn: prepare to be charmed (or to be charming). Sagittarius, Virgo, and Pisces: it's okay to be indecisive, but it will be more convenient for all if you say you don't know, versus changing your convictions.

### New Moon in Sagittarius, December 18

A time for humor and for appreciating the education that you have earned, in or out of school. This could be an accident-prone time when avowals turn into reversals. Stick with folks who help you laugh, particularly Sagittarius, Capricorn, Leo, and Aries. Gemini, Pisces, Cancer, and Virgo: you could be lead down the garden path—so don't go. Libra, Aquarius, Taurus, and Scorpio: ask yourself—what is the fair decision? And then act.

### About the Author

*Sally Cragin is the author of* The Astrological Elements *and* Astrology on the Cusp, *which have been translated and sold overseas in a half-dozen countries. She serves on the Fitchburg (MA) school committee, teaches in the adult education program at Fitchburg State University, and is available to speak to about readings, astrological or tarot. Visit "Sally Cragin Astrology" on Facebook or email sally@moonsigns.net.*

# 2017
# Moon Sign Book
# Articles

# Lunar Meditations

*by Dallas Jennifer Cobb*

Meditation can improve well-being, lessen stress, and increase positive focus in life. Research has been documenting and reporting the positive effects of meditation in myriad areas of our lives.

Building on these general good effects, we can tap into specific energy to enhance meditation and tailor our practice to maximize a particular effect. By understanding the influences that are illuminated by the Moon as it transits through each of the astrological signs, you can find out what areas of life are enhanced by each sign. Lunar illumination can be used to bring light into these areas of your life.

Imagine the exponential result of combining the positive effects of meditation with the energy and focus of the Moon in a particular astrological sign.

## The Positive Effects of Meditation

With the growing understanding of the effects of meditation and the increased money and interest pouring into neuroscience research, the documentation of the positive effects of meditation is vast. A quick Internet search produces thousands of articles and scholarly journals touting the physiological, psychological, and spiritual benefits of meditation.

The physical effects include lowered heart rate and blood pressure, improved oxygen efficiency, enhanced immune response, and an enhanced capacity to heal (which includes neurogenesis, the growth and development of new neurons). Psychologically, the positive effects include increased levels of serotonin; a reduction of depression, phobias, and fears; and increased emotional stability and resilience. Meditation improves our learning ability and memory, develops intuition, and facilitates communication between the two hemispheres of the brain. Meditation develops emotional maturity and increases sociable behavior (which both result in improved social relationships) and helps us to feel good.

On the spiritual level, meditation can increase our feelings of oneness with the Divine and enable us to feel happiness, peace of mind, and compassion. Meditation can help facilitate a deeper understanding and acceptance of ourselves while aiding us in cultivating a deeper relationship with spirit and the Divine. Meditation connects us with our own deeper meaning and purpose and reminds us that we are not alone.

## The Power of the Moon

One of the two luminaries that influence our seasons, cycles, and daily lives, the Moon affects us enormously. The magnetic energy of the Moon affects tides and weather, mental health and emotional fluctuations, fluids in the body, and the emotions and subconscious. Some of the earliest forms of astrology were observations of lunar phenomena and their effect on menstrual and fertility cycles.

The Moon is known as the Queen of the Night, and it astrologically represents what our heart knows to be true. It governs intuition and other aspects of trans-rational perception, and the Moon connects us with all the things we know but can't prove. The Moon governs the soul, feelings, love, social conscience, and meditation.

The Moon's cycle lasts twenty-nine and a half days. Emulating the cycle of all life, the Moon is born, waxes to fullness, wanes slowly into darkness, and then prepares to be born again. Each phase of the Moon has specific energetic effects, but for the sake of brevity, this article focuses more on the position of the Moon in particular astrological signs and the qualities that are illuminated.

## Moon Meditations

Moon meditations are used in many cultures and many practices. In the yoga tradition, there are specific Full Moon chants and meditations and yoga sequences that honor the Moon.

In the Rinzai Zen Buddhist tradition, hands are held in a full moon shape with the left fingers cradled in the right fingers, and both thumbs touch to form a moon-shaped circle. The hands surround the belly button (the Moon), and the arms round out slightly from the body, their shape also representing the Moon.

The Roshi Kyozan Joshu Sasaki taught Moon meditations to his students in order to teach them the temporality of the ego and to dissolve the individual self. The Moon, in its cyclic and repeating nature, is the perfect metaphor to contemplate and dissolve falsely held concepts of dualities and boundaries like inner and outer, self and other, good and bad, and light and dark.

These Moon meditations enabled students to align the mind with an image that expresses and symbolizes a full and complete cycle that includes all aspects of being.

# Meditation

Meditation can be done in a stationary position or as a movement. Stationary meditation can be done lying down, sitting supported in a chair, sitting cross-legged without support, leaning against a wall with legs out, or kneeling. For many of these sitting postures, pillows or meditation cushions offer more comfort and adjusted support. Movement meditations include Zen-style walking meditation, a Pagan/Celtic labyrinth walking meditation, or even slow, mindful yoga or Pilates.

Common meditation techniques include visualization, mantra meditation, focused meditation (looking at an object or into a candle flame) movement meditation (awareness—allowing your thoughts to arise and simply observing them without judgment), and guided meditation.

Try a variety of physical positions and different meditation techniques to discover what works best for you. I learned as a beginner that each kind of meditation had commonality: I first created stillness in my body, breathed deeply and regularly, relaxed and let my muscles soften, and created symmetry in my body by placing my hands in the same position (by surrounding my belly button, palms down on my thighs, or in a yoga mudra with index finger and thumb touching.)

Regardless of the type of meditation I undertook, these steps helped me to slow down and observe, engage with myself, and begin the process of meditation.

## The Influence of Astrological Signs

Understanding the energy related to each astrological sign will enable you to comprehend what is specifically being illuminated by the Moon in each sign, allowing you to consciously engage that particular energy through your meditation practice. To check where the Moon is in astrological terms, consult the Moon Tables in the *Moon Sign Book*.

Moon in Aries illuminates getting stuff done. Don't make excuses. Feel the support of the Moon for starting new things, developing new habits and practices, or even making a fresh start. Take time to affirm.

The following is a meditative breathing exercise:

Inhale deeply and quietly, intoning "I am…"
Exhale slowly, intoning "happy."
Inhale: I am…
Exhale: safe.
Inhale: I am…
Exhale: healthy.
Inhale: I am…
Exhale: peaceful.

Repeat this cycle, setting your intention.

Moon in Taurus illuminates our desire for calm, peace, and comfort. Focus on safety, security, and serenity. Use Moon in Taurus to practice awareness meditation.

Be present in your body, in touch with its sensations, and take notice of what it feels like to truly relax. Consider using music to facilitate your meditation when the Moon is in Taurus. Music can transport us and free us from our deep-felt wants, enabling us to sensually be present in the moment.

With the Moon in Gemini, harness the restless energy and get ready to move. Today is a great day for a walking meditation, for the body to move and process the often frenetic kinetic energy of Gemini.

Consider the following during a walking meditation: Let your attention be focused on walking. With each step, simply be aware of the heel touching the ground, the roll through the foot, and be aware of how the toes push off of the earth and how the leg follows through. With each step, immerse yourself in the simple mechanics of walking.

In Cancer, the Moon illuminates feelings. Dive deep into your inner space. Give yourself the gift of peace and quiet where you can find belonging and nurturing. The Moon rules the sign of Cancer and feels at home here—full of emotion, intuition, and a need to feel safe. There is the potential for great healing while the Moon is in Cancer.

Try the following: With each inhale, intone "Bless this…" With each exhale, name an emotion you find within, like "hurt."

"Bless this…sadness. Bless this…rage." Take time to be in touch with your deepest self, and allow the deeply held feelings to arise. Release them in tears (if need be). Bless them and let them go.

When the Moon is in Leo, the need to perform and stand out in public and spotlight beauty is illuminated.

Practice mindful creativity to draw, paint, or collage your vision. Use song or chanting to express yourself, or use dance or drama to move your spirit on the world's stage. Even more than the need to be seen and heard, know that we also need to be acknowledged and affirmed. With that outside reflection, we can cultivate pride in our own gifts.

With the Moon in Virgo, practicality is illuminated. This is a time to take care of business, set things right, and to organize and make lists and plans. Moon in Virgo favors structure, routines, attending to details, and organization and practicality. Mental pursuits, service to others, health, and work are goals in focus.

Try the following solving meditation: Call to mind a problem you are facing. See it as a mass of knotted wool. As you breathe and relax, see a loose end, a thread you can pull on. As you gently tug on the loose end, allow the knot to unravel, dissolving the problem you have struggled with.

Moon in Libra is a time to suffuse your environment with balance and beauty. Pleasing interactions, diplomacy, problem solving with peace in mind, and seeing both sides of an issue are illuminated by the Libra Moon. This is a time for relationship and partnership meditation, leading to improved communication, peace, and beauty between parties. Harmony, beauty, and close personal ties are deeply satisfying during a Libra Moon.

Facing your partner, sit cross-legged with knees touching. Place your right hand on their heart; let them place their right hand on your heart. Cover their hand with your left hand, and ask them to do the same. Looking deeply into one another's eyes, breathe deeply, and let your eyes convey your love, trust, joy, and faith in your partner.

When the Moon is in Scorpio, personal emotions can be intense. We feel deeply and passionately, and this is an ideal time to go to the heights and depths of our feelings. Intuition and instinct aid us, and we can get to the bottom of things, resolving long-held issues and uncovering our own power.

Use this time to practice a guided meditation that releases fear, limitations, and bad habits. Profound healing can come from weeding out the deep roots of our issues.

With the Moon in Sagittarius, the illuminated energy is upbeat and optimistic. We embrace new vision and look for our own truth. We tend to take a big-picture focus, and we tend to not get too caught up in the details.

Anything is possible now: you have faith, hope, and the courage to take chances. Sit quietly and focus on your breath. Inhale thinking, "I am…" Exhale thinking, "…that I am." As you repeat this mantra, internalize the knowledge that you are loved and you are perfect as you are.

Moon in Capricorn helps us become planners, putting structure and timelines in place to support our dreams. We are aware of reality and the effect of time. We know we need the structures to support our desire for success. Achievement, success, and manifestation are important to us, and we become determined and resourceful. We have the time, energy, and resources to pursue our dreams.

Try this accomplishing meditation: Still yourself, and slow your breath. With each breath affirm the following: "I have enough time, energy, wisdom, and money to accomplish all that I desire."

When the Moon is in Aquarius, we are more intellectual than emotional, more impersonal than personal, and we are attracted to unusual, radical, new, and out-of-the-box ideas. We are inspired to improve ourselves, and we enjoy brainstorming in groups and developing ideas with input from others.

Use the power of the intellect to visualize a luminous white light floating six inches over your head. As you breathe, feel the light flowing into the top of your head, spreading into your skull, and breathe it into your brain. See the white light flowing out from your brain and into your nervous system. Let it spread throughout your body as you visualize this healing white light touching every part of your physical being.

As the Moon enters Pisces, we feel dreamy, a little spacey, and disinclined to face reality. It's important to allow the wistful, intuitive, and sensitive self to be honored in this time. Allow your imagination free rein. Let boundaries and limits dissolve, and let your energy merge and blend to form something new. Let go of the little details, and let the process of transformation guide your dreamy thinking.

Throughout the day, practice miniature visualizations that pull the strong, stable energy of the earth up through your chakra system and cascade it out the top of your head, surrounding you in protective, healing white light. Allow yourself to dwell in dreaminess, knowing you are protected and safe. Let your imagination run wild.

## Developing a Practice

We are all different, so experiment with a variety of meditation practices until you discover what works best for you. I initially started with a morning practice because I could wake early, do my meditation, and then wake up my daughter and start the busyness of the day. After several months, I noticed so many profound effects of meditation—increased calm, a profound sense of well-being, better sleep patterns, and a sweet feeling of "everything is well in my world" after meditation. Because of these, I decided to add an evening meditation.

In the morning I meditate lying down in the quiet of my home. I have set up a small sacred spot reserved for meditation. The creation of habit seems to have helped me, and my sleepy self knows what the routine is, slipping easily into meditation in that spot and time frame.

I do my evening meditation outdoors, sitting cross-legged, on the shore of the lake that I live near. It has provided me with a profound connection to the natural world and the elements. Each day as I leave the beach, I feel full with the blessings of having communed both with my highest self and with nature. I feel loved and connected to this higher power.

I write this in early autumn, and I realize that as the seasons shift, it may become impossible to continue this practice during the winter in this way. I long to stay outside because of the profound spirit connection I feel outdoors, but I know that I may end up indoors in the cold, dark season. Because we each need to find what works for us, to figure out our own time, place, and tools for meditation, know that I will be adjusting my evening meditation practice—perhaps as you are reading this and developing your own meditation practice.

## About the Author

*Dallas Jennifer Cobb practices gratitude magic, giving thanks for personal happiness, health, and prosperity; meaningful, flexible, and rewarding work; and a deliciously joyful life. She is accomplishing her deepest desires. She lives in paradise with her daughter, in a waterfront village in rural Ontario, where she regularly swims and runs, chanting, "Thank you, thank you, thank you." Contact her at jennifer.cobb@live.com or visit www.magicalliving.ca.*

# Healing with the Moon

*by Amy Herring*

Someone once said that we are not really able to heal another person, but we can support them in healing themselves. Just as a nurse might sew up a wound to help our body heal, so can a friend provide a listening ear and open arms to help our heart heal itself. Whether it's our turn to carry the stretcher or lie down on it, we often call on the Moon when it's time for healing.

No matter what hurts, healing requires vulnerability; if we do not expose the wound, we will never be able to apply the healing salve where it's actually needed. The Moon represents the most vulnerable part of us. It is our heart and hearth fire; it is stronger than it seems but also most susceptible to wounding. The Moon in our natal chart is the vulnerable part of us that we often protect from harm, and it is this part of ourselves that we draw from when caring for another. When we heal with the Moon, we instinctively offer our own brand of care through nurturing and empathizing in our own style.

## Nurturing

One of the most universal archetypes linked to the Moon is the image of the mother. No matter what our personal experience with our mother has been, the universal symbol of mother or mothering is associated with loving attention, protection, and nurturing: to protect someone or something that is vulnerable and encourage growth.

Whether we have children of our own or not, and whether we are male or female, when we give heart-centered shelter and care to a creature—two-legged, four-legged, or root-legged—we are engaging the "Mother Moon" archetype. The way we choose to show this nurturing instinct will shine through the sign in which the Moon lies in our natal chart.

## Empathy

It's from our lunar instinct that we draw an innate sense of empathy. How we express that empathy, how quick we are to surrender to it, and the ways we try to give comfort draw from our Moon sign. When we empathize with someone, we are engaging with them on a heart-centered level. A compassionate response to another's suffering in general or the suffering of people in the world at large is often (though not exclusively) governed by Neptune—where Neptune lies in our natal chart describes the ways that our spiritual empathy is most easily invoked. But there's a difference between openhearted sympathy for human plight and the very personal, irrational, and often primal empathy that is invoked when someone we care for is in pain. Of course, when Neptune is linked with the Moon or any of the personal planets in our chart—Mars, Venus, the Sun, or the Moon—the range and intensity of our empathetic response doubles!

## Self-Healing

When we need healing, we may seek out the help of someone we deem qualified: a friend, parent, lover, therapist, physician, shaman—the list can go on. However, we are always ultimately in charge of our own healing, and we can look to our natal charts for clues about how to fulfill our needs and heal our wounds. In most cases, the Moon will not only tell us about our emotional needs and the nature of the wounds we acquire but also how we seek out comfort. Not all wounds are deep—sometimes all we need is a little retreat so we can regroup. Our Moon sign can indicate what feels most comforting to us—for some, it might be a fun night out with friends; for others, it might be a quiet evening and a bubble bath.

## Too Much of a Good Thing

Although the Moon sign can reveal one's healing tools, everyone will use them differently and not always to their best ends. Additionally, one person's healing tonic is another's poison. When a Sagittarius Moon makes a joke to lift spirits, a Cancer Moon might feel ridiculed, like their feelings aren't being taken seriously. When a Capricorn Moon calmly offers practical suggestions, it may have an Aries Moon feeling anything but calm. Sometimes we comfort others the way we would want to be comforted; other times, our own discomfort at another's pain can bring out our defense mechanisms. One size does not fit all, so when in doubt, read the warning label and use as directed!

### *Aries*

You have an innate gift to rouse and rile others, a tonic that can be very healing when someone is hurting because they've let themselves be mistreated, abused, or overlooked. You foster an attitude of empowerment over the defeatist attitudes or martyrdom, so you aren't likely to throw anyone a pity party. You encourage others to get back in the game.

2016 © 5 second Image from BigStockPhoto.com

**Self-Healing:** Find something to fight or something to do. You don't do well feeling weak or defeated; remind yourself of your strength in some way to feel better.

**Warning label:** Be patient if someone doesn't bounce back as quickly as you or if they're not ready to take up arms right away.

### *Taurus*

You heal by providing a sense of grounded calm. When emotions are turbulent and hurts rage out of control, you instinctively try to find a way to dial down the intensity. You have a knack for getting to the heart of a problem that seems overwhelming or complex. You nurture with simple solutions, whether it's offering the comfort of a warm cuppa or straightforward advice.

**Self-Healing:** Slow down and back out of demands. When something blindsides you, you can feel thrown over—find a way to steady yourself until you feel like you regain your balance.

**Warning label:** Don't oversimplify by minimizing the effect of the wounding event or your patient may feel like their pain is being trivialized.

## *Gemini*

Your innate healing talent lies in your ability to turn anything around by offering another perspective on what ails someone. You know that attitude is everything when it comes to matters of the heart, and when a heartfelt story or another viewpoint fails, make 'em laugh. You have a quick wit and are playful at heart, which can lift another's spirits.

**Self-Healing:** Humor is not only the best medicine you have in your healing arsenal, but a heavy dose for yourself can also work wonders. You can benefit from informal talk therapy to help you gain new perspectives on what troubles you. You can also benefit from simply engaging your mind elsewhere.

**Warning label:** Offer another point of view, but not seven or eight, or your patient may just feel more overwhelmed.

## *Cancer*

One of your best healing qualities is your understanding that it's okay to hurt. You can love and comfort someone while they are hurting without pressuring them to get over it. Your strong sense of loyalty and heightened sense of empathy make you the ideal healer, and in fact, many of those born under your sign find themselves in the healing professions as an outlet for this predisposition. You instinctively take others under your wing until they are ready to fly again.

**Self-Healing:** You tend to hide in your shell when you are hurt; make that shell comfy with all of your favorite things, but when you dare, allow someone you love and trust to comfort you. Receiving care instead of only giving it can heal you surprisingly quickly.

**Warning label:** Avoid pouring so much of yourself into healing another that you become the patient! Be mindful of situations that you can help most by not helping and allowing others to find their own strength again after healing.

## Leo

Although pop astrology often accuses you of hogging the spotlight, you excel at instinctively knowing how to turn it on others. You have the ability to make someone feel special when you are charming and sincere. Your time and attention are your most generous offerings. You can encourage others to find their way back to a sense of dignity by helping them rise above insult or injury.

**Self-Healing:** Spend time with someone who knows your worth and can remind you how to shine.

**Warning label:** Misery may love company, but if you share your own experiences, strive to do so from a desire to reflect another's feelings rather than the urge to take your turn at the microphone.

## Virgo

Your instinctual healing style will prompt you to immediately figure out how you can be as helpful as possible. You easily step into a supportive role; offering practical advice is second nature to you, which is sometimes just unobtrusively taking care of mundane tasks when someone needs a break or is in crisis.

**Self-Healing:** You are most susceptible to wounding when you perceive you've fallen short of expectations or failed in some way; get some perspective by seeking out and acknowledging your accomplishments to balance the strength of the inner critic.

**Warning label:** Be careful about jumping straight to problem-solving mode. Offer practical advice tentatively and be sure it's welcome, or your help may feel anything but helpful.

## Libra

Your natural ability to mirror another's point of view, even if you don't always agree with their perspective, is your most powerful healing ability. You know how to make others feel understood and valued in their own right, which can help them drop their defenses. Your natural talent in mediation can also come in handy if the source of the wounding pain involves relationship conflict. (As long as the conflict doesn't involve you.)

**Self-Healing:** Restoring your emotional equilibrium is top priority when you are wounded, using any means of comfort or beauty that offers peace. A one-on-one with a close friend can provide a sounding board for your feelings.

**Warning label:** Depending on the intensity of the situation, sympathize but avoid outright lying in the effort to make another feel validated. If the relationship is a significant one, you may both feel compromised if the truth comes out later.

## Scorpio

While some people shy away from feeling or expressing strong emotions, you are able to handle the hotter emotions such as fear, anger, and jealousy, which heal through liberation. Your ability to say out loud what no one else dares can give others permission to admit the things they are afraid to, allowing them to speak truths from the heart that may have been long buried or denied. You know the wisdom of admitting when things are bad, and you make it okay to not be okay. You can offer comfort by allowing others to be their messy, imperfect, real selves.

**Self-Healing:** When you hurt, you can benefit from giving yourself the space and time to rage, cry, or do whatever else strikes your fancy. You may sometimes suppress those feelings for fear that others around you won't be able to handle it, but for you, the only way out is through experiencing those feelings.

**Warning label:** Not everyone is ready for the punch of truth, especially when they are vulnerable. Be careful about how much force you use and whether your own agenda is too much at work.

## Sagittarius

Most of all, you heal through hope and humor. You can be quite the jester and you are quick to make someone laugh—especially when they are taking themselves or life too seriously. Whether it's helping someone find the meaning in painful events, or encouraging them not to dwell on what can't be changed, your contagious positivity is your instinctual healing gift. You tend to encourage others to move on quickly by seeing the possibilities inherent in every moment.

**Self-Healing:** In general, you can quickly bounce back from upset when you can find a reason to smile again. A bit of easy fun and goofing off with someone whose company you enjoy can help you shake sadness off. You know the wheel is always turning!

**Warning label:** Laughter may be the best medicine, but timing is everything; don't skip to the punch line if your patient isn't ready.

### *Capricorn*

Your level-headed approach and practical attitude make you highly valuable in times of need or crisis. You have the ability to divide and conquer unlike any other sign, delegating tasks and taking care of the highest priority items with grace and expediency. You help others heal by showing them how they can help themselves—by taking responsibility for what they can do and helping them see just how capable they are. Your grounded wisdom can also provide reassuring guidance.

**Self-Healing:** You are the ultimate self-cleaning oven when it comes to taking care of your own problems—you can make a list and check it off but when apathy or depression creep in, your tendency to prioritize duty over relaxation can create an emotional deficit that feels overwhelming. Work can lift your spirits, but see that it's fulfilling on a personal level or you may be running on empty.

**Warning label:** You don't tend to be a hand-holder, as you usually require both hands to take care of business! You know that falling apart just because someone else is won't get the job done, but you may feel at a loss when there's nothing to be done.

Be mindful of falling into problem-solving mode when simple understanding and love are what's needed.

## Aquarius

Your nurturing style is most apparent in what you don't do. While you can have strong opinions philosophically or mentally, you don't tend to be overbearing when it comes to matters of the heart, and you usually don't make heavy emotional demands on others. You instinctively offer others the space and freedom to be, say, or do whatever is most natural and true for them, and you will defend their right to be, say, or do it. Your detached style may seem overly cool to some, but you nurture by offering validation for others' independence. You can help others know their own heart by cutting through the expectations of others.

**Self-Healing:** You may find that the best way to heal is to focus outward, rather than inward. Mental or easygoing social stimulation may help you recover from emotional upset better than navel-gazing. Alternatively, time spent alone without worrying about fitting in or pleasing others can do a world of good, when you are free to be yourself.

**Warning label:** Be careful that you don't give another so much space that they feel alone or mistake your coolness for indifference.

## Pisces

You are naturally empathetic, so kindness is often your strongest healing gift. You are instinctually gentle and giving with others, especially when it's obvious they are in pain or in need of comfort. You seek to lift the hearts of others in your healing style, whether it's helping them find the silver lining, recapture hope and optimism, or find lighthearted humor.

**Self-Healing:** You are often in a state of emotional openness, so retreating to an activity or place that nourishes you without the distraction of the needs of others can be the best medicine.

**Warning label:** Your tender touch doesn't often get misapplied, but some signs may find your touch a little too light. Avoid too much whitewashing in an effort to skip over pain.

## About the Author

*A graduate of Steven Forrest's Evolutionary Astrology program, Amy has been a professional astrologer for twenty years. She has written numerous articles and two books on astrology,* Astrology of the Moon, *and* Essential Astrology (2016). *She especially enjoys teaching and writing about astrology. Visit HeavenlyTruth.com for readings, classes, and educational videos.*

# The Eight Phases of the Moon

*by Charlie Rainbow Wolf*

Our ancestors knew that the Moon controlled the tides. They understood the lunar rhythms and the influence that those rhythms had on the earth's living things. More and more people are returning to that wisdom to learn the secrets of the Moon and employ them in their daily lives. To live within the rhythms of the Moon is to live within her power.

There's some controversy about when the Moon cycle starts. Some cultures mark it from the Full Moon, while others will mark the start of the cycle as the New—or Dark—Moon. This is what makes the most sense to me, for it is more in harmony with the cycle of life. We emerge from the dark of the womb, and we return to the dark of the earth when our lives have ended.

## New Moon

The New Moon phase is exactly as it sounds, the time when she's starting her cycle of light. It lasts just under three days, and it's the first phase in the lunar month. It's impossible to see the Moon just as it turns to new, because it rises and sets with the Sun. This is called the Dark Moon by some people, for obvious reasons. It is only as it starts to age that a thin crescent of light will appear in the western sky. The New Moon encourages newness, and it's a great time for starting new projects. It is now appropriate to commence any ritual work that will help to draw things to you—a money spell, for example. People born at this time tend to have a natural childlike wonder about them. Even though they can be eager, they can lose interest in projects before their completion. They're likely to achieve things at quite a young age but will have to learn how to keep that momentum going during the rest of their lives.

## Waxing Crescent

The waxing crescent is the second point in a lunar month, and it is the period between the New Moon and the first-quarter Moon. Sometimes called the waxing crescent, this Moon appears in the western sky early in the evening. Its energy is similar to that of a New Moon, but here it's more controlled. There's a natural curiosity during this time that goes along with the ability to look at problems from a different perspective. This is still a good time to bring new things into your life or plant seeds that bear their fruit above ground. People born under this phase of the Moon are sometimes conflicted between following traditions and trying new things. They're likely to be very dynamic in their late twenties and early thirties, or near the time of their first Saturn return.

## First-Quarter Moon

Mental agility and self-expression come easily during the first-quarter phase, which is halfway between the New and Full Moons.

This is the half-disc Moon that can often be seen during the day and brightly shining during the first half of the night. It is the third of the eight phases of the Moon. Enthusiasm is likely to abound, and you'll be able to concentrate on the tasks at hand. The plans that you've made and the energy you're using to draw things into your life could now be coming to fruition. Those who are born during a first-quarter Moon are naturally inquisitive, and they are often very adept at finding new ways of dealing with old problems or issues. Their late thirties and early forties—the years leading into the Uranus opposition—are likely to be their most productive years.

### Gibbous

Gibbous is the term used to describe the moon phase between the first quarter and Full Moon. It is fourth in the phases of the lunar calendar. Often the Moon will look full at this time because it shines so brightly, but if you look closely, you'll see that it's still a bit ovoid. This Moon rises in the afternoon and sets well before dawn. It can be very tempting to rush ahead during this time, but patience should still be exercised. This is a great time for hard work, especially when it comes to cooperation and teamwork. It's important not to follow philosophies and tenets blindly, but rather to test them and make sure they are valid—it's that patience thing, again. People born under this Moon usually have something helpful to contribute, whether to society as a whole or just to their immediate social circle. They're most likely to make their mark in their mid- to late forties, after their Saturn opposition.

### Full Moon

Most would consider the Full Moon the middle or apex of the lunar phase: moonrise is at sunset, and moonset is at sunrise. This is the moon phase when things can come to fruition. This is a time when emotions are heightened, and there can be a rise in passion—both intimacy and anger. This is a great time to project

new ideas into the future so they can manifest. Enthusiasm and reason and creativity and practicality are balanced. It's an excellent time to focus on teamwork and strive for harmony with other people. Some people hold their celebrations during Full Moons in order to take advantage of the lunar energy being at its brightest. People who were born during Full Moons are often intuitive. They often have the potential to be good at linking the past to the future in a positive and constructive way—although they may need to guard against nostalgia. The years leading up to age fifty, and the Chiron return, are likely to be the most constructive.

### Disseminating Moon

The disseminating Moon is a term to describe the phase between a Full Moon and last-quarter Moon. It rises just after sunset and sets just after sunrise. During this time, sowing seeds and sharing ideas and knowledge are appropriate. It's a time for others to learn from your experiences—and for you to learn from your past and the experiences of others. Communication and the lessons that go with your past experiences are highlighted. It's a time to start letting go of what isn't working. The disseminating Moon is also the moon phase that starts the period when root crops—anything that is tuberous or which grows below the ground—should be planted. It's a time to start reflecting and slowing down the energetic activities that the Full Moon may have inspired. Those born under this Moon are likely to add interest and intrigue to life, although they may need to backpedal a bit and remember to consider the needs of other people. They're most likely to shine in their midfifties, after their Chiron return.

### Last-Quarter Moon

The last-quarter Moon is a reconciling Moon, the time when advice should be given or taken, when projects need to be brought to a conclusion, and when problems need to be solved. During the first-quarter Moon, the energies were on the increase; during the last-quarter Moon, they're on the decrease. This Moon rises about halfway through the night and sets around noon. It's the penultimate phase in the lunar calendar. This is an appropriate time to downsize and get rid of things that are no longer desired. It heralds the arrival of endings. People born during this phase may find they are natural counselors and advisors. They may be prone to nostalgia, and they may dwell on the past rather than focusing on the here and now. It's in their late fifties and early sixties when they're liable to realize their full potential.

### Balsamic Moon

The balsamic Moon is an introspective Moon, the last one before the darkness of the New Moon. In fact, the Moon is rarely seen during this phase—the last of the lunar calendar—for it's just a thin sliver of light, visible right around dawn. This phase is a suitable time for meditating, contemplating, and pondering things in order to prioritize them for the next lunar cycle. It should not be a time for drastic changes, nor should it be a period when new activities are undertaken. It's a time to take a break as one cycle comes to a natural close, so that the next cycle can begin. Those born during a balsamic Moon may find themselves quite introverted, intuitive, and perhaps even somewhat mystical. Spirituality will often be important for them, too. For these people, it is their later years, rather than early in their lives, when they are likely to find their highest happiness and their greatest success.

## Conclusion

The Moon has much wisdom to impart for those who walk in harmony with its rhythms. It is because of the Moon that Earth stays stable on its axis. The Moon influences the behavior of nocturnal animals, and it pulls the ocean tides back and forth. It helps us understand cycles and seasons. Its light can give atmosphere and enhancement to ceremonies and rituals. Most of all, though, when we work with the energies and the influences of the Moon, we can know that we are connected to those who have done so before, and that we are leaving behind echoes for those who will follow us in years to come.

### About the Author

*Charlie Rainbow Wolf is happiest when she is creating something, especially if it can be made from items that others have cast aside. Pottery, writing, knitting, astrology, and tarot are her deepest interests, but she happily confesses that she's easily distracted, because life offers so many wonderful things to explore. She is an advocate of organic gardening and cooking and lives in the Midwest with her husband and special-needs Great Danes. You can find her at www.charlierainbow.com*

# Ornamental Edible Landscaping with Stone Fruits

*by Mireille Blacke, MA, RD, CD-N*

As a registered dietitian, I can give you plenty of reasons to eat stone fruits—peaches, nectarines, apricots, cherries, and plums—but are there just as many benefits to growing them in your own backyard?

Moving to my current residence in Connecticut three years ago was an overwhelming experience. The property consisted of a Queen Anne Painted Lady home along with Victorian-style gardens that the former owners had painstakingly maintained. It made economic sense for homeowners in the Victorian era to blend stone fruits (or drupes) into their garden landscapes. Why not? Most of them had staff to maintain them all! Aesthetically, stone fruit trees complement strawberries, blueberries, blackberries, and raspberries (otherwise known as bramble fruits or drupelets) colorfully clustered across a garden. Stone fruits are not large trees, and they fit well into the diverse arboreal landscape, easily interspersed among the massive trunks of mighty white oaks, the graceful canopies of fragrant lilacs, and the vibrant hues of elegant Japanese maples.

While it made sense for Victorian homeowners to plant ornamental edibles like stone fruits in their backyards, is it still a wise option? I learned from experience that stone fruits provide significant challenges and rewards for those who maintain them. There are numerous books written on stone fruits, but I recommend a cost-benefit analysis to decide if a home orchard works for you.

## Benefits

The benefits of growing your own stone fruits include improved health, saving money, food safety, avoiding pesticide residue, increased flavor, ecological landscaping, and sustainable practices.

Will growing your own fruits increase your daily consumption? Stone fruits are low in calories, saturated fat, cholesterol, and sodium, and they are a good source of dietary fiber, vitamins A and C, and the mineral potassium. The high amounts of antioxidants found in stone fruits offer a spectrum of health benefits, including vision support, anti-inflammatory properties, heart disease and cancer prevention, nerve and muscle function, boosting immunity, and collagen formation (important for hair, skin, and nails). Insoluble fiber from the fruit skin helps prevent constipation, and soluble fiber promotes healthy glucose control and cholesterol regulation.

Health benefits involve more than just nutrition. If your life swirls into chaos at times (like most of ours), working in the garden can provide time to unwind, some exercise, and opportunities for your choice of time alone, with a significant other, or for family activities.

If stone fruits top your list of favorites, and you tend to buy more in peak season (June through September), it might make financial sense for you to grow your own, considering you can guarantee your own food safety and enjoy the increased freshness and flavor of home-grown foods. Because healthy, mature trees may yield hundreds of pounds per year, your initial investment is minimal compared to future dividends.

Peaches and nectarines are prime examples of reasons to grow your own, given their high placement on "The Dirty Dozen," a list published annually by the Environmental Working Group. According to this list, peaches rank second highest in pesticide residue in fruits and vegetables, and nectarines are third. In these cases, it makes sense to either splurge for organic peaches and nectarines, which are less likely to contain pesticide residues than conventional produce, or grow your own. (Cherries are listed at seventeenth and plums eighteenth on the extended list.)

Creating an ornamental landscape by incorporating edible stone fruits alongside or instead of other flowering trees and shrubs has functional, aesthetic, and sustainable planting benefits. The stunning blossoms on my cherry tree have created as much joy as the fruit it has produced. This backyard ecology has broader impact; the fuel saved to transport fruit around the country and globe is another reason to appreciate a home orchard.

Limited space or a small lot does not rule out growing stone fruits. Dwarf fruit trees exist, often bearing within three years, and many can be planted in containers for porch or deck placement.

## Pitfalls

Stone fruits face several challenges to survive and thrive: soil conditions, water and nutrients, sunlight, spacing, pollination, climate, and protection. My experiences, though challenging, are in no way exhaustive; see my references for more comprehensive reading suggestions about detailed stone fruit growing, including pest control, cold-hardiness, pruning specifics, and climate recommendations.

Let's face it: stone fruits can be a bit fussy, regardless of climate. When I first moved into my Victorian home, I thought there was a typo on the real estate listing indicating there was a peach tree on the premises. The short, leafy, and seemingly healthy tree that was plopped next to an impressive flowering cherry tree in the backyard produced what resembled oversized green and fuzzy almonds. The cherry tree, meanwhile, produced more than 150 pounds of sour (tart or pie) cherries, which were either promptly eaten fresh, made into baked goods and other delights by family and friends, or frozen. I then learned from research that a peach tree needs between three to four years to bear edible (or in this case recognizable) fruit. This tree was at least that old.

So I had two stone fruit trees of roughly the same age sitting next to each other, but they could not differ more in terms of vigor and yield. Let's review that "thrive and survive list" again.

Each tree needs soil that can accommodate its root system as it grows to maturity, in terms of nourishment and drainage. Water and proper nutrients must be available and provided in appropriate amounts to give the root system enrichment from nitrogen, potassium, phosphorus, and other minerals. Stone fruit trees need full sun: at least eight hours of sunlight per day, which is necessary for photosynthesis. They must not be crowded or spaced too closely to shade trees, roadways, buildings, or overhead wires. However, tree spacing must also be close enough to allow certain insects, usually bees, to cross-pollinate with self-unfruitful (self-unfertile, self-incompatible) varieties. Wait, there's more! Select stone fruit cultivars suited to your climate, adequate chilling periods to your location, and appropriate hardiness. Be mindful of protection from the elements, wildlife, insects, disease, machinery, and humans (e.g., neighborhood children).

## The Dirt

Backyard stone fruits are not typically planted from seeds or pits. Peaches and nectarines are usually grafted onto seedling peach tree roots and grow rapidly. A small grafted apricot or plum tree may start producing fruit in three years. Sweet cherries bear in five to seven years, and sour cherries in three to five years.

Base your stone fruit tree selection on your climate and soil conditions, unless you want to risk the disappointment of a non-blooming tree. Planting on small mounds in well-drained soil, with adequate spacing to receive full sun, will work well for most of the stone fruits. While peach trees are notoriously fussy about soil moisture and fertility, apricots are more easy-going, tolerating soil variety and drought better than most other fruits. Peaches, nectarines, and apricots, unlike plums, are intolerant of heavy, cool soil. Generally, cherry trees are considered to be the most difficult stone fruits to keep alive. For best results, a cherry tree's soil cannot be saturated for long periods during dormancy or during the growing season. Extremely wet weather may cause fruit cracking and disease, but cherry trees also need sufficient water to prevent their roots from drying out. Thick, cool mulch will help protect them in areas of frequent drought, especially in sandy soil. Sweet cherries prefer a lighter, sandier soil, while sour varieties tolerate heavier soils with good drainage. Cherries also have a high chilling requirement and are very susceptible to a number of diseases (brown rot, bacterial canker, and several viruses).

## For the Birds

Cherry trees are beautiful ornamental trees, with generally two home-growing options: sweet and sour (tart, pie) cherries. Sweet cherries are usually considered best for fresh eating while sour cherries are used for cooking, baking, and processing (canning, jams, and preserves). However, I can attest that plenty of people prefer a more tart taste and like to eat sour cherries fresh off my tree. As do the majority of birds in Connecticut.

Birds love cherries more than other orchard fruits, and probably give the home orchardist the most grief. Unlike other stone fruits, cherries do not ripen off the tree. This doesn't make a difference to the birds, who will pilfer them at any stage of ripeness. The kamikaze-diving and aerial antics of the birds, and squirrels, vying for this cherry tree's juicy red treasures amuse me for a few days before that sentiment twists into seething rage. I suggest netting your cherry tree, if possible, or introducing a "scare-eye" balloon, dummy owl, or repurposed aluminum pie plates, unless you intend to share your crop with the birds.

Life is a bowl of cherries? Not with the birds in my neighborhood.

## Princess Peach

Peaches and nectarines are fussy about climate and soil conditions, so what do they need to thrive? Their soil must be well-drained and provide the root systems with high amounts of nitrogen. They prefer dry, sandy soil that thoroughly warms and full sun and loads of water during summer months. They are susceptible to peach leaf curl and brown rot, but I saw no evidence of disease on my tree. Pollination wasn't an issue because peaches and nectarines are self-fruitful and do not need partnering trees to produce fruit. This tree was producing, but the resulting fuzzy orbs were just tiny, green, and riddled with holes.

To grow peaches successfully, you must have the appropriate climate for cold-hardiness, chilling hours for mild climates, and a long frost-free season. Avoid planting peach trees in low areas, due to greater risk of frost pockets. But these princesses of the stone fruits require something else: ample attention! The missing puzzle pieces were fruit thinning and heavy annual pruning: this peach tree needed both and had received neither. Mystery solved!

## Chop Chop

Proper pruning leads to fewer but larger fruits, encourages annual bearing, and helps prevent breakage by eliminating weaker limbs. Regular pruning creates a nicely shaped and productive tree that is easier to work with. Annual pruning will stimulate new growth. If the tree is already vigorous, don't prune too much. If it appears weak, prune more severely to stimulate growth.

Peaches, nectarines, and Japanese plums need to be pruned heavily after maturity. Apricots, cherries, and European plums require light pruning. Take care not to remove the spurs that cherries, plums, and apricots need to bear their fruit, unless they are old or numerous.

Early summer brings the need for pruning, and summer is also the time to thin developing fruits by at least half. Although thinning reduces the number of fruit and total yield, it improves the size and quality of the remaining fruit. This process results in fewer but larger fruits, and some contend that thinning increases the sugar content of individual fruits so they taste sweeter. Thinning can also reduce the spread of some diseases (due to moisture and air movement) and, like pruning, decrease the total load on branches to lessen the risk of branches breaking.

Despite such benefits, many home gardeners are conservative about fruit thinning. Leaving too much fruit on the tree by not thinning or thinning too lightly will decrease the tree's ability to form flower buds the following year. The process of thinning is easier to accept if you remember that only seven to eight percent of the tree's flowers are needed to produce a full crop of fruit.

As with pruning, thinning needs differ among stone fruits. Peaches and nectarines benefit from extensive thinning, while cherries, plums, and apricots require minor thinning, if any— thin excess fruit when they are less than one inch in diameter. With peaches and nectarines, begin at one end of a branch and systematically remove fruit, leaving one fruit every six to eight inches. Apricots and plums should be four to six inches apart along the branch. Be sure to remove doubles, two fruits fused together, as they provide homes for insects and diseases; it's also important to clear out small, disfigured, or damaged fruit to provide the benefits I mentioned earlier (as with thinning).

## The 12–18 Rule

My peach tree was impaired because it needed heavy pruning, thinning at the appropriate time, and the correct type of fertilizer in the right amount.

To determine if your stone fruits need fertilizer, use "The 12–18 Rule." Observe the most recent growth at the tips of the branches. If a mature tree, one of bearing age, produced less than twelve inches of growth in the past year, fertilize more. If you see twelve to eighteen inches of new growth, it is receiving enough nutrients; continue to fertilize as you have been. If your tree produces more than eighteen inches of new growth, don't fertilize at all.

Over-fertilizing will produce a tree that grows too fast, bears poorly, and is more susceptible to winter injury and disease.

Underfeeding typically reduces fruit-bearing ability. Fertilize a peach or apricot tree only if it needs it, and then only early in the spring. When in doubt, don't fertilize, or practice "less is more." Fertilizing in the late summer is a mistake because it will stimulate tree growth when it should be getting ready for winter. Peaches need nitrogen-rich fertilizers more than other fruit trees; blood meal, bone meal, and calcium ammonium nitrate are suitable. Nectarines may just need an application of annual compost. By comparison, cherry trees need very little fertilizer but still need enough nitrogen to form fruit buds.

## Pollination Vexation

My Japanese plum trees looked healthy and lush but produced nothing. Physiological problems may prevent a tree from producing fruit: lack of pollination, frost injury to flowers, too much shade, too much fertilizer (especially containing nitrogen), and improper pruning. Thinning, pruning, shade, and soil conditions were not the culprits here. There were no signs of common diseases like black knot, bacterial spot, or brown rot. I looked to pollination problems next.

Most peaches, nectarines, and apricots are fully self-fruitful and do not require a genetically different tree to provide pollen. Most sweet cherry varieties are self-unfruitful and require two different sweet cherry varieties to provide effective pollen. Even though sour cherries and European-type plums are considered self-fruitful, they often produce better when several are planted together. Pollination of sweet cherries with sour cherries is unlikely because they bloom at different times. To be on the safe side, planting three different cultivars of the same plum or sour cherry type is recommended.

My Japanese plums are self-unfruitful, but I had two different cultivars of the same plum type to cross-pollinate and produce fruit, and I made sure the cultivars bloomed at the same time.

There was no shortage of bees, the primary pollinators of fruit trees. In terms of spacing, plum trees should be planted within eighty feet of each other, but half that distance is recommended if the plums must compete with other pollen sources.

Oops.

That explained it. My plum trees were too far apart for adequate pollination, if only by a margin of about ten feet. The solution seemed to be to either uproot one plum tree and move it closer to the other one or add a third tree between the two plum trees.

## Stone Fruit Fortification

In attempting to identify pests or diseases and their associated damage, it is first necessary to recognize pest control problems as distinct from activities of non-harmful and beneficial organisms. This is in addition to problems resulting from improper cultural care. For example, bacterial spot is an infectious disease that occurs in the peach, nectarine, plum, and apricot, as well as in sweet and sour cherry trees. In contrast, bark splitting on stone fruit trees and fruit cracking in sweet cherries may be mistaken for diseases but are actually physiological problems.

Brown rot fungus may be the most common cause of fruit rot in stone fruit trees. Upon fully ripening, peaches and nectarines should be picked or processed promptly, as perishability increases susceptibility to brown rot. Similarly, if cherries or plums have split skin, process them or eat them quickly to avoid brown rot spore invasion.

In addition to brown rot, black knot is also common among sweet and sour cherries (and also plums). Sour cherries are highly susceptible to cherry leaf spot, a fungal disease which may be difficult to control. Despite this susceptibility, many home orchardists choose not to spray their cherry trees and don't have a problem. Greatly reduce the overall risk of disease by removing infected fruit, leaves, and branches, keeping stone fruits at a safe distance from any nearby infected wild cherries.

As peaches are the most demanding stone fruit in a number of ways—pruning, climate needs, susceptibility to pest problems and disease—plant only the number of peach trees you can realistically manage.

Diseases and insects can be controlled through the periodic applications of the proper insecticide or fungicide. But take special care to protect your pollinators! Spraying flowering trees with insecticides will kill pollinator bees. Instead, preemptively look for disease-resistant varieties. Recognize natural enemies like spiders and beetles that can handle most of your pest control for you. Because chemicals can disrupt the habitat of many pests' natural enemies, the drawbacks of insecticide use in many backyard situations outweigh any potential benefits.

## The Final Analysis

Does your cost-benefit analysis indicate your own stone fruit orchard would be worthwhile?

Stone fruits provide compact, appealing "ornamental edibles" for your landscape. They provide colorful, fragrant flowers in early spring, and they often yield enough fruit to share. Increased fruit consumption provides significant health benefits, and growing your own stone fruits allows greater food safety, most notably in terms of pesticide use. Of utmost importance to many homegrowers, they offer unmatched taste and quality compared with supermarket counterparts.

Yes, growing your own stone fruits takes work. You will have to weed weekly and manage wildlife and pests throughout the summer months. Patience is required, both in terms of years to bear and sometimes in solving problems. An early or short winter may negate your efforts. You will face competition from birds, mammals, insects, fungi, bacteria, and perhaps other humans for your fruit.

Some stone fruits are more difficult than others, but be sure to consider all relevant factors involved in growing and maintaining them within your own garden or orchard setting. You may be blessed with the ideal climate and soil conditions for the fussy and demanding peach. You may live in an arid region that reduces the likelihood for most pests and diseases. You may decide that a well-maintained orchard may add to your home's value. Or you may just enjoy a challenge and want to learn about sustainable landscaping. If not, logic dictates that the produce section at Stop & Shop or Whole Foods might save you some aggravation.

As for my stone fruit challenges, the sour cherries remain in fine shape (just ask the birds), and the peaches are definitely showing improvement. A third Japanese plum tree was added to bridge the pollination gap between the other two. An apricot tree will soon join the stone fruit congregation and hopefully toss plum-apricot hybrids (such as plumcots, pluots, apriums) into the mix, assuredly with new sets of rewards and challenges. But then, I'm not one to run from aggravation.

## About the Author

*Mireille Blacke, MA, RD, CD-N, is a registered dietitian, certified dietitian-nutritionist, and addiction specialist residing in Connecticut. She is obsessed with the city of New Orleans and the various works of Joss Whedon. Mireille adores her three Bengal cats, which dominate her life. Mireille worked in rock radio for over two decades before shifting her career focus to psychology, nutrition, and addiction counseling. She has been published in* Llewellyn's 2016 Moon Sign Book, Today's Dietitian, *and* OKRA Magazine. *Mireille is presently penning* Life and Times of the RadioWitch *and works as a Bariatric Dietitian at Saint Francis Hospital in Hartford, CT. Follow Mireille on Twitter @RockGumboRD and read her irreverent blog posts at rockgumbo.blogspot.com and radiowitch.com.*

## References

Blacke, M. "Just Peachy! The Health Benefits of this Favorite Fruit." *OKRA Magazine*, accessed August 8, 2015. https://okramagazine.wordpress.com/2013/04/10/just-peachy-the-health-benefits-of-this-favorite-fruit/.

Environmental Working Group. "Dirty Dozen." Accessed August 31, 2015. http://www.ewg.org/foodnews/dirty_dozen_list.php.

Hill, L. and L. Perry. *The Fruit Gardener's Bible: A Complete Guide to Growing Fruits and Nuts in the Home Garden*. North Adams, MA: Storey Publishing, 2011.

Ingels C., P. Geisel, and M. Norton. *The Home Orchard: Growing Your Own Deciduous Fruit and Nut Trees*. Richmond, CA: University of California Agriculture and Natural Resources, 2007.

Marrotte, E.L. "Insect, Disease and Mite Control for Peaches." Accessed August 8, 2015. http://www.ladybug.uconn.edu/factsheets/tp_05_insect_peaches.html.

Marrotte, E.L. "Why Fruit Trees Fail to Bear." Accessed August 8, 2015. http://www.ladybug.uconn.edu/factsheets/tp_05_fruittreesfailtobeal.html.

Merwin, I. "Growing Stone Fruits." Accessed August 29, 2015. http://www.gardening.cornell.edu/factsheets/ecogardening/growstone.html.

Pennsylvania State University Extension. "Stone Fruits." Accessed August 8, 2015. http://extension.psu.edu/plants/gardening/fphg/stone.

Walter, J. "Stone-Fruit Season." *Just Peachy*, accessed August 16, 2015. http://www.takethemagicstep.com/coaching/beginners/nutrition/stone-fruit-season-just-peachy.

# Many Moons

*by Bruce Scofield*

Imagine looking up in the sky one night and seeing a half-dozen or more moons. A few are big and appear as a disk, but others are smaller and, while bright, look more like the planet Venus. One of them zips through the skies, rising in the west and setting in the east! One pair of moons are in resonance—they meet up at the same time every few days. Another moon rises at the same time every day. These weird sightings are not so far out; things like this do happen on other planets. One wonders what astrology would be like if Earth had a multitude of moons.

Our single Moon fascinates us all. It's a shape-shifter—changing form over the course of the month as its angle with the Sun changes. Yet we never see the back of the Moon. This is because the Moon and Earth are tidally locked. We know about ocean tides on Earth that are pulled by the Moon (there are also much smaller land tides), but imagine how much tidal force the much bigger Earth exerts on the Moon. Over very long periods of time, the Earth's gravitational pull on the Moon has distorted it, causing one side to bulge and lock in direction to the Earth, and there it has stayed. Tidal locking is common in our solar system, as we will see in our tour of the moons.

The process of moons orbiting planets came about in different ways. One is similar to the way the entire solar system formed. A spinning dust cloud shaped like a disk, called a protoplanetary disk, slowly condenses to form a planet. Condensing dust farther out from the planet forms moons. Moons formed this way more or less orbit in a flat plane and are called regular moons. Other moons may be bodies captured by the planet's gravity. These moons can have a variety of orbits and are called irregular moons. Earth's moon doesn't exactly fall into these categories and appears to be the result of a collision. The leading hypothesis today argues that long, long ago, a body half the size of Earth, called Theia, smashed into Earth, creating a debris cloud made up of Theia and a large part of the outer layers of the Earth. This debris coalesced into the Moon we see today.

### Mars

Mercury and Venus have no moons, but Mars has two small ones— Phobos (fear) and Deimos (terror). Asaph Hall discovered them by telescope in 1877, but in a way they were "inadvertently predicted" one hundred fifty years earlier by none other than Jonathan Swift, in his book *Gulliver's Travels*. These moons were named after two characters in Greek mythology who fought wars with their father Ares (the Roman name is Mars). Phobos is the larger moon but is not spherical; it is oblong, measuring about 17 × 13 × 3 miles across. It is very close to Mars and moves through the sky faster than Mars rotates, so Phobos actually rises in the west and sets in the east. Phobos eclipses the Sun periodically, but it is too small to create a total eclipse. Phobos is further distinguished by a massive crater on one side that Hall named after his wife Angeline (who was a suffragist and abolitionist). Phobos's density is very low, prompting speculation that it is hollow or possibly artificial. It's most likely made up of more ice than rock.

Mars's other moon is smaller, under four miles in diameter, and more distant—appearing more like a very bright star. Its orbital period is not much longer than the Martian day of about twenty-five hours, so it will rise in the east and take almost three days to cross the sky and set in the west. Both Phobos and Deimos are tidally locked to Mars. Based on their composition, both moons are most likely captured asteroids, but this is not settled. An alternate hypothesis is that a large impact threw big chunks of Mars into orbit and all but two fell back to the planet. Regardless, Phobos will crash into Mars in about fifty million years as its orbit slowly decays.

### *Jupiter*

Jupiter has an abundance of moons—sixty-seven as of this writing. Most of them have been named after characters associated with Zeus (the Roman equivalent of Jupiter). With Jupiter, we have eight regular moons that have more or less circular orbits in the plane of Jupiter's equator, along with many irregular moons. The irregular moons are very small and have extreme orbits, suggesting that they are captured objects, probably asteroids. The eight regular moons most likely formed when Jupiter did. These include four small ones: Metis, Adrastea, Amalthea, and Thebe. They orbit Jupiter closely, circling the planet in under one Jupiter day, which is really fast—about ten hours. The other four, farther from Jupiter, are the well-known Galilean moons: Io, Europa, Ganymede, and Callisto. They were simultaneously discovered in 1610 by Simon Marius in Germany and Galileo Galilei in Italy.

Galileo published first and received credit for the discovery, but later astronomers decided to use the names that Marius proposed. These are big moons—all nearly two thousand miles or more in diameter.

We have learned a great deal about Jupiter's moons from the Galileo spacecraft that was launched by NASA in 1989 and arrived in Jupiter's neighborhood in 1995.

Io was named for the mythological priestess of Hera who was one of Zeus's lovers. It's known for its incredible volcanic activity—it has at least 400 active volcanoes. Io also has rugged mountains, some taller than Mt. Everest. These features on Io have been named for characters and places from the Io myths and also from Dante's *Inferno*. The intense geological activity that produces these features stems from tidal friction—the friction produced as Io experiences extreme tides from massive Jupiter. Io is Jupiter's closest Galilean moon.

Farther out from Io comes Europa, a bit smaller than Earth's Moon, but still the sixth-largest moon in the solar system. It was named after the queen of Crete, who was also a lover of Zeus. Europa, orbiting between Io and Ganymede, is locked into orbital resonance with them. For every two orbits of Europa, Io makes four orbits and Ganymede makes one. But the most astounding feature of Europa is that its surface is smooth, though with many cracks. It appears that its icy crust is riding on a subsurface salty ocean that may be over 60 miles deep. That's a lot of water—about twice the volume of all of Earth's oceans. Speculations abound as to whether or not this ocean may harbor life. We will learn more when NASA's Europa Clipper and the European Space Agency's Icy Moon Explorer reach Europa in the mid-2020s.

Ganymede, the next moon out, is big—about 3,300 miles in diameter and 8 percent larger than Mercury, though not as dense, as it is made up of light silicate rock and ice. It was named for the youth who was abducted by Zeus and made cupbearer of the gods. Like Europa, it may have layers of liquid water and ice, though its surface has both smooth and cratered sections. Ganymede has polar caps and its own magnetic field.

Callisto is just behind Ganymede in size at around 3,000 miles in diameter. It was named for a nymph who was associated with the hunter goddess Artemis, daughter of Zeus. Callisto is tidally locked to Jupiter, rotating once every revolution and showing the planet only one face. As the farthest of the Galilean moons from Jupiter, it is not tidally heated and receives less radiation, so it may be the best choice for a future human base. It is not dense, but its surface is heavily cratered.

### Saturn

Moving farther out from the Sun, we arrive at Saturn with its 62 moons. Of these moons, 24 are regular and the rest are orbiting in all directions. But let's not forget Saturn's rings, which are composed of millions of tiny satellites, sometimes called moonlets, that range from the size of dust to the size of a football field.

Saturn's most famous moon is Titan, discovered by Christiaan Huygens in 1655. By 1684, Giovanni Domenico Cassini discovered four additional moons orbiting Saturn, and in 1789, William Herschel discovered two more. Herschel proposed naming the Saturn's regular moons after the Titans, the brothers and sisters of Cronus (the Roman equivalent of Saturn). Later, when NASA's Voyager 1 and Voyager 2 passed Saturn, even more moons were discovered, and the names of Inuit, Gallic, and Norse giants were used for these irregular moons. In 1997, NASA launched the Cassini Mission to explore Saturn and its moons. It reached Saturn in 2004 and began orbiting the ringed planet and sending back data. Its mission has recently been extended, and Cassini will continue to explore until at least 2017. In early 2005, Cassini deployed the Huygens probe, which parachuted to the surface of Titan and sent back data during its descent and pictures of its landing.

Titan is unique among our solar system's moons—its orange color is due to its thick atmosphere, which is mostly nitrogen and some methane. It's a big moon, larger than the planet Mercury and second only to Ganymede as a moon. Titan is tidally locked with Saturn and its orbit is highly inclined, which suggests that there were serious collisions early in its history. We have learned from Cassini and Huygens that Titan is made of ice and rock, and the moon even has seasons, though it's cold—about minus 180 degrees F. Titan has a methane cycle in which methane, a gas at Earth's temperatures, changes from liquid to gas and back to liquid. Liquid methane collects in lakes on Titan's mostly smooth surface; it flows like rivers, evaporates, and then rains back down. A large, dark area of Titan, called the Xanadu region, is mountainous and may be geologically active. The Huygens probe landed on a plain and took pictures of eroded ice rocks; ice that is as hard as rock. Some scientists see Titan as an analog for a very early Earth, though much colder.

While Titan is Saturn's only large moon, there are many other interesting bodies in the Saturn system. The moon Rhea is under 1,000 miles in diameter and is mostly ice with some rock. Its surface, heavily cratered, is an ice crust that breaks at the edges and slides downhill into slumps. Iapetus, roughly the same size as Rhea, is also heavily cratered and has some huge impact basins. It has an odd equatorial ridge, like a wall, that is about 12 miles high and 800 miles long. Iapetus is tidally locked with Saturn and has two distinct hemispheres—one light and one dark. Tethys, a bit smaller, is mostly ice and highly reflective. It has a massive crater named Odysseus that is almost 300 miles across. Tethys also has a massive valley, called the Ithaca Chasma, which is 2 miles deep and wraps around three-fourths of the moon. Mimas is a small moon, only about 250 miles in diameter, but it has a giant impact crater, named Herschel, making Mimas resemble the Death Star in *Star Wars*.

Enceladus is a small moon of Saturn, only about 300 miles in diameter, but it has been getting a lot of attention. Its northern hemisphere is cratered, but its southern hemisphere has long cracks, called "tiger stripes," from which tidally-heated geysers and cryovolcanoes erupt and spew liquids and gases into space. Cryovolcanoes exist on very cold planets and release not hot magma, but water, methane, and ammonia. The Cassini probe has made several close passes to Enceladus and has recorded the contents of its eruptions, mostly water vapor with some organic compounds, leading to speculations about the possibility of life on this little moon. Two other moons of Saturn are Dione, which is locked in a resonance with Enceladus, and Phoebe, which is an irregular moon.

### Uranus

Uranus, the next planet out from the Sun, has 27 moons that are either named for characters in Shakespeare's plays, or from the poetry of Alexander Pope. Herschel, who discovered Uranus, also discovered two moons, Titania and Oberon, in 1787. More moons were discovered in 1851 by William Lassell and are named Ariel and Umbriel. Miranda, discovered in 1948 by Gerard Kuiper, is named after Miranda from Shakespeare's play *The Tempest*. Miranda has a close orbit to Uranus and is tidally locked with it. This moon also has some extreme topography with canyons and escarpments.

Uranus has only been visited by Voyager 2, which added to the list of moons orbiting Uranus. But what's really different from other moon systems is that Uranus has an extreme tilt to its axis, causing the regular moons to orbit at right angles to the plane of the solar system, which then causes extreme seasonal cycles.

Titania, named after the queen of the fairies in Shakespeare's *A Midsummer Night's Dream*, is Uranus's largest moon at a diameter of about 1,000 miles. It's about half rock and half ice, and it may have a subsurface ocean since it is tidally locked with Uranus. As a result, the surfaces change over relatively short periods of time and resurface ancient craters. Oberon, a bit smaller, is the outermost regular moon of Uranus and is very heavily cratered. It was named after the king of the fairies in *A Midsummer Night's Dream*. Umbriel is named after a character from Pope's poem *The Rape of the Lock*, as is Ariel after both Pope's poem and Shakespeare's *The Tempest*. Both are similar in size, about 700 miles in diameter. Ariel is cratered and has some rugged terrain.

### Neptune

Neptune has 14 known moons that are, appropriately, named after water deities. As with the other planets, there are regular and irregular moon. Neptune's rotation is about 13 hours and all but the outer two moons in this list orbit synchronously with its rotation. The irregular moons have both prograde and retrograde orbits and were probably captured by Neptune's gravity. Of the irregular moons, Psamathe and Neso have very large orbits that take them 25 years to orbit Neptune.

Triton is Neptune's largest moon, with Proteus being Neptune's second-largest moon. Triton is much bigger than the rest of Neptune's moons combined, having 99.5 percent of the combined mass of these moons. It was discovered in 1846 by William Lassell, but it wasn't seen up close until Voyager 2 passed through the Neptune system in 1989. Triton has a retrograde orbit, which means it orbits in the opposite direction to Neptune's rotation. This strongly suggests that it is a captured body, probably coming from the Kuiper Belt. Triton is slightly larger than Pluto and from what Voyager 2 found, it is similar in composition and surface features to Pluto—flat plains of frozen nitrogen and ice with few impact craters.

### *Pluto*

With Pluto, we come to the end of the solar system as we have known it. While Pluto has been downgraded from official planet status into a new category of dwarf planets, it is still one of the most compelling bodies to orbit the Sun. Pluto is small, not even as big as Earth's Moon, and a bit smaller than Triton, yet it amazingly has its own collection of moons. These moons are, in order of distance from Pluto, Charon, Styx, Nix, Kerberos, and Hydra. Charon, the ferryman of Hades in Greek mythology, is the largest of these, about 750 miles in diameter and about half the size of Pluto itself. Charon's gravity is such that Charon and Pluto are more like a double planet, each orbiting a point in space that lies between them. They are tidally locked and together form the gravitational center that the other moons orbit. Four small and elongated, non-spherical moons orbit farther out in the same plane as Charon. The shifting gravitational fields from Pluto and Charon cause these moons to rotate erratically. Nix, named after the mother of Charon, and Hydra, the nine-headed serpent that fought Hercules, are small moons with diameters of about 29 and 37 miles, respectively. In between them, Kerberos—named after Cerberus, the dog that guards the underworld—is in orbit. Kerberos is roughly 10–15 miles in diameter. Styx, Nix, and Hyrdra are in a complex orbital resonance, which suggests the moons were formed as a result of a collision. Pluto's moon system is really quite weird.

Our tour of the moons of our solar system ends here, but what a strange trip it has been. There is much to explore and no doubt some extraordinary discoveries will be made as humans make their way into the outer solar system. Today, many scientists believe that if there is life in the solar system outside of Earth, it will not be on a planet—it will be on a moon.

**About the Author**

*Bruce Scofield holds a PhD in geoscience and is the author of fifteen books and numerous articles on astrology, science, archaeology, hiking, and travel. He maintains a private practice as an astrological consultant, speaks at conferences, and teaches for Kepler College.*

# Saving Seeds—A Way of Saving the Earth and Yourself

*by Penny Kelly*

Deciding to save seeds from your garden is often the mark of an experienced gardener, although it can be done by beginners or anyone who loves plants and growing things. Most seed savers begin quite casually or even unintentionally. They notice that the lettuce planted in early spring bolted, flowered, and went to seed in the heat of summer. Then, in September, they notice dozens of tiny lettuce plants growing around the base of the original lettuce plants, which are now old and decrepit-looking. Voila! A new crop of lettuce is growing! In this case, they didn't lift a finger. It was Mother Nature who "saved the seeds" and, in effect, planted them right where they fell! The realization dawns… Ah,

I could collect some of those seeds and save the cost of new seed packets from the hardware store or plant nursery.

My first venture into deliberately saving seeds was a disaster. I carefully collected seeds from a variety of plants—tomatoes, melons, cucumber, lettuces, beans, zucchini, and others. I put them into envelopes and put the envelopes into a series of file folders labeled with pertinent information such as type of seed, Latin name, year planted, date collected, and whether I had selected for size, early or late germination, or other characteristics.

In the following spring I went to the cupboard containing the folders, all neatly arranged in baskets, where I had so carefully stored the seeds. To my dismay, I discovered they were all stuck together and covered with the various molds that had destroyed them. Lesson number one: seeds need to be very dry before you put them in storage!

The next year, I collected another set of seeds, dried them for weeks, and put them into new envelopes and file folders, once again labeled with the relevant information. When I went to get them out of the basement the following spring, I discovered that a mouse had gotten into the baskets, eaten through the paper envelopes, and enjoyed the nicely dried seeds. The husks and a lot of mouse droppings were all that remained. Lesson number two: seeds need to be stored in glass or metal containers if you want to make sure they are safe from the critters, moths, and bugs that make their way into hidden places and feast on anything offering good nutrition, and seeds are loaded with nutrition that is meant to feed the little plant when it germinates and begins its journey into feeding us.

This led directly into my third year of lessons in seed-saving. I was in a hurry to be done with the garden, and I had not collected seeds from the various veggies that ended up on my table. So I ran out to collect what I could in a last-minute way. I dried them carefully, put them in glass jars, and planted them the next spring.

As I planted them, I noticed that most of the seeds were quite flat and thin, but this meant little to me until almost nothing came up in the rows I had planted. Drat! Those thin, flat seeds were not capable of sustaining the germination process!

The nutrients in the seed are called the "germ," thus I learned of another factor to be aware of when saving seeds. When you pick fruits or vegetables too soon, the plant will not have had time to fill out the seed with life-giving germ. Mature seeds will be fat and rounded when they are filled with germ, and this is like money in the bank for the future plant that will grow from it. It gives the new seedling a leg up when growing conditions are less than ideal at the time of germination.

## Healing Seeds

A seed is a tiny living system that is very quiet yet waits expectantly for the right conditions to sprout and give its gift to the world. On its journey, it will face many challenges: bacteria, molds, and viruses will force it to defend itself. It will encounter environmental challenges such as excessive heat or intense cold.

A fully mature seed filled with germ

An immature seed without enough germ

It will have to face the prospect that there might be too little or too much water, too little sun, too much shade, damaging winds that cause mechanical stresses, or the daunting effects of chemicals. And if the soil has collapsed and has no life in the form of various microorganisms to keep the soil fluffy and friable, our tiny seedling may spend most of its energy digging through compacted layers of dirt, all in a search for the minerals and nutrients it can use to build a beautiful structure from which to hang its vegetables or fruit.

One of the things discovered in my work with biophysicist William Levengood at his lab near Ann Arbor, Michigan, was that people—especially healers—could dramatically affect every aspect of the life of the seed. This included germination, resistance to cold, heat, drought, excess moisture, bacteria, molds, mildews, rate of growth, amount of fruit produced, the taste of that fruit, and the keeping quality.

We brought people into the lab, gave them a handful of thirty seeds, asked them to face east (direction matters!), and then we asked them to focus their consciousness on the seeds in their hands until their hands felt warm and they could feel what might be described as energy flowing through them. After a few minutes, usually no more than ten minutes, we took the seeds from them and allowed the seeds to rest for at least half an hour because the threshold for energetic changes to thoroughly impact the seeds was about twenty minutes. Then we put the seeds in germination paper and put them in a germination chamber along with thirty control seeds that had not been "treated." The seeds that were treated by healers consistently germinated more quickly, had a bigger root mass, grew more quickly, and were resistant to all of the trials and tribulations that seeds normally encounter.

When I finally achieved success in collecting seeds from my own garden and conducting a few seed tests of my own, I was astounded to discover that the plants coming from my seeds were *twice* the size of the plants grown from purchased seeds planted at the same time. I realized that the mother plants were not just growing tomatoes, pumpkins, or lettuces for consumption, they were also collecting information about the environment and encoding that information into the tiny seeds they were producing! Just like all good parents, the mother plants wanted their offspring to have every advantage in being successful when it was their turn to produce. Thus, they had optimized their seeds for perfect, rapid, and healthy growth in the same soil where they originated. The new plants were ready to deal with the moisture, wind, sun, bacteria, and microorganisms in their motherland. They did not have to waste time overcoming unexpected conditions or the short supply of various nutrients or antioxidants.

Deciding to save seeds from your garden is the mark of a committed gardener. It requires knowing which plants produce seeds the same year they're planted and which are biennial, meaning they don't produce until the second year. It demands that you think ahead in terms of garden design. The plants that won't produce seed until their second year—parsley, cabbage, carrots, beets, and others—need to be planted in an area where they will not be inadvertently tilled under the following spring when you are preparing your garden for new plantings. If they are scattered all over your garden, you'll have a problem. The simplest solution to this problem is to plant an area just for seed saving, and then mulch it well toward the end of summer. If you have carrots in the ground, you might have to put chicken wire or hardware cloth over them for the winter. One fine spring day I came out to inspect my second-year carrots to see if they were growing yet. I discovered an entire row of slender holes where the carrots had been. It must have been a very good year for the local rabbits and deer!

Once you begin collecting seeds, you are likely to realize that people are just like seeds. Every seed, if it is to become what it was born to become, must be ready to let go of its compact form and open outwardly to become something new and totally different. The tiny seed must put out a root system and begin feeding from its local environment in order to get its head above the soil and open its leaves to begin collecting sunlight. So it is with humans. If we are to become what we were born to become, we must be ready to let go of our compact form and open to become something new and different.

Look at the amazing structures that some seeds become—a cucumber vine, a flavorful marjoram or basil plant, a sprawling tomato, a towering stalk of corn, or a small onion with the intense power to make us weep. Imagine the forms we might take if we recognize that we are also individual seeds of life! In the same way that plants anchor themselves in the soil, we must begin nurturing ourselves in ways that anchor us in the surrounding fields of energy. We must begin drawing in love and light from the realms of energy that we usually ignore. Only then will we trigger the lock that springs open to reveal the hidden structure within us, a structure that is akin to the oak tree hidden within the acorn. This ancient hidden structure within the human used to be called the Tree of Life. When it unfolds, we become something more than we have been and, like all evolved seeds, begin to nurture life. May you discover the joy and power of saving seeds and enjoy all the wisdom that comes from doing so. We are all seeds in the realms of life!

## About the Author

*Penny Kelly is a writer, teacher, author, publisher, consultant, and naturopathic physician. After purchasing Lily Hill Farm in southwest Michigan in 1987, she raised grapes for Welch Foods for a dozen years and established Lily Hill Learning Center where she teaches courses in Developing Intuition and the Gift of Consciousness, Getting Well Again Naturally, and Organic Gardening. She has been deeply involved in community gardening in Kalamazoo and Battle Creek, MI, through grants from the Kellogg Foundation. Penny holds a degree in humanistic studies from Wayne State University and a degree in naturopathic medicine from Clayton College of Natural Health. She is the mother of four children, has cowritten or edited twenty-three books with others, and has written seven books of her own. Penny lives, gardens, and writes in Lawton, Michigan.*

# The Hawaiian Lunar Calendar

*by Michelle Perrin*

In Europe and North America, the standard calendar used by governments and most people is the Gregorian, or Western, calendar. It is a solar calendar, meaning it is determined by the position of Earth as it revolves around the Sun, which takes approximately—but not exactly—one year. Every four years, on a leap year, a day is added in February to make sure the calendar stays calibrated to the actual position of the Earth to the Sun.

As the Earth rotates around the Sun, the Moon is also rotating around the Earth, and, as it does so, we see different parts of the Moon illuminated from our vantage point. Moon phases are what we see when the Sun, Earth, and Moon align differently during their rotations. For example, when the Earth is between the Sun and Moon in a straight line, we have a Full Moon, but when the Moon comes between the Earth and the Sun, we have a New

Moon, when the Moon is black because the Sun is not illuminating the side we can see.

The Hawaiian Calendar, called the *Kaulana Mahina*, is based on the moon phases as visible by the naked eye. The solar calendar requires calculation by astronomers, as the Earth's rotation around the Sun cannot be viewed by the average person, but the lunar calendar can be tracked by almost anyone gazing up into the night sky. While the solar calendar keeps a rigid organization of our days, the lunar calendar brings us closer to the changing cycles of nature.

The Western calendar is divided into months—a word derived from the term "moon"—but it is not determined by moon phases, given that the New Moon and Full Moon fall on different times each month. In a lunar calendar, however, time itself is marked by lunar phases. In the Kaulana Mahina, when there is no Moon in the sky, it is *Muku*, which is the last day of the month for every month.

### Kaulana Mahina: The Hawaiian Lunar Calendar

In the Western tradition, we have eight moon phases, starting at the New Moon, when the Moon is dark. Then there are two quarter Moons and the Full Moon, with four sub-phases in between. There are thirty moon phases based on the shape of the Moon in the Hawaiian lunar calendar. There are four nights of Full Moon, each with a different name, which are known collectively as *nā pō mahina kōnane*, or "the nights of bright moonlight."

Each month is divided into three weeks, or *Anahulu*; the first week is called *Hoʻonui*, or growing bigger; the second is named *Poepoe*, meaning round or full; the third week is *Hoʻēmi*, the Hawaiian term for "decreasing." Each Anahulu has ten days, just like your fingers, which could have been a useful counting technique in a culture that had no writing system. In fact, the word for week is comprised of the words *ana* (count) and *hulu* (an archaic word for ten).

In Hawaii, twelve 30-day months make for a 360-day year. The actual lunar month, or *malama*, lasts about twenty-nine and a half days, so every three to six years a thirteenth month, a *malama pili* (leap month), is added. This thirteenth month is not always added at the same time like leap day in the Gregorian calendar, and its name varies by when it is added into the calendar, as well as by regional differences. In fact, the thirteenth month has at least fourteen names. Moreover, the *Mauli* moon phase, the phase before the New Moon, was sometimes eliminated to calibrate the calendar. Different practices were observed throughout the islands.

The Hawaiian calendar is also a heliacal calendar that uses the rising of a constellation over the horizon as means of marking time. When the Pleiades rise on the eastern horizon at sunset, it marks the beginning of the *Makahiki* season, which occurs sometime in October or November. The Hawaiian New Year is celebrated on the first New Moon (*Hilo*) after this celestial event, during the month of *Welehu*, which occurs in the Western month of November or December.

## Makahiki: The Four-Month-Long New Year's Party

Makahiki was an extremely important period of the Hawaiian year—a three- to four-month period of celebration. War was declared *kapu*, meaning forbidden, and all unnecessary work ended except for the preparation and serving of food. Since the Hawaiians did not use money, land taxes were collected through offerings in each *ahupua'a* to the god of agriculture, Lono, whose spirit was embodied in a pole draped in *kapa* cloth and carried around the island. For the ancient Hawaiians, the gods could manifest throughout nature, so this effigy was not a symbol but an actual incarnation of the divine.

Once the offerings were collected, the next phase of Makahiki started: the numerous strict kapu were lifted and the people

# Anahulu Hoʻonui

| | | | | |
|---|---|---|---|---|
| Hilo | Hoaka | Kūkahi | Kūlua | Kūkoli |
| Kūpau | ʻOlekūkahi | ʻOlekūlua | ʻOlekūkolu | ʻOlepau |

# Anahulu Poepoe

| | | | | |
|---|---|---|---|---|
| Huna | Mohalu | Hua | Akua | Hoku |
| Mahealani | Kulu | Lāʻaukūkahi | Lāʻaukūlua | Lāʻaupau |

# Anahulu Hoʻēmi

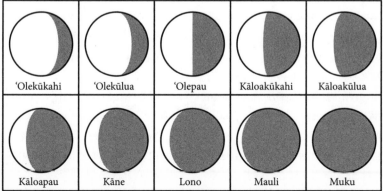

| | | | | |
|---|---|---|---|---|
| ʻOlekūkahi | ʻOlekūlua | ʻOlepau | Kāloakūkahi | Kāloakūlua |
| Kāloapau | Kāne | Lono | Mauli | Muku |

enjoyed an extended period of games, dancing, sports, peace, rest, and celebration. During this period, people in each ahupua'a lived off stores of food that people shared. Many of the traditions of this special time are unknown to us because there was no written record in ancient Hawaii. Makahiki ended when the Lono pole was again marched through the island to close the ceremony and return to a more formal way of life.

When Captain Cook first arrived in Hawaii, it was during the Makahiki season, which is one of the reasons the Hawaiians first welcomed him as the arrival of Lono, who returns during this period in different manifested forms.

Makahiki and the kapu system were abolished after the death of the King in 1819 before the arrival of the Christian missionaries. Makahiki has been making comeback in recent decades, however. To many people, it symbolizes an opportunity to honor their past ancestors and traditions as well as heal the many sufferings brought upon the culture through Western contact.

## *The Year and the Seasons*

In the past, North American planters had a special name for each of our twelve months based on what was going on with the Moon, such as the Grain Moon, Sap Moon, or Harvest Moon. The names of the Hawaiian months also give clues to each period's conditions and accompanying activities. It is also interesting to note that each Hawaiian month name is also used as a name for a star in Hawaiian astronomy.

The months can differ by name from place to place in Hawaii, and different islands will use the same names but in a different order; fishermen and farmers also often use different names. Starting in the 1960s, a renewed interest in the lunar calendar led to efforts to standardize the calendar. Old newspapers were reviewed and elders were interviewed. Most of those interviewed, however, were from the Big Island of Hawaii, so that is why the

Big Island system of naming and order is the most prevalent today.

The Hawaiian year is divided into two seasons: *Ho'Oilo*, the Wet Season (or winter), and *Kauwela*, the Dry Season (or summer.) The two seasons could shift based on the side of the island you were on and the climate of that particular place.

### Ho'oilo: The Wet Season

During the first three months, it is rainy and soggy and not much work can be done. This is the festive Makahiki season. Agricultural work resumes in *Kaulua*.

**Welehu (sifting ashes):** November to December. The first month of the New Year. Fires were needed for keeping warm. Makahiki was celebrated and no formal work was done.

**Makali'I (little eyes):** December to January. The first shoots (or eyes) of various plants begin to show. Makahiki continues.

**Ka'elo (drenching, soggy):** January to February. Thunderstorms and rain. The final month of Makahiki. Too muddy for planting.

**Kaulua (indecisive, of Two Minds):** February to March. The Hawaiian equivalent of "In like a lion, out like a lamb." The "Two Minds" alternate between rain and sun, wind and calm. Planting starts again.

**Nana (animate, initiate):** March to April. This is the time of year when nature springs alive. Things begin to grow heartily and nature is blooming and green.

**Welo (tail, also fluttering):** April to May. An auspicious time for farmers when plants send up shoots that resemble tails. The end of the Wet Season, things will be calmer and easier from this point. Red kapa flags are hung on temples to mark the start of strict ceremonies for *Kū*, the god of war and daily activities.

### Kauwela: The Dry Season

Days and nights are warm, days are long, and plants grow quickly.

**ʻIkiʻiki (sticky, uncomfortable):** May to June. High humidity. Very favorable for planting and food production.

**Kaʻaona (rolling along):** June to July. Pleasant weather and a good period for pruning.

**Hinaiaʻeleʻele (dark clouds toward the mountains):** July to August. Hot and stormy. This is a period when fruit is getting dark and heavy and is easy to pick off the trees.

**Mahoe Mua (first twin):** August to September. Weather starts to turn rainy and windy. Productive growing and harvesting.

**Mahoe Hope (twin coming soon after):** September to October. The weather this month is so similar to the previous one that they are like twins. Productive growing and harvesting.

**ʻIkuwā (loud voice):** October to November. The beginning of Makahiki. The last good month of the season. Everything needs to be harvested and stored before the rain comes toward the end of this period. A white kapa cloth was hung on temples to signify the arrival of the New Year.

## Moon Phases

The predictability of the moon phases gave a never-wavering structure to daily life, representing the cycle of birth, growth, maturity, decline, death, and an ultimate rebirth. This, in turn, gave rise to an efficient and predictable calendar based on observations following the Moon. The Moon imparted knowledge, energy, and resources, and because of this, it was seen as the provider for mankind.

The Moon and its phases dictated when all aspects of Hawaiian life could take place, such as fishing, farming, planting, gathering, harvesting, healing, mending, worship, ceremonies, and cultural activities. During the kapu era, many activities were restricted or banned during certain phases; on some nights, nothing could occur at all except for praying in a temple.

The Hawaiian "day" began at sunset, and that moon phase set the tone for all activities until the next sunset. Night was considered the period of the gods, and day was considered the period of mankind. Moreover, the darkness was not a place of fear but a place of creation. While Hawaiians used a lunar calendar based on the phases of the Moon, most of their planting took place during the daytime, but agriculture could also be done at night to garner the creative, spiritual rays of the Moon.

## Special Periods

For each month in the Hawaiian calendar, there were special multi-day phases that were named after certain gods, others that were unproductive days for rest and repair, and some were kapu.

### *Sacred Periods*

Certain lunar nights were dedicated to the four major Hawaiian deities: *Kū, Lono, Kanaloa*, and *Kāne*. While the kapu system was in place, planting was restricted or forbidden on nights sacred to these gods, and instead, men had to go to the temple. After 1819, farmers experimented with varying crops and, through observation and experimentation, deduced which to grow on these nights.

The Nightmarchers comprise a ghostly procession of ancient Hawaiian warriors, ancestors, gods, goddesses, and living chiefs. The Nightmarchers were said to roam between dusk and dawn on these sacred nights while carrying torches, chanting, and playing drums, often appearing to accompany a dying person to the spirit realm. It was said that if you looked upon a Nightmarcher, you would die immediately, so it was wiser to leave the area, hide, or lie prostrate to avoid detection. Nightmarchers would also appear on the night of the Full Moon, *Akua*.

The only god to receive human sacrifice was *Kū*, the god of war. Most sacrifices in ancient Hawaii were done by voluntary drowning in the ocean.

## The Four Kapu Periods

*Kapu-Kū*—Dedicated to *Kū*, the god of war and certain crops. Took place during the first week of the waxing Moon. This was a strictly observed ceremonial period spent at temple and no one fished or planted. Human sacrifices occurred. The *Kapu-Kū* occurred on the first four nights of the month: *Hilo, Hoaka, Kūkahi,* and *Kūlua.*

*Kapu-Hua*—Dedicated to the god of procreation, *Kāne,* and the god of agriculture, *Lono.* It was forbidden to eat *hua* (fruit) and offerings were left to the gods, who were roaming the lands. Takes place during the second week on *Mōhalu, Hua,* and *Akua.*

*Kapu-Kāloa*—Dedicated to Kanaloa, the god of the seas, the underworld, and magic. Only certain crops were planted. Occurs on the third week on *'Olepau, Kāloakūkahi,* and *Kāloakūlua.*

*Kapu Kāne*—Dedicated to the god of procreation and the dawn, sun, and sky. Fishing and planting were restricted. Occurs on the last four days of the month, during the third week on *Kāne, Lono, Mauli,* and *Muku.*

## The 'Ole Nights: Unproductive Periods of Rest

'Ole is the Hawaiian word for "without" or "none." During these periods, nothing was planted and new things were not started, as it was seen as inauspicious. There were four 'Ole days in the first week and three 'Ole days in the last week. These were days to stay at home, mend, make repairs, and relax. They were also good periods for pruning or weeding, since it would take longer for the weeds to grow back.

## The Kū Phases: Tall and Strong

There are four nights in the first week named after the god *Kū.* The word *Kū* also means to stand upright, erect, and firm; plants sown on these days will possess these qualities. *Kū* nights are also

the best periods to build a fence, roof, or house, as they are sure
to have solid foundations and stand tall.

## The Four Full Moon Nights

Hawaiians believed that there were four "nights of roundness,"
and they believed the light was brightest under the first three.
During these nights, there were many activities, rituals, and
ceremonies. People would dress up, make *leis*, and ceremonially
weed as a family.

## The Lāʻau Phases: A Time for Healing

*Lāʻau* means tree, plant, bush, wood, timber, healing, and herbs,
including those that can be used for medicine. During these
phases in the second week of the month, the horns of the crescent
Moon appear again. This period is especially good for gathering
medicinal herbs, as the Full Moon pulls the liquid out of the earth
and into the plants, filling them with sap and making them their
most potent. Planting certain types of plants was discouraged
because they could grow to be woody instead of tender. Over
three hundred plants were used for medicine in Hawaii. These
were also days for healing in special buildings dedicated to recuperation.

## The Kāloa Phases

There are three nights in the last week named after the god
Kanaloa. The focus was on nourishing and healing people to keep
them from dying. The Nightmarchers would walk these nights
seeking relatives to accompany them back to the underworld.
*Loa* means "long," so these are good nights to plant anything with
long stems, long vines, long leaves, or to make rope.

### About the Author

*For ten years, Michelle Perrin, aka Astrology Detective, has built
a reputation as one of the world's most trusted and sought-after
astrologers. Her work has appeared in some of the most influential
titles online and in print, making her one of the few astrologers*

who has garnered respect from both a mass audience as well as the astrological community. Her horoscopes have appeared on the website for Canada's W Dish Network, Tarot.com, and Dell Horoscope Magazine, among others. Her writings have also been featured in The Mountain Astrologer, the leading trade journal for the astrological community.

# Weekly Tips Provided by:

**Penny Kelly** is a writer, teacher, author, publisher, consultant, and naturopathic physician. After purchasing Lily Hill Farm in southwest Michigan in 1987, she raised grapes for Welch Foods for a dozen years and established Lily Hill Learning Center, where she teaches courses in Developing Intuition and the Gift of Consciousness, Getting Well Again Naturally, and Organic Gardening. She is the mother of four children, has cowritten or edited twenty-three books with others, and has written seven books of her own. Penny lives, gardens, and writes in Lawton, Michigan.

**Nicole Nugent** lives in Minneapolis with her husband, young daughter, and several sadly overfull bookcases. She has contributed to Llewellyn's annuals from behind the scenes for eight years. In her spare time, Nicole enjoys gardening, cooking, and exploring the Twin Cities via parks and trails.

**Robin Ivy Payton** is Portland, Maine's Yoga Intuitive. Astrologer for The Portland Phoenix and Robin's Zodiac Zone, Robin also writes about yoga, meditation, health, and the powers of music, color, and nature. Robin created RoZoYo®, a fusion of astrology and yoga based on the relationship between the Moon, Sun, planets, and our physical and energetic bodies. She teaches classes and workshops in the Portland, Maine, area and leads special practices at festivals such as Love Yoga Fest in Hyannis, Massachusetts. Robin appears on radio broadcasts including Ultrasounds on WMNF Tampa, Florida. Follow her at instagram.com/robinszodiacyogalife and www.RoZoYo.com

**Charlie Rainbow Wolf** is happiest when she is creating something, especially if it can be made from items that others have cast aside. Pottery, writing, knitting, astrology, and tarot are her deepest interests, but she happily confesses that she's easily distracted, because life offers so many wonderful things to explore. She is an advocate of organic gardening and cooking, and she lives in the Midwest with her husband and special-needs Great Danes. Follow her at www.charlierainbow.com.